Recent research into a self-taught tradition of English rural poetry has begun to offer a radically new dimension to our view of the role of poetry in the literary culture of the eighteenth century. In this important new study John Goodridge offers a detailed reading of key rural poems of the period, examines the ways in which eighteenth-century poets adapted Virgilian Georgic models and reveals an illuminating link between rural poetry and agricultural and folkloric development. Goodridge compares poetic accounts of rural labour by James Thomson, Stephen Duck and Mary Collier, and makes a close analysis of one of the largely forgotten didactic epics of the eighteenth century, John Dyer's *The Fleece*. Through an exploration of the purpose of rural poetry and how it relates to the real world, Goodridge breaks through the often brittle surface of eighteenth-century poetry, to show how it reflects the ideologies and realities of contemporary life.

CAMBRIDGE STUDIES IN EIGHTEENTH-CENTURY
ENGLISH LITERATURE AND THOUGHT 27

Rural Life in Eighteenth-Century English Poetry

Rural Life in Eighteenth-Century English Poetry

JOHN GOODRIDGE

The Nottingham Trent University

CAMBRIDGE
UNIVERSITY PRESS

Published by the Press Syndicate of the University of Cambridge
The Pitt Building, Trumpington Street, Cambridge CB2 1RP
40 West 20th Street, New York, NY 10011–4211 USA
10 Stamford Road, Oakleigh, Melbourne 3166, Australia

First published 1995
Reprinted 1997

Printed in the Great Britain by Biddles Ltd, Guildford, Surrey

A catalogue record for this book is available from the British Library

Library of Congress cataloguing in publication data

Goodridge, John
Rural life in eighteenth-century English poetry / John Goodridge.
p.   cm. – (Cambridge studies in eighteenth-century English literature and thought; 27)
Includes bibliographical references and index.
ISBN 0 521 43381 9 (hardback)
1. English poetry – 18th century – History and criticism.
2. Rural conditions in literature.
3. Literature and society – Great Britain – History – 18th century.
4. Pastoral poetry, English – History and criticism.
5. Agricultural labourers in literature. 6. English poetry – Roman influences.
7. Country life in literature. 8. Agriculture in literature.
9. Farm life in literature. 10. Virgil – Influence.
I. Title. II. Series.
PR555.R87G66   1996
821'509321734 – dc20   95–7156 CIP

ISBN 0 521 43381 9 hardback

For Alison

Contents

Preface

The study of eighteenth-century poetry has experienced major advances in the past decade or so, and the present work is offered as part of a much larger process of rediscovery and reassessment. Many thousands of poems about rural life were written between 1700 and 1800, and I have chosen to look closely at a small number of texts rather than embarking on a comprehensive survey. The poems I have selected for attention may be seen as representing wider trends, as well as being of individual interest; but the main reason I have focused my attention so closely is in order to give the texts the kind of detailed treatment which (I would argue) is the only way by which they yield significant meaning. Part of what I want to do, indeed, is to assess the degree to which an interdisciplinary and detailed reading can enable us to rediscover the poetry of the eighteenth century, without on the one hand condescending to or apologising for it, or on the other losing sight of our own concerns and interests, our reasons for reading. I have for similar reasons focused my resources on two topics, concentrating on the related themes of rural labour (Part I) and agricultural prescription (Part II). Rural labour seems to me to have been the most important aspect of rural life in the period, for the rural population as well as for the more thoughtful of the poets; while agricultural prescription was a central preoccupation of the eighteenth century, one which tells us a great deal about the period and its psyche. The two themes also inter-relate in a number of ways, as we shall see.

The help and encouragement of others has been essential, and I would like to thank some of them here. Claire Lamont encouraged and guided me tirelessly in the doctoral phase of my research, and I am very grateful to her. I am blessed with a supportive family: Pete Goodridge gave invaluable and extensive help with agricultural and shepherding matters, Meggie Goodridge advised on textile history, and Gill Goodridge played a vital role in helping me to shape and revise the book. The subject matter and the basic impetus for the project were first suggested by my father, Frank Goodridge (1924–1984).

Helen Boden offered important comments at an early stage in my research, urging me to give Mary Collier a full role in my plans, for which

I am especially thankful. Carolyn Williams kindly supplied information on the background to Dyer's anti-French sentiments. The librarians at the University of Newcastle upon Tyne, in particular Robert Firth and Dr Lesley Gordon, have patiently tolerated my demands on their time and resources, as have the staff of the British Library. C. M. Cowan of the Gilchrist Library in the Faculty of Agriculture at Newcastle University kindly sought out early agricultural books for me. I should like to thank the Dean and Chapter Library, Durham, and its Librarian, Roger Norris, for kindly allowing me to transcribe and quote from Dyer's 'Commercial Map' manuscripts, from the library's Longstaffe Collection. I am grateful to the Audio-Visual Department at the Nottingham Trent University for preparing materials for the front cover illustration, and to Barbara Taylor for compiling the index.

I have received the encouragement and help of many people, often over a number of years, and I would like to thank Anne and Karen Antonelli, Rowena Burrell and Quentin Seddon, Don Feasay, Desmond Graham, Neil Hairsine, Ernst Honigmann, Peter V. Jones, Kaye Kossick, Pete Sampson, Kelsey Thornton, Bob White, my students and colleagues at Newcastle and Nottingham Trent, and friends in the eighteenth-century and Clare communities. Above all I have been helped by the encouragement and support of my partner, Alison Ramsden, to whom the book is dedicated with love and thanks.

Errors of fact and judgement are my own. I have allowed myself to be led by the interdisciplinarity of the eighteenth-century poets into areas and disciplines in which I am an enthusiastic amateur, and I shall be especially grateful to have my shortcomings in these areas drawn to my attention.

The Nottingham Trent University, December 1994

Abbreviations and conventions

Agrarian History	Joan Thirsk, G. E. Mingay *et al.* (eds), *The Agrarian History of England and Wales* (vols. I–VIII, Cambridge, 1967–85).
Camden	William Camden, *Camden's Britannia [1598], Newly Translated into English with Large Additions and Improvements*, trans. and ed. William Gibson (London, 1695).
'Commercial Map'	John Dyer, unpublished manuscript notes, plan and related materials for a 'Commercial Map of England', Longstaffe Collection, Dean and Chapter Library, Durham (cited by folio number).
Defoe	Daniel Defoe, *A Tour Thro' the Whole Island of Great Britain [1724–6]*, ed. G. D. H. Cole (two volumes, London, 1968).
DNB	*The Dictionary of National Biography*, ed. Leslie Stephen, Sidney Lee *et al.* (reissued edition, twenty-one volumes, London, 1908–9; Supplement, 1909; Second Supplement, three volumes, 1912; Corrections and Additions, 1966).
Drayton	Michael Drayton, *Poly–Olbion. or A Chorographicall description of Tracts, Rivers, Mountains, Forests, and other Parts of this renowned Isle of Greate Britaine [1613–22]*, in *The Works of Michael Drayton*, ed. William Hebel, vol. IV (Oxford, 1933).
GM	*The Gentleman's Magazine* (1731–1907).
OED	*The Oxford English Dictionary* (compact edition, two volumes, Oxford, 1979; Supplement, 1987).
TE	*The Twickenham Edition of the Works of Alexander Pope*, ed. John Butt, Maynard Mack *et al.*, vols I–X (London and New Haven, 1939–67).

Quotations from poems under discussion normally have specific book and line references in brackets after the text. Letters are normally cited using the formula (*Sender–Recipient*, date). Biblical references are to the *Authorised*

xiii

Version of the Bible (1611). Shakespeare references are to the text as edited by Peter Alexander (1951).

Textual note

There are problems in selecting a working text for three of the four main poets discussed, Mary Collier, Stephen Duck and John Dyer. I have used the following, for reasons I shall briefly explain:

The Thresher's Labour by Stephen Duck, The Woman's Labour by Mary Collier, Two Eighteenth Century Poems, ed. E. P. Thompson and Marian Sugden (London: The Merlin Press, 1989);

John Dyer, *Poems*, ed. Edward Thomas (1903 [reprinted in facsimile, Lampeter: Llanerch Enterprises, 1989]);

James Thomson, *The Seasons*, ed. James Sambrook (Oxford, 1981).

The Thomson is a standard edition. The Collier/Duck edition is conveniently available and is the most textually alert. The reasons why the 1730 text of Duck (printed in this edition) is to be preferred to the 1736 text more usually used by editors are set out by Thompson and Sugden in an editorial note (pp. 27–30), and by Peter J. McGonigle in 'Stephen Duck and the text of *The Thresher's Labour*', *The Library*, sixth series, 4 (1982), 288–96. I have corrected one error in the Thompson/Sugden text of Collier (which is based on the first edition of 1739): 'find linen' to 'fine linen' (p. 20).

Dyer presents far greater problems, since no text is entirely satisfactory, and the best edition produced so far exists only as an unpublished thesis (by J. G. E. Davies, 1968). I have therefore chosen a conveniently available edition, the 1989 reprint of Edward Thomas's 1903 edition. Significant or substantive textual variants from other major editions of this text (as with the texts of Duck, Collier and Thomson) are recorded in my notes. In quoting the Dyer text I have silently corrected to the text of the first edition (1757) the following, apparently typographical errors:

I, 57: 'seas' (1989), corrected to 'sees'
I, 143: 'bate' (1989), corrected to 'bait'
I, 209: 'curl' (1989), corrected to 'curls'
I, 346: 'six' (1989), corrected to 'sixth'
I, 348: 'they 'ave' (1989), corrected to 'they've'
I, 399: 'flight' (1989), corrected to 'fright'
I, 399: 'left' (1989), corrected to 'lest'
II, 111: 'wood' (1989), corrected to 'wool'.

For other texts used, see *Select bibliography*. See also *Abbreviations*.

Introduction

Thou wilt not find my Shepherdesses idly piping on oaten Reeds, but milking the Kine, tying up the Sheaves, or if the Hogs are astray driving them to their Styes. My Shepherd gathereth none other Nosegays but what are the growth of our own Fields, he sleepeth not under Myrtle shades, but under a Hedge, nor doth he vigilantly defend his Flocks from Wolves, because there are none, as Maister *Spencer* well observeth.   (John Gay, 'Proeme', *The Shepherd's Week*, 1714)

There are, as Gay says, no wolves in the English countryside. The Scottish poet James Thomson had to let his muse wander as far as the mountains of southern Europe, to find wolves for the machinery of sublime terror in his poem 'Winter'. But their absence from the British Isles is not just of literary significance; it played a key part in the nation's history, for the wealth on which the rise of England as an economic power was based came above all from wool; and one of the first conditions for successful sheep husbandry is the absence of *Canis lupus*, the most destructive predator of sheep in temperate and subarctic areas. By isolating the absence of wolves, and patting Spenser on the back for having noticed this, Gay means to mock the drawing together of history and literature, and the assignation of literary value according to economic and patriotic criteria.[1]

The context of his remarks is an introduction, which has been aptly described as 'preposterous', to a set of mock-pastorals he wrote in 1714.[2] Their intention was to satirise the writings of a group of Whig writers who had decided that the time had come to jettison the Mediterranean conventions of neo-classical pastoral poetry, in favour of something more British. It was the misfortune of this group to be represented by Ambrose Philips (1674–1749), whose mawkish imitations of Spenserian diction, principally his *Pastorals* (1709), made him an easy target for the more talented Scriblerian satirists. The result of this has been that Philips is remembered, not as the founder of an English school of pastoral, but as a somewhat ridiculous figure.

Yet despite its ill-starred beginnings, and the wit of Gay's mock-earnest insistence on what is 'real' in the countryside, the movement towards a

1

revived native pastoral, a more engaged and realistic kind of rural writing, was to be as important to the culture of the society which was quickening in the early eighteenth century, as the absence of wolves had been to its economy. From Newcastle upon Tyne where 'Mountains, of Coals' were being 'dug up at every pit', to Bristol where the 'very parsons talked of nothing but trade, and how to turn a penny', the rising mercantile society sought new cultural forms to express new values.[3] The significance of the novel in this process has been well-documented; the role of rural poetry rather less so. Raymond Williams has provided one model; and John Barrell has produced a substantial body of work exploring the movement from comic to exemplary, pastoral to georgic. (I shall be drawing on this work extensively in this book.)[4]

English literature in the seventeenth century had, according to James Turner, 'lost any sense of the countryside as a "field full of folk"'. Considering what he calls 'The Vanishing Swain', he continues:

Virgilian pastoral thrives, but true Georgics are hard to find. The world of work is no longer thought fit for poetry, except in eccentric and popular verse. Like a new colony, the land is cleared of its troublesome natives and planted with a new and more loyal population – hilarious bumpkins, contented morons, fauns, fairies and demigods.[5]

Turner's allusion to a 'field full of folk' implies that we must go back three centuries, to the time of Langland's *Piers the Plowman*, to find the rural labourer decently portrayed. How far, then, would we need to go in the other direction? One answer might be, to 1798 and *Lyrical Ballads*, in which what Wordsworth called the 'necessary character of rural occupations' achieved a new level of engagement and significance.[6] However, Turner implies that 'true Georgics' (were they to be found) might yield something more edifying than the cast of rural inhabitants he mockingly lists; and he exempts 'eccentric and popular verse' from the literary forms which excluded rural labour. Both hints are useful, for if we move forward a little from the seventeenth century, we find new poetic traditions, both 'georgic' and 'popular', in which rural life and labour are strongly present. I am thinking in particular of two forms related to the pastoral tradition: the English mixed georgic; and the proletarian anti-pastoral poem. Both came to prominence in the eighteenth century, and both reflect the new, mercantile society. In this book I shall be examining some examples of the two forms, and tracing in them a number of aspects of rural life and labour. First I would like to look briefly at the forms themselves, and consider their context a little further.

There has been a tendency either to over- or under-define what we mean by 'pastoral'. Literally meaning 'of shepherds', it can easily be assumed to include – taking a well-known modern example, William Empson's *Some Versions of Pastoral* (1935) – subjects such as proletarian literature (ch. I), Elizabethan double-plotting (ch. II), *The Beggar's Opera* (ch. VI), and *Alice in Wonderland* (ch. VII). Indeed, as David Nokes has written: '"pastoral" has become a word of almost infinite elasticity. It is now applied to anything from a pretty landscape picture to the responsibility for attempting to dissuade young people from committing suicide'.[7] Nokes's two examples are obviously designed to show the bizarre expansion of the word's meanings; but they may also serve to delineate a central tension in pastoral, one that helps to account for the fuzziness in our understanding of the word. Pastoral is a manifestation of an apparently universal, pre-conscious, human desire for an ideal and simple world. Because this desire cannot usually be fulfilled in the 'real' world it is the natural territory of art and literature. But, one way or another, the real world always seems to intrude on the fantasy. The intrusion may be direct or indirect, inside or outside the text. It is direct, for example, in Sir Philip Sidney's *Arcadia* (1590), where King Basileus hopes to escape from politics and the responsibilities of kingship into an Arcadian retreat, but cannot avoid bringing his problems with him. Here the pastoral machinery only serves to emphasise the inescapability of reality. Sidney was aware that the pastoral was a kind of illusion or game, and the far-from-innocent plotting of *Arcadia* (the cross-dressing, inappropriate sexual and social behaviour, and so on) serves humorously to acknowledge this.

Indirectly, the real world intrudes through critical hostility to pastoral. This may take the form of critical attacks, as for example when Shakespeare's early critics attacked what they called the 'fantastical' in his plays. Or it may take the form of attempts to modulate the fantasy element of pastoral, by demanding that it adopt a position more overtly related to the 'real world', and especially to the 'real' countryside. We are familiar with this last response to pastoral as an aspect of the modern preoccupation with 'realism'. In the eighteenth century, the demand was not so much for realism as for what might be termed 'responsibility'. Pastoral poetry could justify its existence, and the reader's attention, if, in addition to its traditional ability to satisfy the imaginative need for ideal simplicity it could also, to use a modern phrase, 'earn its keep', by teaching and moralising, by being 'useful'. The English mixed georgic poem offered just such a combination.

There had long been a didactic tradition in English verse; *Piers the Plowman* has been mentioned, and there were many kinds of didactic poetry in the Medieval and Renaissance periods.[8] But it was in the period after 1650 that the factors which were to promote the rise of the English georgic began to appear. Durling describes them as a complex mix of neo-classicism, didacticism and a general increase in interest in theoretical and practical learning.[9] In 1697 Dryden's translation of Virgil appeared. In it the *Georgics* were accompanied by Joseph Addison's 'Essay on Virgil's *Georgics*', in which Addison prophetically delineated those characteristics of the poem which would ensure its appeal, and the success of its imitators, in the eighteenth century.

Virgil's poem, Addison noted approvingly, was written in the 'middle style' (p. 1). The eighteenth-century georgic-writers would construct their own version of this style, principally from two Miltonic elements: the Latinate epic style of *Paradise Lost*, and the more anglicised style of Milton's pastoral poetry, especially 'L'Allegro' and 'Il Penseroso'. In this way they were able to employ certain features of the epic and pastoral genres, without having to work within those genres. This was especially important, not only because of a need, which I have touched upon, to modulate the indulgence and fantasy of pastoral, but also because, as Margaret Anne Doody has shown, epic was distrusted in this period; indeed there was a general distrust of set genres. As Doody says, the 'route to all traditional genres was, like the road to the epic, visibly signed "no entry"'.[10] Thus Addison celebrated the freedom the digressive georgic form offered, taking care to distinguish it from the artifice of pastoral, and emphasising its didactic usefulness. Comparing Virgil's *Georgics* with his *Pastorals*, he writes:

> though the scene of both these poems lies in the same place, the speakers in them are of a quite different character, since the precepts of husbandry are not to be delivered with the simplicity of a plowman, but with the address of a poet. No rules, therefore, that relate to pastoral can any way affect the *Georgics*, since they fall under that class of poetry which consists of giving plain and direct instructions to the reader.   (p. 1)

There is in the *Georgics* none of the pastoral simulation by which the poet pretends to be a rustic, to Addison's obvious relief. But neither is georgic, as the phrase 'plain and direct instructions' might suggest, a dull, earth-bound kind of writing. Addison insists on its poetic qualities, finding it the ideal medium for instruction precisely because it is poetry, and so 'addresses itself wholly to the imagination' (p. 2). Virgil's poem, he considers, is:

> altogether conversant among the fields and woods and has the most delightful part of nature for its province. It raises in our minds a pleasing variety of scenes and landscapes whilst it teaches us, and makes the driest of its precepts look like a description.   (p. 2)

This was the perfect combination the new society sought, a poetry which could maintain its traditional lyricism, and its interest in nature and rural life, while also offering, by a kind of sleight-of-hand, moral and practical instruction. The genre could now be defined: 'A georgic, therefore, is some part of the science of husbandry put into a pleasing dress, and set off with all the beauties and embellishments of poetry' (p. 2). Addison continues his essay with a more detailed examination of the techniques Virgil uses to blend didacticism and poetry; and his praise of the way Virgil 'breaks the clods and tosses the dung about with an air of gracefulness' (p. 6) has been much quoted. If the eighteenth-century sensibility required its rural poetry to be purposeful as well as poetic, this was not to be achieved at the expense of decorum; and the need for georgic-writers to maintain the 'high' style alongside the 'low' aspects of the georgic would have an important influence on the progress of the form. It may be seen, for example, in the tendency of early georgic-writers to offset the 'lowness' of the form by the distancing procedure of including an element of burlesque or mockery in their georgics.

A good example of this is John Gay's series of georgics (*Wine*, 1708; *Rural Sports*, 1713; *The Fan*, 1714; *Trivia*, 1716). In these poems, the teacherly function of the georgic is subtly undercut by elements of humour, parody, burlesque, and deliberate inappropriateness. The 'lowness' of georgic is made a part of Gay's creative mixing-up of styles, purposes and generic expectations. This kind of approach was especially characteristic of the Scriblerian writers, but we also find it in other georgic-writers of the period, for whom the Addisonian view of georgic held strong. Thus the most successful of the early georgic-writers, John Philips (1676–1709), prepared the way for his georgic poem *Cyder* (1708), by writing burlesque Miltonic verses (*The Splendid Shilling*, 1701), and a mock-georgic (*Cerealia*, 1706). In *Cyder* itself, Philips luxuriates in the richness of his neo-Miltonic diction, purposefully allowing its excesses to offer a humorous antidote to the more earnest elements of his poem.

Philips's was an attractive model, much plundered by Pope and other contemporaries, and routinely praised in the text of later georgics. *Cyder* showed the potential richness and variety of English georgic poetry. The genre could encompass a number of different styles, including pastoral and epic, panegyric, topographic, epistolatory and meditative verse. It could address philosophy and the sciences, geography and history, politics and trade. Its tone could range from the humorous to the serious, its manner from the satiric and polemical to the lyrical. Agricultural prescription provided a unifying central focus for these diverse styles and subjects.

Later writers would pursue its diversity into different areas. It could be used to address a particular facet of rural life. William Somerville's poem *The Chace* (1735), for example, was the best of many georgics devoted to hunting, fishing and field sports. Different kinds of agriculture inspired georgics on specialist subjects, such as Christopher Smart's *The Hop-Garden* (1752). Further afield, James Grainger addressed Caribbean agriculture in *The Sugar Cane* (1764), as did several other poets. The georgic could instruct in other areas of knowledge, too. John Armstrong's extraordinary verse account of the circulation of the blood and the operation of the digestive system, in *The Art of Preserving Health* (1744, see especially Book II, lines 12–95), is a good example of the widening of the georgic's subject matter, in one of a number of georgics on the subject of health. John Gay (*Trivia*, 1716) was the first of many to take the georgic into the city; while John Dyer, whose poem *The Fleece* (1757) we shall be examining, included for the first time industrial locations and processes. Erasmus Darwin (1791–89) used the genre to teach botany, with digressions to his many other scientific and philanthropic interests. By the end of the eighteenth century the form had been used to teach or to discuss an impressive range of practical and philosophical subjects.[11]

Nor was the georgic restricted to didacticism. For some of the most successful georgic-writers of the century, the practical instruction which was the form's major characteristic was merely a stepping-stone to greater poetical purposes. Pope, for example, used the georgic form in *Windsor Forest* (1713) to convey his political and historical ideas, drawing heavily on the patriotic potential of the form, and using elements of pastoral, topography and mythology to focus the poem. More ambitiously still, James Thomson united many different themes and styles into a coherent four-part seasonal structure, in *The Seasons* (1730), the most influential and important of the eighteenth-century georgics.

We shall be examining one of Thomson's themes, rural labour, in some detail, and comparing it with two contemporary poetic treatments of the subject, Stephen Duck's *The Thresher's Labour* (1730), and Mary Collier's *The Woman's Labour* (1739). I have used the phrase 'proletarian anti-pastoral poem' to characterise these last two poems, and I shall have something further to say about their 'anti-pastoral' quality and its literary sources when we examine the poems. Here, we may very briefly consider their place within the developments we have been discussing.

Labour is a characteristic theme of the English georgic, in contrast to the pastoral, in which labour is normally hidden. The georgic presents a positive, and even a heroic view of labour, as a pleasurable and a socially progressive activity. Poets such as Duck and Collier place labour at the centre of their poems, in the georgic manner; but their proletarian background, and their first-hand experience of labour led them to take a harsher, more negative view than is usual to georgic. They indeed responded to the new interest in labour as a subject for poetry, and participated in the georgic tradition; but at the same time theirs was effectively a counter-movement, refuting not only the idealisation of labour in the georgic, but the whole edifice of pastoral verse and pastoral attitudes. A satisfactory title for their genre has not been formulated, partly because their work has been rather neglected in the past, though it seems to me to represent an important response to the georgic tradition.

I have stressed the Virgilian georgic tradition here; but there were, of course, many other kinds of rural poetry in the eighteenth century. The pastoral eclogue found new forms and themes; loco-descriptive and topographic poetry became increasingly popular (there was always a good supply of unsung prospects and localities to celebrate, and an interest in the local and the particular). The Horatian forms were also very popular, inspiring numerous variations on the themes of 'town versus country' and 'the happy man'. All these kinds of poetry, and other, less common forms, are of interest.[12] We shall, however, be concentrating, in what follows, on poetry which derives from the tradition of Virgil's *Georgics*. This is not only because, in the words of a modern critic, the *Georgics* 'occupied a unique position as the perfect poem' in the eighteenth century;[13] but because Virgil in many ways set the agenda for the period's most serious attempts to tackle the subject of rural life, whether we consider the work of Thomson or Dyer, Duck or Collier, Cowper or Crabbe.[14]

PART I

'Hard Labour we most chearfully pursue'
Three poets on rural work

Thomson, Duck, Collier and rural realism

Jonathan Swift's complaint that *The Seasons* are 'all Description, and nothing is doing' reflects a fundamentally negative view of rural life as a serious subject for pastoral and georgic. The man credited with the idea of a 'Newgate Pastoral, among the whores and thieves there' could not perhaps be expected to find stimulation in *The Seasons*, for at the heart of James Thomson's vision is a view of the rural world that has little in common with the literary manipulations of Scriblerian pastoral and mock-pastoral.[1] For Thomson the rural world is not only the traditional Horatian alternative to the corrupt city, but also the model for his particular philosophical views. James Sambrook divides the concerns of the poem into categories: 'devotional', 'scientific', 'georgic', 'geographical, historical and narrative', 'descriptive' and 'subjective'. The poem is a 'portmanteau' of themes and genres, one strand of which I shall be extracting for critical attention in what follows. But it also has a central theme, a single informing idea: Sambrook's comparison with Lucretius' *De Rerum Natura* is helpful in this respect. Each 'season' has a central 'force'. In 'Spring' it is the 'Soul of Love' (line 582), the restorative and renewing power of that season. In 'Summer' it is the sun, the 'powerful King of Day' (line 81) that dominates. In 'Autumn' the controlling image is more diffuse, as the poet moves between a warm benevolence reminiscent of summer, and a more forbidding environment that anticipates winter. The 'weighty Rains' (line 738), and the cycle of water Thomson describes (lines 736–835) perhaps give a central image. 'Winter' focuses closely on the sublimity of the season's 'Cogenial Horrors' (line 6, 'Congenial' in some later editions). Each of these four forces is for Thomson the manifestation of a deity: this is expressed directly in 'Summer' in the description of the sun as 'Soul of surrounding Worlds! in whom best seen / Shines out thy Maker!' (lines 95–6).[2]

The movement in *The Seasons* typically progresses upwards ('progress' and 'upwards' are two favourite words in the poem) through a pyramidal hierarchy. We can see this in 'Spring', for example, where first plant-life, then birds, then man emerge into the new season (see lines 17, 22–5, 33–7). Man, on earth at least, is at the top of the hierarchy. His emergence from savagery through industry and learning is much rehearsed – though the pastoral-based idea of a descent from a golden age is contradictorily present too, while the praise of Newton ('Spring', lines 203–17) shows a typically economic Thomsonian melding of the praise of God's creation (the rainbow) and of man's ingenuity in interpreting it (Newton).

The poem is carefully orchestrated to illustrate and illuminate a single theme, and Johnson's accusation of 'want of method' in the poem, in his 'Life' of Thomson, is in this respect misleading.[3] The tone and message of that theme is one of triumphant harmony. We need to be aware, in extracting a single strand from the poem, that this tone and theme constitute the major context for all the individual elements of the poem, including the set-piece descriptions of rural labour which will be our principal concern here. The poem has a unitary purpose, and what it says about any individual issue is ultimately guided by that purpose.

Like Thomson, Stephen Duck is ultimately concerned with a single theme, but his theme strikingly opposes Thomson's. *The Thresher's Labour* was commissioned by Duck's local patron, the Reverend Mr Stanley, as a poem 'on his own Labours'.[4] Duck uses a method and a genre which are as focused as Thomson's, and in their way just as original. In the poem the seasonal and agricultural cycle, traditionally used (not least by Thomson) as a model of harmony and of pleasing *concordia discors*, becomes a dehumanising machine, controlled by 'The Master', and driving the farm workers relentlessly through a never-ending cycle of backbreaking work. It is, as the editors of the *Penguin Book of English Pastoral Verse* acknowledge, an 'anti-pastoral'.[5] But the fact that it is the first anti-pastoral in their anthology is interesting. Our information about Duck's education and development as a poet make it surprising that he would pioneer a new kind of poetry. His chief literary influences, read in the time he could snatch from his farm work, were mainstream texts such as Addison's *Spectator*, Milton's *Paradise Lost* (read with the help of a dictionary and a book of grammar), and Edward Bysshe's *The Art of English Poetry* (1702). His sources seem conventional, and the frequent use of often rather forced epic similes in *The Thresher's Labour* gives some indication of the constraints and inadequacies of his self-education.

Anti-pastoral was available in the early eighteenth century, notably in William Diaper's *Brent* (1726). Diaper's main anti-pastoral device is to attack the English weather, but he also finds time to complain about food, drink, and many of the features of the English countryside. Duck sometimes hits a similar note, seen for example if we compare Diaper's 'No joyous birds here stretch their tuneful throats' with Duck's 'No cheerful sound diverts the list'ning ear' (p. 4), though we have no evidence he had seen Diaper's poem, or indeed any anti-pastoral.[6] It seems that he has independently thought of the idea of creating an unrelievedly negative picture (though we will see some relenting in this when we look more closely at his poem). Certainly his central idea of turning the farming year into a malevolent and merciless machine is, as far as can be established, his own original contribution to the genre.

So Thomson seeks harmony and what he calls 'social Glee' ('Summer', line 370) in rural labour, while for Duck 'Tis all a dull and melancholy Scene / Fit only to provoke the Muses' Spleen' (p. 4).[7] The third poem I want to look at here is also primarily an anti-pastoral, and at first sight has an easily defined relationship with that genre: *The Woman's Labour* was written in response to *The Thresher's Labour*, as its author, Mary Collier, wittily explains in the autobiographical 'Remarks of the Author's Life', which preface the 1762 edition of her works. When she was a washer-woman in Petersfield: 'Duck's Poems came abroad, which I soon got by heart, fancying he had been too Severe on the Female Sex in his Thresher's Labour brought me to a Strong propensity to call an Army of Amazons to vindicate the injured Sex: Therefore I answer'd him to please my own humour.'[8] Collier's first purpose, then, was to refute Duck's accusation of idleness in women, which she does with vigour, answering him point for point. However, her methodology and genre are more complex than those of Duck's poem. Generically her poem has some Thomsonian, portmanteau-like qualities. It is, for example, both an imitation and a parody of *The Thresher's Labour*, extending some of that poem's themes and methods into new areas. Collier echoes and extends Duck's complaint of a hard working life by describing a working life some degrees harsher than his, and comparing it in detail with his. Whereas Duck's dreams are haunted ('Our Labours ev'n in Sleep don't cease', p. 11), Collier replies that 'we have hardly ever *Time to dream*' (p. 20), which 'trumps' his complaint, and raises the anti-pastoral stakes. She highlights each echo/reply to Duck (as here) with italics, to emphasise her imitation of, reply to and parody of each element in Duck's vision. It is a method worthy of the Scriblerians in its double-edged irony.

She also imitates and mocks the rather heavy classicism of 'great Duck', as she calls him, notably in an opening burlesque passage written in the manner of neo-classical 'decline of' poetry:

> *Jove* once descending from the clouds did drop
> In show'rs of gold on lovely *Danae's* lap;
> The sweet-tongu'd Poets, in those generous days,
> Unto our Shrine still offer'd up their Lays:
> But now, alas! that Golden Age is past,
> We are the objects of your Scorn at last. (p. 16)

The splendid classicism of this writing is striking, and I shall discuss some of its mythology later. There is at least a hint, too, of eighteenth-century patriotic panegyric, as when she rails against Duck's hostility to women talking:

> In this, I hope, you do not speak your mind,
> For none but *Turks,* that I could ever find,
> Have Mutes to serve them, or did e'er deny
> Their Slaves, at Work, to chat it merrily.
> Since you have Liberty to speak your mind,
> And are to talk, as well as we, inclin'd,
> Why should you thus repine, because that we,
> Like you, enjoy that pleasing Liberty?   (p. 17)

The 'Liberty' here is the traditional liberty of 'God's Englishmen', celebrated in Thomson's poem *Liberty* (1735–6) and elsewhere, and signalled by Collier's chauvinistic contempt for the unenlightened 'Turks'. Women, of course, were not numbered among 'God's Englishmen', and Collier ironically undercuts the patriotic rhetoric she has set up when she suggests that she and her fellow women workers are 'Slaves'.

There is also in the poem a range of humorous and satirical devices, notably the Popean zeugma she uses to show mock-sympathy to Duck's complaint against women, and:

> Those mighty Troubles which perplex your Mind,
> (*Thistles* before, and *Females* come behind).   (p. 19)

Collier's poem includes elements of heroic and mock-heroic, panegyric and satire. It is also both pastoral and anti-pastoral: as we shall discover when we look more closely at her description of labour, there are ways in which she takes up pastoral ideas present in Thomson's poem, as well as the anti-pastoral ideas from Duck.

We find in these three poems a cross-section of approaches to rural labour, including elements of idealism and realism, pastoral and anti-pastoral, humour and seriousness. The perspectives range from the visionary overview of Thomson's poem, to the minutiae of conditions and tasks catalogued by Duck and Collier. There is a good deal of contrast and contradiction, as well as areas of agreement and similarity between the three poets. A number of critics have made comparisons between the images of rural life presented in *The Seasons* and *The Thresher's Labour,* and it has become a familiar approach for introductory work on both Duck and Collier.[9] There are obvious reasons for this. The poems appeared in the same year, 1730. They offer contrasting views of rural life and labour, both of which seem more original and more intensely expressed than anything written earlier in the century. Thomson and Duck seem to have had some influence on each other; and *The Seasons* became a touchstone for later rural poets, and was especially cherished by the self-taught poets who emerged in increasing numbers following Duck's success.[10] And although their backgrounds were very different, Thomson and Duck were close contemporaries (Thomson was born at Ednam, Roxburghshire, in September 1700, Duck at Charlton, Wiltshire, in 1705). Their major successes occurred in the same year (also 1730).

If comparisons between *The Woman's Labour* and the Thomson and Duck poems have only recently begun to be made, it is because Mary Collier had until the last few years been entirely forgotten. The modern rediscovery of her dates from 1974, when Sheila Rowbotham printed an extract of *The Woman's Labour* in her book *Hidden from History*; Mary Chamberlain included a passage in her *Fenwomen* the following year. Now that she has been rediscovered, comparisons do spring to mind, and have been made, particularly with *The Thresher's Labour*, which Collier's poem directly addresses and replies to; but also with *The Seasons*, which offers a contemporary poetic view of rural labour, including women's labour. Some biographical similarity may be seen between Collier and Duck: fifteen years, and the county of Hampshire, separate their dates and places of birth, but nothing separates their social class – both received only rudimentary education, Duck in a Dame School, Collier with her mother. And if the sharpness of *The Woman's Labour* suggests a gap between the two, Mary Collier's declaration that she 'soon got by heart' Duck's poems suggests a strong empathy with him; and the elegy his suicide moved her to write is clearly heartfelt.[11]

That comparisons between the three poets should focus on their description of rural labour is equally unsurprising: the subject is central to Duck and Collier, and Thomson's vignettes of rural work provide important focusing points in his poem. Descriptions of rural labour are not common in the early eighteenth century, either in poetry or in prose. John Barrell shows that significant interest in what he calls 'more actualised images' of rural life by those who purchased books and paintings was a phenomenon of the later part of the century. The degree to which writers presented 'actualised' rural labour in the early part of the century (implying some degree of central attention and focus as well as a more 'realistic' approach) was limited.[12] The three descriptions of rural labour offer some interesting contrasts: between the approaches of a professional poet and of two labourer-poets; between male and female writers; between pastoral and anti-pastoral. These factors make comparison between these texts of historical as well as literary interest.

Clearly the comparison is worth making, and it has often been made, though never in very much detail. Rayner Unwin (1954) makes three short comparisons of work-description between Thomson and Duck. Alan Warner (1967) quotes parallel passages of *The Seasons* and *The Thresher's Labour* on haymaking, and briefly discusses them. H. Gustav Klaus (1985) quotes an abbreviated version of the Thomson haymaking passage, noting Duck's 'break' from its sensibilities, and the significance of Collier's 'courageous reply to Duck, who quite obviously did not include the female agricultural worker in his "we"'. Donna Landry (1990), in the fullest and most theoretically alert reading of *The Woman's Labour* to date, makes a number of comparisons and contrasts with Duck and Thomson; and John Barrell (1992) compares the harvests of Duck and Thomson, making some reference to Collier. The editors of both the modern 'back-to-back' editions of *The Thresher's Labour* and *The Woman's Labour* take up the comparison in their Introductions, dealing on the whole sympathetically with both writers and both sets of experiences.[13]

These comparisons raise important critical issues about the relationship between poetry and history, and we may look briefly at these issues here. All the critics I have cited tend to make comparative decisions about the veracity of the three accounts. A clear division, for example, is made between Thomson and Duck, in terms of historical 'truth'. Unwin (p. 62), contrasts Thomson's 'Arcadia with verisimilitude' with Duck's 'unimaginative statements of fact'. Klaus (p. 13), distinguishes between the 'view expressed' by Thomson, and the 'unadorned presentation of agricultural labour' by Duck. For Warner (pp. 40–3), Thomson's description is a 'generalised literary picture', Duck's 'an authentic picture of cutting the hay'. Landry (pp. 68–9), finds Thomson to be a 'disembodied, disinterested observer rather than a participant in the labor and hardships being described', his poem 'the production of a privileged leisured observer'. Collier's poem by contrast has 'vivid simplicity'.

The theoretical issues raised by such critical contrasting of authenticity and inauthenticity, and the privileging of texts written by those deemed to be more engaged with rural labour, are complex. By their rarity, and the fact that they engage an important aspect of contemporary social life, these poetic descriptions of rural life are naturally of historical interest. But some thought clearly needs to be given as to what kinds of historical information they offer, and how we can judge 'authenticity'. The critics I have quoted all see Thomson's text as primarily 'literary', and Duck and/or Collier by contrast as plain purveyors of truth. One text is a poem; the other two are, effectively, historical documents.

The view of Collier and Duck is the more worrying. A poet is not a social historian, though s/he may incorporate this role; a poem is not merely a statement of fact, a regurgitation of sensuous or statistical information. The processes by which a poet selects from experiences and beliefs, selects genre, imagery, language, and develops all these elements into a literary artefact are sophisticated; and modern literary and linguistic theory teaches us, too, that language is not simply 'transparent' in the way that a direct reading of history from literature may assume. In the case of the Duck and Collier poems, I have briefly considered some of the ways in which they are 'literary' as well as documentary. Duck's poem includes epic similes (noted by Warner), prosody, dramatisation, epithets, alliteration and a coherent, structured anti-pastoral machinery. Collier uses parody, imitation and elements of satire, pastoral and anti-pastoral, heroic and mock-heroic in sophisticated and equally clearly literary ways.

Neither do the biographical accounts of these two writers suggest that their writings are simply concerned with transmitting the truth of their working lives. Duck's interest in literature began with a love of 'P[s]alms & singing, & Ballads', a 'certain Longing after Knowledge', and the unexpected bonus of access to a friend's cache of classical and modern literary texts. Though the content and methods of his poetry were swiftly colonised by his various patrons and discoverers he certainly wrote at least one poem ('On Poverty') unsupervised, and probably others too.[14] Mary Collier likewise recalls that her 'Recreation was reading', in which she graduated from 'any foolish History' to religious tracts. When Duck's poems 'came abroad' she learned them by heart, and wrote her reply 'to please my own humour'.[15] Both were primarily interested in what is now called 'creative writing'. Their social class and labouring experiences are of course a crucial element in all these developments. Literature was not usually available to these writers, who latched on to whatever texts were available, and their natural first subject matter was their 'situation' in society, which dominated their waking lives (their time, resources and opportunities to read and write). But this does not mean that they had no other aspiration than to record the social history of their lives; and even less that their poems are not *poetry*, with all its characteristics of abstraction, idealisation, structural and rhythmic patterns, but merely records. It seems to me these modern readings of the poems are in danger of falling into a fallacy, whereby the fact that these writers were proletarian has become the all-encompassing consideration in reading their poems. Because Stephen Duck was a farm labourer it is assumed too easily not only that what he says about farm work must be true, but that in this truth lies the whole of the poetry's significance.

There are historical reasons for this fallacy. Most importantly, in the case of Duck, it seems to have the backing of George Crabbe, whose attack on the falseness of pastoral poetry, at the beginning of *The Village* (1783), exempts 'honest Duck' from the roll-call of liars, and pledges that he (Crabbe) will, 'paint the Cot, / As Truth will paint it, and as Bards will not' (I, lines 53–4). I would express several reservations about this, however. Crabbe is writing within a poem here, his truth therefore a poetic truth; in any case the eighteenth-century conception of truth in poetry (especially that of Johnson and his circle) is not the same as twentieth-century realism, but is rather concerned with a moral-didactic truth. *The Village* is not a documentary description of a 'real' village, but an abstracted progression of counter-pastoral images designed to prove certain truths which, for Crabbe, pastoral poetry has hitherto neglected or denied. And most importantly, if we put Crabbe's phrase 'honest Duck' back into its context, we can see that he clearly accepts what the critics I have quoted seem to be denying: that Duck is a poet as well as a peasant:

> Save honest Duck, what son of verse could share
> The poet's rapture and the peasant's care?
>
> (*The Village*, I, lines 27–8)

Crabbe specifically highlights here the 'sharing' of the roles, the unique combination that gives Duck's poetry its strength.

By contrast the critics under discussion have little place for 'The poet's rapture' in their accounts of Duck and Collier. Conversely, and very much influenced by the idea of Duck as truth-teller, any pretensions Thomson may have to veracity are put aside. He seems, says Warner, 'to be viewing the scene from the roadside as a tourist or gentleman of leisure' (p. 42). This is a familiar but limiting view; and as with Duck and Collier the issue is class. The professional, middle-class poet may not be trusted to give an accurate view of what farm work is like, because he has probably never done any; a worker is a worker, and a poet is a poet, and neither can write 'out of' their role; social class determines and delimits human capability.

Such an approach reaches its crisis in comparisons between Duck and Collier: for here we have two labourer-poets contradicting each other. Which one is the authentic voice of history? Rayner Unwin (p. 62), as an advocate of Duck, accepts as knowledge Duck's attack on women workers for working too little and talking too much, assuring us that 'Duck knew well that "the tattling croud" had no place amongst Wiltshire harvesters'. Donna Landry, raising the flag for Mary Collier Studies after a 250-year neglect, champions Collier. I should say at once that I think Unwin is palpably wrong in his statement, but my opinion is not based on the accounts of Duck and Collier, but in the fact, easily established 'outside' the texts, in conventional historical sources, that women and men have worked alongside each other in harvest fields throughout history. Analysis of the poetic opinions of Duck and Collier would not provide an adequate substitute for other kinds of historical research in this, even if their accounts agreed, which they do not.

The issue also depends on what kind of historical 'truth' one is looking for. If we look more closely at the central elements of the Collier-Duck dispute we can see that the issue is not simply one of 'facts', but of opinions, priorities, areas of attention, the modulation and presentation of practical and aesthetic concerns, and the construction of poetry. Duck's anti-feminist statement consists of a thirty-line description of the second day of the hay harvest. In the morning the master arrives with a group of women 'arm'd with Rake and Prong' to turn the hay. The poet's constant theme throughout his description is their talk, which he derisively describes as 'prattling', 'noise', 'tattling' and so on. He wishes 'their Hands were active as their Tongues', says they sit around talking when their break is finished, is mock-baffled by the fact that they all seem to talk at once, and so cannot be understood by bystanders, and finally directs a shower of rain on to the field, at which:

> Their noisy Prattle all at once is done,
> And to the Hedge they all for Shelter run.   (p. 8)[16]

I shall have something to say later about the significance of Duck's resentment of their talking; what I want to consider here is his literary purpose in this descriptive passage, which seems to me predominant, and which is made plain by the new verse-paragraph that follows the couplet I have quoted, in which he declares:

> Thus have I seen on a bright Summer's day,
> On some green brake a Flock of Sparrows play.
> From twig to twig, from bush to bush they fly,
> And with continu'd chirping fill the Sky,
> But on a sudden, if a Storm appears,
> Their chirping noise no longer dins your ears;
> They fly for shelter to the thickest bush,
> Their silent sit, and all at once is hush.   (pp. 8–9)[17]

This is a very carefully planned and executed simile, clearly the product of Duck's nights with *Paradise Lost*, Bysshe's *Art of English Poetry* and Addison's *Spectator*, the last of which would have told him that 'the Ancients' in their similes 'provided there was a likeness ... did not much trouble themselves about the decency of the comparison', that the similes of the heroic poets are designed to 'fill the mind with great conceptions', and that Milton 'never quits his simile till it rises to some very great idea'.[18] His primary purpose, in other words, is a literary one; a piece of natural observation of birds falling silent has moved him to try his hand at an extended simile.

Mary Collier's comment on this passage from Duck is that 'on our abject State you throw your Scorn, / And Women wrong, your Verses to adorn' (p. 16). This is astutely perceptive, and recognises the primarily literary intention of Duck's scene of women in the hayfield. Duck is in fact concerned with working two familiar literary devices into the scene: this simile, and a thunderstorm, the latter a familiar georgic device. Like Thomson he is economical with his imagery, and thus he gives his resentment of the women's talk a threefold literary purpose, as an element of his anti-pastoral machinery, as the occasion for the thunderstorm which will silence them, and (as a result) as the focus for his epic simile. Collier's anger at Duck is thus accurately focused on the trivialisation, the 'Scorn' as she calls it, of his making literary capital out of his chauvinistic attitudes; but she recognises that the problem is not primarily caused by the issue of veracity *per se*, but distortions caused by Duck's concern with style at the expense of content. (This of course in no sense excuses his attitude, either for her or for the modern reader.)

Duck is not actually thinking very much at all about what the women are doing in the hayfield. Collier recognises this, and her counter-version of the hayfield scene, in which she draws on her own remembered experience of haymaking, locates a telling inconsistency in Duck's account, which she pounces on and wittily quotes against him. Having completed his epic simile Duck is concerned with turning the mood of the poem from one of painful work to the aesthetic satisfaction of completion:

> But better Fate succeeds this rainy Day,
> And little Labour serves to make the Hay;
> Fast as 'tis cut, so kindly shines the Sun,
> Turn'd once or twice, the pleasing Work is done.
> Next day the Cocks appear in equal Rows,
> Which the glad Master in safe Ricks bestows.   (p. 9)

To which Collier gleefully replies:

> For my own part, I many a Summer's Day
> Have spent in throwing, turning, making Hay;
> But ne'er could see, what you have lately found,
> Our Wages paid for sitting on the Ground.
> 'Tis true, that when our Morning's Work is done,
> And all our Grass expos'd unto the Sun,
> While that his scorching Beams do on it shine,
> As well as you we have a time to dine:
> I hope that since we freely toil and sweat
> To earn our Bread, you'll give us time to eat.
> That over, soon we must get up again,
> And nimbly turn our Hay upon the plain,
> Nay, rake and prow it in, the case is clear,
> Or how should *Cocks in equal Rows* appear?   (pp. 16–17)[19]

Duck's pleasure in the 'equal rows' is closer in spirit to William Shenstone's aestheticising *ferme ornée* ideas of 'throw[ing] all your haystacks into the form of pyramids', than to the realities of a working hayfield; and in focusing on the pleasure of (his) completion he has casually marginalised the women's work.[20] The hay is 'turn'd once or twice' – by women of course, though Duck makes it sound as if the sun is doing the 'pleasing' Work; and the haycocks 'appear', as Collier cannily notices, in an apparent act of self-creation, though she knows that it is the women who build them. We are faced here not simply with the question of veracity, but with literary and aesthetic issues, which Collier's reply shows she is well aware of. We cannot simply ignore the literary elements in this kind of writing, which are as important as the accuracy of its social history (for Duck in this instance *more* important), and in any case are inextricably linked with it.

Of course it would be foolish to suggest that there is no basis for the idea that Duck and Collier generally exhibit a greater concern with the harsh realities of rural work than Thomson, that they know more about it, and that Thomson is concerned with a more 'idealistic' vision than those of the two self-taught poets. A farm labourer like Duck and a working woman like Collier are by the nature of things likely to be better chroniclers of what rural labour feels like than a professional writer like Thomson; and the grand overview of Thomson's poem is equally likely to lead him to describe things harmoniously and ideally. What I would challenge is the reductive notion that the two 'labour' poems are purely factual, and the injustice it leads to in its failure to acknowledge what (after all) was the central aspiration of Duck and Collier: to write poetry, to be poets. Another kind of patronage hovers about this approach, with its talk of 'vivid simplicity', 'unadorned presentation' and 'unimaginative statements of fact', however much it lionises the veracity of the self-taught poets. Similarly if we strip these poems of poetry, and ascribe that quality solely to Thomson, he is bound to look excessively literary, though of course Duck, Collier and many other self-taught poets, from Robert Tatersal to John Clare, were also literary in their theory and their practice. We cannot simply 'dredge out', in Pat Rogers's graphic expression, 'a little inert social history' from these poems, if their essential life as poems and as historical documents has been extinguished by our refusal to take their authors' intentions seriously.[21]

What can we then learn from a comparison of these poetic accounts of rural life? E. P. Thompson's introduction to *The Thresher's Labour* and *The Woman's Labour* perhaps gives a hint. He takes a mildly ironic approach to the Duck-Collier controversy, firstly setting up Duck's authority: 'Men had long known about the deficiencies of female labour, and Duck's poem confirmed this knowledge. Who, after all, would know better than a Wiltshire thresher?' But then offering another rhetorical question to answer the first one: 'Well, perhaps a woman labourer might?' This leaves the reader to decide, but also accepts both views as 'historical', not in the way I have attacked, of making one or both 'true' in a documentary way, but in the sense that they reflect the views of the historical figures, Stephen Duck and Mary Collier. The information they provide is not a substitute for historical research, but a potentially important element of it.[22]

It seems to me that what is most 'real' about a poem like *The Woman's Labour* is the way in which it seeks and finds a literary expression for Collier's feelings about her experience of haymaking: her pride in it as part of her personal history, her righteous anger at what she feels is Duck's misrepresentation. Like Duck, she feels the experience in terms of hard work. Like Thomson, her portrayal of haymaking is essentially optimistic, though in a more tempered way. Where his optimism is sustained by pastoral idyll, and the idea of 'social glee' (a togetherness that makes work pleasurable), hers (though also suggesting that idea) is centrally sustained by the idea of 'nimbly' conquering the work. Duck also seeks to conquer the work, though his is a more competitive, less sociable work-ethic than those of Thomson or Collier. There are similarities and differences between the three accounts of haymaking; but the way they connect with the 'real world' is through the particular experiences, social roles, education, temper, literary purposes and techniques of the three writers: their ideas and their ideologies, their dreams and their realities.

We cannot understand fully their significance in eighteenth-century culture, or to eighteenth-century rural life, by arranging them into rigid hierarchies of realism, or by casting their authors into class-based preconceptions of what they can and cannot be (the diminutive use of 'Stephen' for Duck, by several critics, is ominous in this respect). Thus the comparison between images of rural life in *The Seasons*, *The Thresher's Labour* and *The Woman's Labour* that follows does not attempt just to weigh the relationship between the poems and the 'reality' of rural life (though this is of course considered); but examines them also as poetry, and in terms of the ideas and attitudes their words and images express. If this is a longer and more tentative route to learning from them something about the early eighteenth century, it is perhaps fairer to the writers and more appropriate to their procedures and intentions than earlier comparative studies.

2

Initiations and peak times

Going to work

The distribution and organisation of labour in rural poetry is a helpful indicator of the concerns of the poet. How is labour initiated? In Milton's portrayal of Eden, Eve attempts to divide rationally the work between herself and Adam:

> Adam, well may we labor still to dress
> This garden, still to tend plant, herb, and flow'r,
> Our pleasant task enjoined, but till more hands
> Aid us, the work under our labor grows,
> Luxurious by restraint ...
> Let us divide our labors.   (*Paradise Lost*, IX, line 205 ff.)

Eve's primitive socialism suggests much more than it seems to. For the cautious Adam, Eden is a place of dangerous temptation, where 'I should mind thee oft, and mind thou me' (IX, line 358), and their separation, for whatever practical reason, is potentially hazardous. A simple division that makes sense to Eve symbolises a serious ideological disunity, which leads to disaster. The subtext that Satan may have put this idea in her head is slightly remote (her dream is five books earlier), but the important point is that for Milton labour, its division and its implementation, so important in the Puritans' world-view, is the natural territory of ideology, and of ideological conflict.

For Alexander Pope, by contrast, it is not, and rural labour in his *Pastorals* is initiated with studied lassitude. The speaker in 'Summer' says 'Let other Swains attend the Rural Care' (line 35), while in 'Spring' Strephon says to Daphnis, 'Sing then, and Damon shall attend the Strain / While yon slow Oxen turn the furrow'd plain' (lines 29–30). The lurking pun on 'strain' reflects the separation of function between these swains, whose only duty is to sing and to listen, and the labouring world – 'other swains' and 'oxen' – for whom strain means toil. We can see in this a reflection of Pope's strongly idealistic conception of pastoral, as a place where 'we are not to describe our shepherds as shepherds at this day really are'.[1] His intention is to recreate a 'golden age', and his golden age turns out to be rather more laid-back than Milton's Eden.

These two examples indicate the extremes of ideological significance that may be attached to the deployment and initiation of labour. Eve's attempt to divide the labour rationally may be read as a response of 'free will' to the question Adam has framed, of 'How we might best fulfil the work which here / God hath assigned us' (IX, lines 230–1); but which demonstrates for Milton the double-edged quality of free will. Pope's swains are artfully arbitrary about work because work is not a significant factor in the ideology and aesthetics of Popean pastoral.

In different ways Thomson, Duck and Collier offer very much more ordered modes of labour initiation than these two earlier poets, and in doing so show the ways in which they see work as an important social function. Thomson's first scene of rural labour begins:

> Forth fly the tepid Airs; and unconfin'd,
> Unbinding Earth, the moving Softness strays.
> Joyous, th'impatient Husbandman perceives
> Relenting Nature, and his lusty Steers
> Drives from their Stalls.   ('Spring', lines 32–6)

At first sight it seems that something like Eve's free will is the initiator: the husbandman apparently makes an independent decision on the basis of a change in the weather. The earth has thawed and dried out sufficiently to become workable, and Thomson dramatises what every farmer knows: that seasonal tasks are best begun the moment that time and weather (forces which are both constantly present in this poem) permit. The husbandman, by whom (as the emergence of the 'Master' later in this passage makes clear), Thomson means the farm labourer, is simultaneously 'joyous' and 'impatient', which gives further impetus to the idea of him as self-motivating. But the principal mover in the passage is nevertheless 'Nature', for whose 'relenting' the husbandman has to wait. In Robert Bloomfield's popular imitation of Thomson's poem, *The Farmer's Boy* (1800), in a slightly different seasonal context, 'Nature herself invites the Reapers forth', which provides a nice gloss to Thomson. Nature, or rather its controlling seasonal cycle, is the manifestation of the deity, the 'varied God' of Thomson's poem, and the deity is seen as ultimate controller of the work, and of its initiation.[2] Thomson's constant theme in *The Seasons* is the harmoniousness of things, and the husbandman's joyousness may be read as the first of many instances of optimistic, forward-looking initiations, which set the pitch for this harmony. The poet uses his privileged position within the conventions of georgic prescription to provide social motivation to the human side of this initiation, directly advising the swain to 'be patient' ('Spring', line 137), broadening his address in order to tell his countrymen to 'venerate the Plow' ('Spring', line 67), and so on.

Duck's overall purpose is of course entirely opposed to Thomson's, and the benevolent arbitrariness by which, for Thomson and his imitators, 'Nature herself' calls the workers to the land is very different from the despotic arbitrariness of Duck's initiator, invariably 'the Master'. Another kind of urgency rules this work:

> Soon as the Harvest hath laid bare the Plains,
> And Barns well fill'd reward the Farmer's pains;
> What Corn each sheaf will yield, intent to hear,
> And guess from thence the Profits of the year;
> Or else impending Ruin to prevent,
> By paying, timely, threat'ning Landlord's rent,
> He calls his Threshers forth. (p. 1)[3]

There follows a series of commands:

> As he directs, to different Barns we go;
> Here two for Wheat, and there for Barley two. (p. 3)[4]

And finally some pre-emptive bargaining by the Master:

> So dry the Corn was carried from the Field,
> So easily 'twill thresh, so well 'twill yield.
> Sure large day's Work I well may hope for now. (p. 3)

The contrast with Thomson could not be more strongly apparent. Thomson's 'joyous' husbandman, prompted by Nature, moves harmoniously into action, and the spring tasks begin easily: thus in the same passage of 'Spring' the Master appears ploughing, the Sower appears casting grain, the harrow follows along. The opening of 'Spring' has aptly been called a 'theatrical invocation', and the field work here begins as if set in motion by a curtain's rise.[5] Harmony is immediate and pervasive.

The most striking difference we find in Duck's work initiations concerns motive. In calling the workers to work, which he does three times in the poem, the Master has usurped the function of Thomson's 'Nature'. He has done so not with any concern for 'harmony', but only with profit in mind. Weather, which is a part of the great balanced harmoniousness of things for Thomson, is for Duck's Master a purely utilitarian subject, which he can use in his preliminary bartering with the threshers to demand maximum output. Neither is he concerned with the importance of human roles. In Thomson's 'Spring' initiation, each person has an individualised role: as 'Husbandman', 'Master' and 'Sower', each is a distinct 'actor' in the drama; whereas in Duck, only the Master has a role, the others being literally numbers to divide up arbitrarily.

The motivations of the workers themselves are rather more diffuse in

Duck's poem. Living in what the poet clearly shows to be hardship, they are opportunistic about the work, constantly in search of the small advantage that will make life bearable. They cannot choose, and wherever the Master commands them to go they go. Thus at the dividing up at the beginning (pp. 1–2) they simply go where they are sent and begin work. The Master's second command (p. 5) evokes a positive response: they have been stuck in a suffocating barn for months, and the Master's appearance is 'welcome', for it means the 'grateful Tidings' that they can now move to the summer fields. This work, of course, becomes in its turn strenuous and tedious, and they remember the 'kind Barns with friendly Shades' (p. 6). A brief pleasure is registered at the completion of the haymaking (p. 9), and they return with mixed feelings of relief and foreboding (for they will be called out again shortly) to the barns. In sum, they are precluded from the independent pleasure in pursuing seasonal tasks which seems to be available to Thomson's 'swains'; their lives are ruled by a mixture of fearful and hopeful memories and anticipations. Some pleasure is shown in the success of the haymaking and the harvest (pp. 9 and 11), though the physical commitment they have had to make to it gives this response some overtones of relief.

Collier's labour initiations are different again. Concentrating firstly on her rebuttal of Duck's slur, she plunges into her memories of haymaking *in medias res* (p. 16). Her purpose is to show a continuous round of work, caused by the 'double shift' of a working-class woman's life; so we see the female worker in the middle of a day of haymaking, then going home ahead of her husband to start her 'second shift' of housework. What is shown is a continual round of activity, with less emphasis on starting and stopping than there is in Duck. Later in the poem there are two initiations of labour. The first is the corn harvest:

> When Harvest comes, into the Field we go,
> And help to reap the Wheat as well as you,
> Or else we go the ears of Corn to glean,
> No Labour scorning, be it e'er so mean,
> But in the Work we freely bear a part,
> And what we can, perform with all our Heart.   (p. 17)

The fact that there are two options here emphasises the variety and opportunism of the women's work, contrasting strongly with the season-driven labour in Thomson, and the profit-driven labour in Duck. The women may reap, they may glean; they do, in fact, any work there is, 'No Labour scorning'. There is an element of pride in Collier's declaration of this flexibility, but it is also the product of necessity. Threshing is, for Duck, a hellishly eternal task, as we shall see, but the fact that it is a year-round occupation has the one positive element to it that the thresher has the security of permanent employment. Mary Collier's working women must take whatever work there is wherever and whenever it is available. By taking a pride in this Collier finds a way of humanising its tyranny, of making a virtue out of what is clearly a necessity.

Collier's final work initiation is of her winter work of 'charring'.[6] Again, this is clearly casual work (they are paid 'Sixpence or Eightpence' at the end of the day, p. 22), taken in winter; and the salient point is that it involves getting up before dawn in order to be able to finish it. Though Collier maintains her stoic optimism about this 'Hard labour we most chearfully pursue' the positive word 'chearfully' is ringed with harshness: it is hard labour; it needs to be pursued, not just 'carried out' but 'sought', 'struggled for'. (The absolute word 'most' may be the rhetoric of grim determination, applied to the harshest part of Collier's work-description, or it may be a typographical error for 'must'; either way, a sense of compulsion is strongly indicated.) Collier uses a piece of disharmony unlike anything else in the labour initiations of these three poems to emphasise the uncertainty and difficulty of this: she has the early-rising charwomen locked out and unable to start their work, as the maid is still asleep, being herself overtired from too much 'Work the day before' (p. 20). It is an effective touch; for the women to find any harmony or pleasure in their work is an uphill struggle, though it is one Collier shows they are determined to achieve.

The start of the working day for Thomson's shepherd, in 'Summer', could not be in greater contrast with Collier's wretched charwomen, wandering around in the cold pre-dawn, and locked out on a winter morning. What actually rouses the shepherd is the cock crowing, but any unpleasant alarm-clock associations are dissipated by Thomson's harmonious description of dawn.

> Brown Night retires. Young Day pours in apace,
> And opens all the lawny Prospect wide.
> The dripping Rock, the Mountain's misty Top
> Swell on the Sight, and brighten with the Dawn.
> Blue, thro' the Dusk, the smoking Currents shine;
> And from the bladed Field the fearful Hare
> Limps, aukward: while along the Forest-glade
> The wild Deer trip, and often turning gaze
> At early Passenger. Musick awakes,
> The native Voice of undissembled Joy;
> And thick around the woodland Hymns arise.
> Rous'd by the Cock, the soon-clad Shepherd leaves
> His mossy Cottage, where with Peace he dwells;
> And from the crouded Fold, in Order, drives
> His Flock, to taste the Verdure of the Morn.
>
> ('Summer', lines 52–66)

If the work in 'Spring' began in a theatrical way, then here we have, as it were, lights and music; a vivid visual rendering of the animate and inanimate elements of the country coming awake, and an overture in the dawn chorus, leading to the cock's crowing. The shepherd's rising is seen alongside, and in conclusion to, the many other 'natural' beginnings of the dawn: he is a 'natural man', his labour a part of the 'natural' movement of the day. The philippic against 'Falsely luxurious' Man who will not get up that follows may rather spoil the effect for a modern reader, but is perhaps Thomson's way of showing that his intentions are sternly georgic rather than (as the idyllic description of dawn might suggest) idealistically pastoral. Either way, this is clearly an artful awakening, describing the best kind of beginning for a day's work, where Collier has described the worst.

Three basic sets of values, then, control the initiation of labour in Thomson, Duck and Collier. The first is based very much on a sense of philosophical purpose: Thomsonian labour is a pleasure because it is harmoniously a part of an ultimately benevolent Nature. Its participants have a role and a purpose, within a socialised framework. Duckian labour is by contrast a question of making the best of a bad job. Motivation is, for the worker, based principally on obeying the Master; and, for the Master, based on extracting profit in the face of a fairly hostile Nature. For Collier's women workers things are clearly hardest of all, with their 'double shift', and their touting for char work on winter mornings. They are excluded from the slight advantage of permanent employment enjoyed by Duck's workers. Pleasure exists for these women in the pride they have in their versatility and determination to 'perform with all our heart' whatever work needs doing; and in the communal experience of their work.

Nature, Thomson's benevolent force, is in the form of heat the enemy to Duck's labourers, in the form of cold, wind, rain and snow the enemy to Collier's charwomen. However, it is an over-simplification of Thomson's view to see his Nature as purely harmonious. The long georgic passage on insects in 'Spring' is evidence of Nature's potential for damage; much of 'Winter' is concerned with a Nature sufficiently hostile to destroy a life, and the storm in 'Autumn' is especially damaging to Man. Thomson typically offers socially-wrought solutions to these problems. Patience is the virtue appropriate to dealing with hostile weather in 'Spring' (lines 137–42), while science – a product of Man's rise – will safely see off such problems as the hostile insects ('Spring', lines 120–36). Industry, above all, hard work, is his ideal, and hence idleness his enemy. Duck's view of hard work is not surprisingly jaundiced by his experiences, and Collier, too, has no illusions about its harshness; and *The Thresher's Labour* and *The Woman's Labour* provide, among other things, an important critique of the Thomsonian view of labour.

Haymaking

Examining the scenes of labour themselves reveals a complex set of relationships between the three texts. The two areas of work the three poets all address are the hay and corn harvests. I want to examine here the various descriptions of haymaking and harvest work, before looking at the more specialised kinds of labour each of the three poets concentrates on. Haymaking and harvesting were 'peak-time' activities, tasks of a sort which involved all hands, so we should not be surprised to find each of these writers dealing with them. They are also similar activities in many ways (though there are important differences in the organisation of their tasks), and I shall to some extent be mixing descriptions of hay and corn harvests in my comparisons. Haymaking, the first major harvest of the year, evokes a varied response. It is the work Thomson describes most idyllically ('Summer', lines 351–70); while Duck gives haymaking a mixed reception (pp. 5–9); and Mary Collier (pp. 16–17) treats it with sprightly energy.

For Thomson, haymaking combines all his ideals. It is a period of intense activity, and it is notable that the haymaking scene follows the latest of a number of attacks on idleness. It is a model of social harmony: 'the Village' joins together in 'happy Labour, Love, and social Glee' (line 370). Its pleasure and healthiness, two powerful Thomsonian positives, are made apparent in its long series of vivid adjectives (jovial, rustic, healthful, strong, ruddy, swelling, fragrant, kind, refreshful, green, dusky, russet, gay, blended, happy):

> Now swarms the Village o'er the jovial Mead:
> The rustic Youth, brown with meridian Toil,
> Healthful, and strong; full as the Summer-Rose
> Blown by prevailing Suns, the ruddy Maid,
> Half naked, swelling on the Sight, and all
> Her kindled Graces burning o'er her Cheek.
> Even stooping Age is here; and Infant-Hands
> Trail the long Rake, or, with the fragrant Load
> O'ercharg'd, amid the kind Oppression roll.
> Wide flies the tedded Grain; all in a Row
> Advancing broad, or wheeling round the Field,
> They spread the breathing Harvest to the Sun,
> That throws refreshful round a rural Smell:
> Or, as they rake the green-appearing Ground,
> And drive the dusky Wave along the Mead,
> The russet hay-cock rises thick behind,
> In order gay. While heard from Dale to Dale,
> Waking the Breeze, resounds the blended Voice
> Of happy Labour, Love, and social Glee.
>
> ('Summer', lines 352–70)

Haymaking is a model of perfection for the poet. Each individual joins in a communal and pleasurable effort, and to emphasise the universal involvement, Thomson includes 'stooping Age' and 'Infant-Hands'.

There is a sense in which Duck is precluded by his own literary purpose even if he wished to share the pleasurable communality of Thomson's haymaking scene, and the overt literariness of his rejection of women workers I have mentioned is a part of this predicament. Having decided to focus on the unremitting hardship of 'his own situation', he cannot admit to taking any pleasure in haymaking. On the other hand, the fact that he does seem to take pleasure, however momentarily, in various other aspects of farm work, including the initial mowing of the hay, perhaps suggests there may be positive reasons for his displeasure. As a 'peak-time' farming activity, haymaking requires outside assistance, and resentment at the presence of 'amateurs' in farm work may inform the passage. Also, of course, the basis of Duck's complaint is documentary as well as literary: it would be superficial not to recognise the hardship of even the most pleasurable of rural work. As he says, 'There's always Bitter mingled with the Sweet' (p. 5).

Duck's account of haytime gives us more detail than Thomson, suggesting more thought about the actual work involved. His haymaking is a two-day process, and his account includes various stages in the work, whereas Thomson is concerned with a single and generalised scene of haymaking, set out pictorially. Warner considers that Thomson's phrase 'tedded Grain' ('Summer', line 361) shows he has confused corn and hay harvests, but Sambrook's gloss on Grain here, as 'grass that has gone to seed' clears that matter up.[7] In fact there is no specific factual misleading in the passage, not even at the level of Duck's apparently self-creating haycocks. If we wish to argue with Thomson's portrayal, it must be on the grounds that he idealises, calls labour 'happy', makes 'love' its motive, buries the hard work in 'social glee'. It is an argument keenly pursued by John Barrell, who uses the generic term 'comic' to characterise Thomson's literary *trompe d'oeil*, and who carefully lays bare some of the associative techniques behind what he calls the 'peculiar alchemy' that converts 'labour itself into leisure, pain into pleasure':

That this is to be a comic image of rural work is established straight away by the phrase 'jovial Mead'; it may be too much to claim that the villagers, prior to a day of back-breaking toil, are jovial, but no-one will bother to deny that the meadow may be, and much the same might be said later in the passage about the haycock (lines 367–8), whose gaiety somehow rubs off onto the haymakers whether or not they feel gay themselves.[8]

The only thing missing here is any sense that there may actually have been some pleasure in haymaking (which common sense, and many first-hand accounts from farm workers, say there is), and that Thomson may be drawing on this in his writing, rather than merely verbally tricking us (which he is certainly doing). Nonetheless this is astute criticism of Thomson.[9]

For Duck haymaking is a more diffuse event. His account has the switchback effect of veering between pleasure and pain. Thus he begins in optimism and 'eager haste' (a rather Thomsonian phrase, p. 5), as the mowers, masters of this new activity, size up the task. In the 1730 version the mood is cheerfully competitive:

> And now the Field design'd our Strength to try
> Appears, and meets at last our longing eye;
> The Grass and Ground each chearfully surveys,
> Willing to see which way th'Advantage lays.
> As the best man, each claims the foremost place,
> And our first work seems but a sportive Race.
> With rapid force our well-whet Blades we drive,
> Strain every nerve, and blow for blow we give:
> Tho' but this Eminence the foremost gains,
> Only t'excel the rest in Toil and Pains.   (pp. 5–6)

But by 1736, Duck has made a number of interesting changes (I italicise them in what follows):

> And now the Field, design'd *to try our Might*,
> *At length* appears, and meets our longing *Sight*.
> The Grass and Ground *we view with careful Eyes*,
> To see which way the *best* Advantage lies;
> *And, Hero-like*, each claims the foremost Place.
> *At first our Labour seems* a sportive Race:
> With rapid Force our *sharpen'd* Blades we drive,
> Strain ev'ry Nerve, and Blow for Blow we give.
> *All strive to vanquish, tho'* the Victor gains
> *No other Glory, but the greatest* Pains.   (1736, pp. 16–17)

Duck has as usual classicised this in the later version, but for once his epic aspirations work to good effect. He seems to have gained rather than lost by the process. It is interesting that at a time when he was blurring the vision of much of the poem with pastoral gentility, he managed actually to sharpen up this description of the most skilled part of his annual work. The poet depicts well the irony of an Olympic competition with only a booby-prize to win, adhering faithfully to his concept of 'bitter' always mingling with 'the sweet', yet taking pride in the description of the work.

There was in fact an economic basis for competitiveness and professional pride among mowers. Paul Brassley records that, in the northeast, an eighteenth-century mower could earn '1s. 2d per day during the hay and corn harvests', while he 'had to be content with 6d or 8d per day for the rest of the year'. And as a nineteenth-century reference book puts it: 'It is an essential point [of haymaking] that the mowers should be good workmen, and perform their work neatly and evenly, making the scythe cut as near the ground as possible, in order to insure the greatest bulk of hay, and facilitate the springing up of the young shoots of the eddish or aftermath.'[10]

However, there is also an interesting literary analogue, in Andrew Marvell's 'Damon the Mower', who is as competitive as Duck's mowers, and seems to be motivated by both 'riches' and heroism. He declares:

> What though the piping shepherd stock
> The plains with a unnumbered flock,
> This scythe of mine discovers wide
> More ground than all his sheep do hide.
> With this the golden fleece I shear
> Of all these closes every year.
> And though in wool more poor than they,
> Yet am I richer far in hay.

Frank Kermode comments, 'The Mower is something of a novelty in pastoral, but rivalry between rustics of different professions is not'.[11]

The heat puts a stop to the competition between Duck's mowers, and they regret they have worked so hard, their tiredness exacerbated by an inadequate meal-break in which, in Duck's punning zeugma, 'the Bottle and the Beer's too small' (p. 7).[12] The ups and downs of haymaking continue through a more sensibly paced afternoon, and into the second day, the account of which contains the notorious 'prattling Females' passage.

Little can be salvaged from what I have portrayed as being primarily a literary error of judgement. The attack on women chattering is soundly condemned by Collier on ideological and factual grounds (pp. 16–17), along with the imputation of idleness that accompanies it. Again, there may be an element of jealousy at the pleasure the women find in the work, Duck and his colleagues having exhausted themselves in their competitive efforts. In Duck's account their talk is a substitute for activity, but Collier sees it as 'The only Privilege our Sex enjoy' (p. 17). It is thus for her what the slight advantages of change, good weather and so on are for Duck: a small mitigation to an otherwise unendurable existence. Earlier, in the barn, Duck has complained that the noise of threshing prevents the threshers enjoying the traditional pastoral pleasures of telling a 'merry tale' (p. 3) and singing (p. 4). Sociability as a means of enduring rural work occurs regularly in literary and anecdotal accounts (Mary Collier's harvest scene on p. 19 – discussed below – is a good example), and Duck's resentment may be fed here by a feeling of being excluded from the sociability the women practise.[13] Perhaps the mowers are simply too tired to talk (they 'but faintly eat' during their break, p. 7). Their competitive approach to the skilled task of reaping, and their hostility to the women mean they cannot participate in the sustaining co-operation the women workers practise. (I think this may be what Donna Landry means when she writes that 'By scorning his female fellow workers, Duck has done violence to their shared occlusion from the bourgeois pastoral prospect.')[14]

Thus Duck's account of haymaking shows a range of feelings about this peak-time activity, from the misery of becoming excessively exhausted to the pleasure of feeling a new and challenging experience at the start of the work. Less powerfully felt, but important nevertheless, are such responses as satisfaction with a more moderately paced work, as 'each again betakes him to his place' (p. 7)[15] (reminding us of Thomson's positioning of his haymakers and reapers, discussed below), the pleasure in the final turning of the hay and the relief at returning to the barn (p. 9). It is certainly a more detailed response than Thomson's, and reminds us of the significance that resides in small details for both the poet and the worker in Duck.

Mary Collier is concerned rather with refuting Duck than with providing a full description of her haymaking. Yet there are important details. The women are, first and foremost, good workers, whom the farmer trusts:

> You of Hay-making speak a word or two,
> As if our Sex but little Work could do:
> This makes the honest Farmer smiling say
> He'll seek for Women still to make his Hay;
> For if his back be turn'd, their Work they mind
> As well as Men, as far as he can find. (p. 16)[16]

This is the preparation for her main defence, which takes the form of the flight of remembered experience I quoted earlier:

> For my own part, I many a Summer's day
> Have spent in throwing, turning, making Hay,
> But ne'er could see, what you have lately found,
> Our Wages paid for sitting on the Ground.
> 'Tis true, that when our Morning's Work is done,
> And all our Grass expos'd unto the Sun,
> While that his scorching Beams do on it shine,
> As well as you, we have a time to dine:
> I hope that since we freely toil and sweat
> To earn our Bread, you'll give us time to eat. (p. 16)

Collier moves smoothly into the historical present tense here. Although she does not fetishise the labour in any Duckian way, her phrase 'throwing, turning, making hay' shows that the 'women's work' of tedding is a major part of the haymaking, and thus as important as the mowing. Other accounts confirm this. Morton devotes a full column to the niceties of tedding, and his account suggests it is a highly skilled task.[17] The hay must be dried as thoroughly as possible, and at the same time can easily be spoiled by rain or by not being turned enough (and thus getting burned). Collier shows her meal break as being timed by the work – the hay must all be turned before they take their meal-break, so that while they eat it is being 'expos'd unto the sun'; whereas Duck's mowers are less ruled by time and weather, stopping simply when they are 'With Heat and Labour tir'd' (p. 7). But in fact R. Bradley's eighteenth-century treatise on farming shows that both mowing and drying were highly skilled and critical tasks; the former dependent on exact timing and physical skill, the latter a balance between too dry and too wet; and both a nimble race with the weather.[18]

Though Duck wants to marginalise the women's part of the harvest labour, Collier will not allow him to do so. Her facetious 'hope' in these last lines neatly unites the women's 'toil and sweat' with their need to 'earn our bread' and to 'eat'. She is subtly reminding the thresher of God's harsh command to Adam and Eve, when he expels them from the Garden of Eden, in *Genesis* (4, 19): 'In the sweat of thy face shalt thou eat bread, till thou return unto the ground; for out of it wast thou taken: for dust thou art, and unto dust shalt thou return.' By doing so she is insisting he remember that women share the same burdens and imperatives, the same postlapsarian legacy, as men.

Harvest

I want to bring into the discussion the descriptions of the second great harvest of the year, the corn harvest. As with the initiations of labour in 'Spring' and 'Summer' discussed above, both Thomson's haymaking and his harvest are initiated in essentially theatrical ways. For the summer haymaking, the participants are carefully placed, as if in a painting. On the one hand there is 'The rustic Youth, brown with meridian Toil, / Healthful, and strong' ('Summer', lines 353–4), and on the other:

> the ruddy Maid,
> Half-naked, swelling on the Sight, and all
> Her kindled Graces burning o'er her Cheek.   (lines 355–7)

We have seen the poet's concern with showing a communality of effort, involving men and women, young and old, the 'village' as a united community. In this sense his 'Youth' and his 'Maid' are not primarily individuals but representatives – symbols and synonyms for 'the men' and 'the women'. Yet the way in which they are presented here allows them to appear at the same time as two individuals, a couple; and as individuals the way we see them here suggests the preparation, not for labour, but for a dance. For the autumn harvest Thomson specifies this more overtly, showing a double line of men and women participants, carefully paired:

> Before the ripen'd Field the Reapers stand
> In fair Array; each by the Lass he loves.

> ('Autumn', lines 153–4)

John Barrell reads this setting up of couples in the two harvests as a purposefully erotic sign of the comic mode, with its intentional beguiling of labour. He is particularly scornful of any pretensions the harvest scene might have to realism, commenting on 'Autumn', lines 151–76 as follows: 'In this delightful fantasy of agricultural work, all the reapers are sorted into courting couples, an arrangement equally conducive to love and labour: the man reaps the corn, the "Lass he loves" binds the "lusty Sheaves" – once again the comic adjective is transferred to an inanimate object.'[19] Again, the one thing missing from this comment, which rightly criticises Thomson's suppression of the hardships of labour, is any sense that an erotic and dance-like stance might be *appropriate* in the description of harvest, and might be based on something (like pleasure in haytime) which existed in reality. I think it *is* appropriate for the reapers to adopt a dance-like stance. I take my cue in this from someone who laboured in many harvest fields, but was also, like Thomson, a lowland Scottish poet: Robert Burns. Burns recalls in a letter to Dr John Moore an incident from his youth: 'You know our country custom of coupling a man and woman together as Partners in the labors of Harvest. – In my fifteenth autumn, my Partner was a bewitching creature who just counted an autumn less . . . a bonie, sweet, sonsie lass.' Burns fell in love, and wrote his first poem to his 'Partner'; and thus, as he says, 'began Love and Poesy'.[20] We see here, and in Thomson's descriptions, a Scottish tradition of dance-like pairing in the cornfield. Burns's love of dancing is of course well documented, as is the Scottish dancing enthusiasm of the period: 'eighteenth-century Scotland', says one Burns scholar, 'danced as it has never danced since'; and two folk traditions may thus be seen as converging in this pairing of harvesters. The connection between harvest pairing and dancing is perhaps further suggested by the fact that there is a country dance called the 'haymakers' or 'haymaker's jig'.[21]

This raises a number of interesting questions: did the pairing have a practical purpose, and if so what was it? Does the fact that we do not find it in the Wiltshire cornfields of Stephen Duck, and the Sussex/Hampshire cornfields of Mary Collier mean it was an exclusively Scottish phenomenon? And was it just a function of the harvest, as Burns's comment suggests; or does it also have a place in haymaking, as Thomson's description in 'Summer' perhaps implies?

As a function of the work and from a practical point of view, the pairing of a man and a woman in the harvest field makes sense, and the practice is shown in some visual representations of eighteenth and nineteenth-century harvesting. In George Stubbs's painting *Reapers* (1785), for example, there are three male cutters, two women making sheaf-ties, and another man building a stook. An explanatory illustration in H. Stephen's *The Book of the Farm*, neatly captions the various processes of harvesting. There are three male reapers, and each has a female gatherer working behind him. Thereafter there is one 'Bandster' binding a sheaf, one 'Man raker' cleaning up loose corn, and two more 'Bandsters' setting a stook. All of these latter figures are male, though the term 'Man raker' perhaps suggests this was more frequently a woman's job.[22]

It requires some consideration of the various processes of pre-industrial haymaking and harvesting to see its purpose. In both hay and corn harvest the work tended to involve 'waves' of workers, following one after another. The sequence of events in the harvest was, in general terms, as follows: reaping, gathering, sheaf-making, stook-building, raking, carting, gleaning. For haymaking this would be, again in general terms: mowing, spreading, turning, building windrows, building cocks, raking and carting. Both processes involve distinct first tasks (cutting the crop) from which all the other processes follow, and which determine their timing.

However, these subsequent processes differed somewhat. Haymaking involved a great deal of raking up and raking out, building, unbuilding and rebuilding haycocks. The grass was actually being processed into hay in the field, which might involve a number of repetitions of the same tasks. Hence pools, or gangs of labourers were needed to carry out these processes as circumstances demanded. These gangs tended to be entirely or predominantly of one gender, and were often women.[23] The corn harvest followed a more rigid sequence. In the eighteenth century most corn was spring-sown, slow-maturing and late-harvesting (hence the impatience to get started in Thomson's 'Spring'). It was cut underripe to minimise the loss by scattering of ears of corn, tied into sheaves and built into stooks, which were often then thatched and left for some time in this fairly weatherproof state to ripen further, before being taken to the rickyard or the barn, built into ricks and finally threshed. Once it was cut, processing was a matter of some urgency: one was not playing hide-and-seek with the weather here, as with haymaking, but trying to outrun it (not always successfully, as Thomson's autumn storm, discussed below, suggests). Because corn was late-harvesting, this was often a high-risk manoeuvre, and it required a means of organising the work as streamlined as a modern production line.

Thus, most importantly, each reaper would 'feed' a gatherer, whose job was to gather the spikes into bundles, and possibly to tie these bundles into sheaves. From that point to the rick-building the organisation of tasks was more variable, but the reaper-gatherer part of the process is the important one from the point of view of the subject of pairing, for it was a two-person team job, involving a traditionally male and a traditionally female task, carried out consecutively. A male-female pairing was thus the obvious choice, and an ongoing male-female pair would be able to develop a joint 'pace' for the task as the work went on. Thus while the poet in Burns could read 'pairing' as a charming folk custom, as a working farmer he would know this to be also a piece of agricultural practicality. In Scotland, at least, its association with dancing, and its formalisation into a ritual allowed it to maintain its charm, but its basis in good farming practice is also clear.[24]

The next issue, then, is why we do not find this pairing in Duck or Collier. The answer is slightly disappointing. Duck (pp. 10–11) has other concerns in his harvest scene than describing the actual work-processes in any detail. First, he is intent on a piece of literary work, an apostrophised pathetic fallacy concerning the 'ruin' of the cornfield:

> Ye Reapers, cast your eyes around the Field,
> And view the scene its different Beauties yield;
> Then look again with a more tender eye,
> To think how soon it must in ruin lie.
> For once set in, where-e'er our blows we deal,
> There's no resisting of the well-whet Steel,
> But here and there, where-e'er our Course we bend,
> Sure Desolation does our steps attend. (p. 10)[25]

This is not the best writing in the poem, and is followed by a fairly uninspired epic simile comparing the warlike devastation of the field with that of countries plundered by '*Arabia*'s Sons'. But the passage is interesting nevertheless. It shows the aesthetic impulse of the rural worker (not only the poet) towards the ripened field. Flora Thompson fleshes out this impulse, describing the 'few days or a week or a fortnight' when 'the fields stood "ripe unto harvest"':

It was the one perfect period in the hamlet year. The human eye loves to rest upon wide expanses of pure colour: the moors in the purple heyday of the heather, miles of green downland, and the sea when it lies calm and blue and boundless, all delight it; but to some none of these, lovely though they all are, can give the same satisfaction of spirit as acres upon acres of golden corn.[26]

Duck's allusion to the 'ruin' of the cornfield also strongly suggests the idea of the killing of the corn king, chronicled in the English folksong 'John Barleycorn' and elsewhere in folk culture, and representing a very deep, pre-Christian cultural attitude to harvest.[27]

However, the 'ruin' theme diverts him from considering the placing of the human actors in the drama. Duck then goes on to make a more personally felt complaint about the extreme severity of harvest work. Between these two concerns we can glean a little. As usual the Master commands and is 'our Guide', his role 'to appoint' and 'we the Work to do'. Women appear, but only as gleaners, as the work begins to get harder, and they fence the reapers between the thistles and themselves. This, as we have seen, much amused Mary Collier; though one should say in Duck's defence that thistles, at least, were a serious problem. Tusser instructs the farmer to 'Give gloves to thy reapers'; and George Ewart Evans helpfully glosses this: 'The reapers used gloves to prevent their hands being pricked by thistles as they curved them round the corn when using the serrated sickle.'[28] (Collier is pricking Duck in quite another way, of course.) Finally, the harvest is completed in a celebratory cacophony of 'Bells and clashing Whips' and 'rattling Wagons' (p. 11). But there is nothing about any task between reaping and carting.

Mary Collier, as we saw, gives reaping 'as well as you', and gleaning, as two of the harvest jobs the women could do (p. 17); but she then chooses the gleaning work for closer description; indeed it is not clear whether by 'reaping' she means the general work of the harvest field, or a more daring challenge to Duck's scything prowess. However, she does provide important evidence that women involved themselves in cutting crops at this time, not so much in the phrase 'reap the Wheat as well as you', but where she writes:

> We cut the Peas, and always ready are
> In ev'ry Work to take our proper Share.   (p. 20)

Flora Thompson – as so often – records the end of the tradition:

One of the smaller fields was always reserved for any of the women who cared to go reaping. Formerly all able-bodied women not otherwise occupied had gone as a matter of course; but by the [eighteen-] 'eighties, there were only three or four, beside the regular field women, who could hand the sickle. Often the Irish harvesters had to be called in to finish the field.[29]

Collier does give one vital clue about male-female teams, when she writes:

> What you would have of us we do not know:
> We oft take up the Corn that you do mow.   (p. 20)

This clearly shows that one of the women's jobs is gathering, but does not necessarily suggest male-female teams. We should be aware, however, that it would suit the literary purposes of neither Duck nor Collier to emphasise such team-work, so we can infer little from its absence. Other sources, however, clearly indicate that there was indeed an English tradition of male-female partnership in the cornfield. For example George Ewart Evans, drawing on Victorian manuscript materials from Sussex, found a harvesting agreement which included the specification 'each man to find a gaveller'. As Evans explains, 'the gavellers were usually women, wives of the harvest workers. Their job was to rake the mown corn into gavels or rows ready for carting.'[30]

This is hardly dressed as romantic folk custom, but the tradition's existence in England is clear enough, though by no means all the sources specify a male-female partnership in the cornfield. Hennell discusses various other combinations, such as the Yorkshire team known as a 'yan', consisting of three shearers and one bander. Thomson and Burns perhaps suggest that Scotland had a stronger tradition in this than England; and Charles Keith's poem *The Harst Rig* (1786) supports this suspicion. The title means both a male-female team, and the strip of field such a team would work. In the poem the male and female workers seem to be fully integrated, with much singing and dancing together in the barn as they wait for the rain to stop.[31]

The final question the Thomson-Burns 'pairing' raises concerns the hayfield, and whether or not a 'pairing' also occurs there, as Thomson seems to suggest. As far as I can establish, the agricultural answer is no. I have touched on the fact that because of the elastic nature of the 'middle' tasks of haymaking between reaping and carting, there is no pairing equivalent to the reaper-gatherer/gaveller team of the harvest. There were by the nature of things, large numbers of men and women in a hayfield, but the teams would be more gender-divided; the men reaping in a line; and the women (principally) raking, turning, tedding and building haycocks.

A contemporary painting, *Country Around Dixton Manor (Dixton Harvesters)* (c. 1730), provides some interesting evidence of gender separation in the hayfield. It shows a side view of a long, large hayfield, and its adjacent fields. Within the main field are some one hundred and twenty human figures, with a further twenty or so in the adjacent areas. The figures are very small, but it appears that many of them are in single-sex gangs, or in gangs with a clear majority of either men or women. Thus in the left centre foreground a gang of twenty-three men are spread diagonally across the field, apparently scything hay; to the left of them a group of four women and two men are raking the hay and building small cocks; in the right centre foreground a gang of five women and one man are raking hay into windrows; in the centre background a gang of nine women and three men have shouldered their rakes and are following an overseer away from the small cocks they have clearly just built; behind them a group of six or eight women are resting; and there are various other such groups in the field. Thomson, however, is vindicated so far as his hint of the dance goes. Not only are many of the individuals and groups in dance-like postures, but there is a line of eight or ten morris dancers dancing out of the field to the right. It is doubtless the artist's conceit that the twenty-three mowers, though they bear scythes rather than handkerchiefs, visually echo the morrismen. John Barrell's reading of the painting as a 'comic' version of the battle panorama, a mock-heroic, designed to 'establish Dixton Manor as a properly merry corner of Merry England' should also be borne in mind: Barrell notes, for example, that there is in the painting a distinctly non-documentary telescoping of consecutive tasks into one scene. It is nevertheless interesting and suggestive that gender separatism and a dance-like aspect are both present in this depiction of the hayfield.[32]

But despite the evidence of gender separation in haymaking work, Thomson's pairing of 'Youth' and 'Maid' for haymaking is significant and appropriate for another reason. As with the harvest, so too the hayfield was traditionally a major place and time of sexual opportunity (and again, one would want to nuance the 'comic' purpose of Thomson's hayfield eroticism, in Barrell's analysis, with some sense that this might to some degree have reflected real feelings and activities).[33] The close proximity of toiling and (as Thomson says) 'half-naked' young people of both sexes, the sense of fertility and well-being associated with harvesting generally, the sense of heat associated with haytime, the interesting possibilities of haystacks and (not least) the advantages of July in terms of a consequent spring birth, provided a unique combination of motives and opportunities. Thomson responds to this human element in the fecundity of hay and corn harvest directly; but, more obliquely, there are ways in which both Duck's haymaking and Collier's harvest descriptions also reveal responses; and I shall conclude this comparison of the three poets' harvests by looking in turn at these three responses.

Thomson's 'ruddy Maid, / Half-naked, swelling on the Sight' and 'Reapers ... each by the Lass he loves' is less purposefully frank than Burns's affectionate erotic memory: there is a noticeably coy streak in Thomson's attitudes to sexuality and to women. He sets up clear implications of sexuality, particularly in the haymaking passage, in his 'pairing' and by the sensuousness of his descriptive work; but Thomson often seems to be frustrated by a decorum that puts his head and his heart at loggerheads. This is noticeable in 'Spring', where he considers the 'Soul of Love' (line 582) and its effects. Rising through the ranks of the animal kingdom, his imaginative powers lead him all too quickly to the 'rougher World / Of Brutes' (lines 790–1); and as bulls and steeds do battle his subject of 'love' becomes overtly carnal, something the poet feels the need to declare a wish to avoid. In an attempt, as it were, to cool the subject off, he plunges us into the topic of the 'Monsters of the foaming Deep' (line 822); but this will not serve to put out the 'Flame' (line 827) the poet has lit, and he admits that he must change the subject,

in a passage sufficiently laden with embarrassment for his modern editor
to suggest self-parody:

> But this the Theme
> I sing, enraptur'd, to the British Fair,
> Forbids, and leads me to the Mountain-brow,
> Where sits the Shepherd on the grassy Turf.
>
> ('Spring', lines 830–3)[34]

His 'resolution fails' (to quote his earlier description of fledgling birds,
lines 741–2) 'at the giddy Verge', and the sense of anxious avoidance is
palpable. The effect of this awkward break in so delicate a structure as *The
Seasons* is to weaken severely the last section of 'Spring'. The verse paragraph where the break occurs leads on rather aimlessly, firstly into a
conventional pastoral sketch (lines 832–40), and then into a historical and
patriotic exclamation (lines 840–8). A third attempt to start anew is less
obviously unsuccessful, and the raging carnality of the rutting season
appears to be subdued at last by thoughts of God, Lord Lyttleton and a
beautiful prospect (lines 849–962). Thus fortified, the poet can finally
tackle the subject of human love, which he divides carefully into unwholesome love (of which 'let th'aspiring Youth beware', lines 983–1112), and
wholesome love, with which the season of spring can be concluded on an
acceptably joyous note.

Because the 'rustic youth, brown' and the 'Maid, / Half-naked' in
'Summer' are amongst a larger group, sandwiched between 'the Village'
and 'stooping Age', Thomson is less perturbed by the eroticism of their
demeanour. The harmony of dancing, this context allows him to imply, is
the model for the harmony of rural work, in which all participate; and the
physical beauty and energy of the representative 'Youth' and 'Maid' –
their erotic and fertile potential – may be appropriated and controlled by
this ethos. The equivalent pairing in the autumn harvest uses a more
familiar mechanism for making gender relations acceptable:

> Before the ripen'd Field the Reapers stand,
> In fair Array; each by the Lass he loves,
> To bear the rougher Part, and mitigate
> By nameless gentle Offices her Toil.   ('Autumn', lines 153–6)

This is cast in the chivalric mode, and Thomson draws on the male-female
reaper-gatherer relationship we have considered to reinforce a familiar
poetic view. However, Hennell gives a piece of information that may make
Thomson's chivalrous reaper more credible: 'Towards the end of the day
the reapers put down their sickles and assist the binders in setting up the
sheaves to dry in stooks or shocks.'[35] This is hardly 'bearing the rougher
part' but does suggest help.

The reaper-lass relationship is more overtly sexual in Thomson's description of the harvest feast, towards the end of 'Autumn'. Here:

> The Toil-strung Youth
> By the quick Sense of Music taught alone,
> Leaps wildly graceful in the lively Dance.
> Her every Charm abroad, the Village-Toast,
> Young, buxom, warm, in native Beauty rich,
> Darts not unmeaning Looks; and, where her Eye
> Points an approving Smile, with double Force,
> The Cudgel rattles, and the Wrestler twines.   (lines 1223–30)

Sexuality is safely expressed here by the mixing of *faux-naif* flirtation, comic sexual display and bathos: Thomson has decided to be humorous about sexuality, and the result is comic and vivid.

A fearless misogynist like Duck has no place in his world for this kind of soppiness, of course, whether it is cast as chivalry or low camp: for him the hayfield and the harvest are places where the fittest survive, and women are a damned nuisance. Yet the competitive vying for position among the mowers I have discussed seems to me to have unmistakable resonances of sexuality. Duck comes swaggering into the field armed with his scythe, which he suggestively describes as 'The Weapon design'd to unclothe the Field'. (p. 5)[36] As the men march to work, Duck says 'a new Life seems in our Breasts to glow'. The mowing is (at first) a 'sportive race' – the primary meaning of 'sportive' here is 'playful', but it is a short step to Marvell's amorous use of 'sport' in the phrase 'Now let us sport us while we may.' The reapers 'drive' their blades with 'rapid force', until eventually they collapse in 'streams of sweat' and with 'parch'd throats', leaving them 'quite o'er-spent'. The word 'spent', like 'sportive', also has a sexual meaning, amply demonstrated in Rochester's poem 'The Imperfect Enjoyment'.[37] Seen in this light, one wonders whether Duck's overt hostility to the 'chattering' women is not simply a disguise for the fact that they are the chosen audience for this display of male physical prowess (and of course if they are busy chattering then they are not paying attention). So we do seem to see a response to the fecundity of harvesting in Duck's poem, though it is one that plays out its sexual theme in terms of a distanced and distancing ritual of gender-war.

Mary Collier's harvest is a different matter. She sensibly ignores Duck's sexual display, echoing only those points she wishes to refute or parody. Mowers' machismo is not amongst them: but I think there is a way in which her poem may be seen to respond to the sexuality of harvest, if we take as our starting point the idea expressed by the feminist art historian Whitney Chadwick, that 'Women's sexuality may extend to maternity.'[38] For Collier builds her own picture of the harvest field, concentrating on an entirely different scale of values, and a rather more nurturing form of human interaction:

> To get a living we so willing are,
> Our tender Babes into the Field we bear,
> And wrap them in our cloaths to keep them warm,
> While round about we gather up the Corn,
> And often unto them our course we bend,
> To keep them safe, that nothing them offend.
> Our Children that are able, bear a share
> In gleaning Corn, such is our frugal care.
> When Night comes on, unto our home we go,
> Our Corn we carry, and our Infant too;
> Weary, alas! but 'tis not worth our while
> Once to complain, or *rest at ev'ry Stile*. (p. 19)[39]

Only at the very end of this passage does she revert to her 'flyting', her mocking echoes of Duck. The rest is her own exemplum, to be set against the lack of solidarity and love in Duck's haytime and harvest. Here she delivers her tribute to the goddess of harvest, not in terms of sexual expression, but equally appropriately in terms of maternal nurture and the care of children. This is perhaps the more striking in that it appears Collier had no children of her own.[40] But in the women's gleaning-field the sense is of a mutuality of concern from which no woman is excluded: all is framed in the undifferentiating first-person plural, 'we'.

I shall have more to say about gleaning later: it was painful, backbreaking and hand-cutting work. Collier finely and poignantly expresses the limits which hardship imposes on the women's ability to nurture their children, when she writes here: 'Our Children that are able, bear a share / In gleaning Corn, such is our frugal care' (p. 19). The whole passage is focused on the care of the children; yet she uses the phrase 'frugal care'. It suggests both that the care is frugal because it cannot extend to saving the older children from the painful task of gleaning, which must be done if the families are to have flour for the year (a matter on which survival through the winter might depend); and the 'frugal' care with which the gleanings are carefully collected and husbanded in order to make nurture possible at all. What we see here is a subtle means of coping with a harsh imperative, gently and compassionately evoked, and thus subtle in poetic as well as in social terms. It contrasts strikingly with Duck's harvest (one does not have much time for cornfield triumphalism with a baby on one hip and a sack of corn on the other), and it offers an illuminating alternative to the sentimental, pastoral view of the harvest-field more usually offered by art and literature.

3

Three types of labour

Threshing

It seems clear enough that haymaking and harvesting are the kinds of labour that may include some areas of pleasure as well as pain, as all three accounts, to different degrees and in different ways, suggest. We may also distinguish between the severity of other kinds of work the three poets portray. Thomson, for example, portrays the obviously pleasurable and light work of nutting in autumn, placing it easily into a pastoral context. I want to look here, by contrast, at an activity that is clearly very hard work indeed. This is threshing, and it is the major work of Stephen Duck's annual cycle.

Threshing differs from 'peak-time' activities like the two harvests, or like lambing and shearing, in that it is an indoor job, and therefore is only controlled by weather to the extent that it is carried out when weather-dominated tasks are not to hand. Evans records that farmers tended to sustain the practice of hand-threshing even after threshing machines arrived, because 'it helped to solve the problem of what to do with their workers in the winter'.[1] It also has a far greater seasonal span, and can be done effectively at any time from the harvest to the following summer. Even if Duck were not known to posterity as the 'thresher poet' we could establish from its recurrence in the poem that he saw threshing as his major employment. It is a task for which only one saving grace can be found, in the negative fact that it gets the labourers out of the sun, which in post-haymaking and post-harvest periods is portrayed as a relief.

The description of threshing is concentrated in a longish passage of fifty-three lines (pp. 3–4), reappearing briefly after the haymaking (p. 9) and at the end of the poem, the morning after the harvest supper (p. 11). Thus it frames the two peak-time activities, and both begins and ends Duck's cycle of toil. The main work description (p. 3) is followed by a litany of its hardships. It is firstly (and, by implication, lastly and interminably) uninterrupted labour:

No intermission in our Works we know;
The noisy Threshall must for ever go.
Their Master absent, others safely play;
The sleeping Threshall does itself betray.   (p. 3)

The task is uninterruptible for two reasons. Firstly, it is never finished. We
need to synthesise the three occurrences of it to confirm this. The first
threshing begins 'Soon as the Harvest hath laid bare the Plains' (p. 1).[2]
The poem then skips to spring (giving no information to suggest other
tasks interrupting the threshing) until the Master calls the labourers out to
cut the hay (the longing here to 'breathe in opener Air', p. 5, also suggests
they have been in the barn all winter). Following haymaking they are
returned to the barn for 'But few days' between hay harvest and corn
harvest (p. 9).[3] Finally, the morning after the harvest home, they return to
the barn 'To labour there for room for next year's Corn' (p. 11). The
threshing is a continuous, year-round process, interrupted only twice a
year for the peak-time activities.

In passing it should be noted (because the fallacy has now begun to
enter the reference books) that Donna Landry's claim that Duck dismisses
the season of winter 'with a single line', allowing her to award the two
male writers dunces' caps for being ignorant of the winter hardship Collier
knows all too well, is misleading. A quick scan through *The Thresher's
Labour* in search of the word 'winter' would perhaps confirm it: but my
synthesis of the three threshing references makes it clear that the threshing,
which is described in great detail, and whose conditions suggest extreme
hardship, is what Duck's labourers do all winter.[4]

The work is uninterruptible secondly because it is noisy, so the farmer
has an automatic and insidious way of spying on the workers to see that
they are busy: 'The sleeping Threshall does itself betray.' The slightly
bitter note in 'others safely play' is filled out with the list of what the
threshers cannot do that follows:

Nor yet, the tedious Labour to beguile,
And make the passing Minutes sweetly smile,
Can we, like Shepherds, tell a merry tale?
The voice is lost, drown'd by the noisy Flail.
But we may think – alas! what pleasing thing
Here to the Mind can the dull Fancy bring?
The eye beholds no pleasant object here;
No cheerful sound diverts the list'ning ear.
The Shepherd well may tune his voice to sing,
Inspir'd by all the beauties of the Spring.
No Fountains murmur here, no Lambkins play,
No Linets warble, and no Fields look gay.

> 'Tis all a dull and melancholy Scene,
> Fit only to provoke the Muses' Spleen.   (pp. 3–4)[5]

This is in many ways the most significant passage in the poem. It explains the motivation for the poem's theme of anti-pastoral, and it does so in primarily literary terms. Whether Duck got the idea of the singing, story-telling shepherds from literature or from village culture; whether it was a truism or a seepage from the world of his reading into the world of his work experience, is not now recoverable. The Theocritean pastoral tradition is pervasive among accounts of shepherding, and it is extremely difficult to find any account of eighteenth-century shepherding not tainted with literary pastoral or Bakewellian improving zeal. However, two good early twentieth-century accounts are recorded by Evans, and they emphasise both the hardship of the life and the prized professionalism and independence of shepherds; the mixture of spartan living conditions, absolute dedication and freedom from the kind of hostile supervision Duck so resents. Other early and later sources tend to confirm these features.[6] Bearing in mind the slight bitterness we find in Duck towards the supposed pleasures of other workers, we can perhaps sympathise with the feeling of a man in a barn, bullied and spied on by his Master, that it is all right for the shepherds. Moving in one direction from this, we see a surprisingly industrial scenario of extreme noise, dust and satanic gloom; moving in another we see a literary interpretation of this gloom, as the enemy of the imagination, the deadener of the fancy. Threshing is for Duck (very pertinently to his current endeavour) the enemy of poetry. A later eighteenth-century poet, the weaver Samuel Law, was able to make the monotony of work entrance him into poetic imagination, meditating, as he says, 'in the sounding loom' (and in the depths of raging winter):

> Tho' round my house, he rag'd with all his pow'rs,
> I musing sat, and sung away mine hours;
> Yes, all day long, and in each evening gloom,
> I meditated in the sounding loom.[7]

Unable to transform his confinement in this way, Duck makes poetry from it more straightforwardly by writing an account of it, in the form of his anti-pastoral poem.

I have noted that Duck allows one negative merit in threshing, in that it gets the workers out of the sun in summer. I think that a certain pride exists in the description of the work too, if only as a subtext to the main theme of how hard it is. Duck writes:

> Divested of our cloaths, with Flail in hand,
> At a just distance, front to front we stand,
> And first the Threshall's gently swung, to prove
> Whether with just exactness it will move.

That once secure, more quick we whirl them round,
From the strong planks our Crab-tree Staves rebound,
And echoing Barns return the rattling sound.
Now in the air our knotty Weapons fly,
And now with equal force descend from high.
Down one, one up, so well they keep the Time,
The *Cyclops'* Hammers could not truer chime,
Nor with more heavy strokes could *Aetna* groan,
When *Vulcan* forg'd the arms for *Thetis'* Son.   (p. 3)[8]

The final simile here borrows its classicism from Dryden's Virgil:

As when the *Cyclops* at th'Almighty Nod,
New Thunder hasten for their angry God ...
With lifted Arms they order ev'ry Blow,
And chime their sounding Hammers in a Row;
With labour'd Anvils *Aetna* groans below.[9]

Again, the careful positioning of the workers, as in Thomson's two set-pieces and in Duck's mowing scene (p. 5), is dance-like. But here the movement, with its careful synchronisation of 'just exactness' and its dramatic build-up to the Cyclops image, is itself dance-like. Duck's picture suggests elements of skill, pride and excitement in the work, and the way in which the rhythmic pace of his poetry leads the build-up of these qualities is impressive. Evans's account of nineteenth-century Suffolk threshers suggests boredom as a reason for their strong emphasis on rhythm:

They also had certain devices for relieving the monotony. If the company were all bell-ringers they stood round the threshing-floor, which was usually made of elm, and they rang the changes with the flail, in exactly the same rhythm as they did in the steeple with the bells, all coming in their proper turn, and changing and changing about at a signal from a leader. From a distance this rhythmic beating of the elm floor made an attractive simulation of the bells.[10]

(Duck mentions the 'strong planks' of the threshing-floor, so presumably his was made of wood, too.)

Later, removed to the dubious reality of Queen Caroline's various sinecures, the poet will revisit a hayfield, and record a renewed yearning for the physical involvement of farm labour:

Breakfast soon o'er, we trace the verdant Field,
Where sharpen'd Scythes the lab'ring Mowers wield:
Straight Emulation glows in ev'ry Vein;
I long to try the curvous Blade again.

Duck humorously changes this into a self-deprecating simile about 'old Gamesters' and 'Young Combatants', but the feeling is clearly enough expressed, and as if to confirm that Duck has lost as well as gained by his removal from farm work, he records that his old patron, Stanley, whom he now visits, is no longer there.[11] It would be quite wrong to overemphasise the pride and pleasure in Duck's work: it is an undercurrent, not the main text, which shows a debilitating and backbreaking routine. Nevertheless an awareness of Duck's feelings of pride and pleasure, here and in the mowing scene, allows us a fuller picture of his ideas about his work, and perhaps also makes Thomson's descriptive work seem rather less excessively literary: dance-like movement informs the images of work for both poets. This is not to say that work was the same as dance – as it is, perhaps, for Thomson. John Barrell is right to draw attention to the distorting modern tendency to idealise past rural labour, for example as 'craft'.[12] But neither should we ignore evidence of skill, pleasure and those areas in which rural labourers were able to reclaim some 'beauty' and quality of life from the harsh circumstances in which they were forced to live.

We may note, finally, the views on threshing of two later poets, Cowper and Clare. First, a description of threshing, from Cowper's *The Task* (1785). Unlike Duck's threshing, this is being done outdoors:

> The grove receives us next;
> Between the upright shafts of whose tall elms
> We may discern the thresher at his task,
> Thump after thump, resounds the constant flail,
> That seems to swing uncertain, and yet falls
> Full on the destin'd ear. Wide flies the chaff,
> The rustling straw sends up a frequent mist
> Of atoms sparkling in the noon-day beam.
> Come hither, ye that press your beds of down
> And sleep not: see him sweating o'er his bread
> Before he eats it. – 'Tis the primal curse,
> But soften'd into mercy; made the pledge
> Of chearful days and nights without a groan.[13]

This poet is clearly an external observer, able to enjoy the 'sparkling' of dust that Duck could only find suffocating (though it was perhaps less unpleasant outdoors); and far too glib about pleasant days and peaceful nights ever to have done any threshing himself. Nevertheless he can share with Duck the rhythmic pleasures of the flail's 'thump after thump', a phenomenon here finely portrayed as an aural satisfaction based on the fact that, though the beat is relentlessly kept up, each time it seems in danger of stopping, each time it seems a surprise. The modern Reggae beat has the same hypnotic effect, almost missing its cue each beat, and yet always falling 'full on the destin'd ear' (as Cowper puts it).

Cowper's reference to 'the primal curse' is also apt, reflecting the sense of sheer hard labour threshing evokes, even to the observer. A later labourer-poet, John Clare, would similarly associate threshing with the Fall, in a way which almost suggests that the 'curse' of threshing (and the inoculation of stoical patience needed to bear it) was passed down from father to son:

In cases of extreeme poverty my father took me to labour with him and made me a light flail for threshing, learing me betimes the hardship that adam and Eve inflicted on their childern by their inexperienced misdeeds, incuring the perpetual curse from god of labouring for a livlihood, which the teeming earth is said to have produced of itself before, but use is second nature, at least it learns us patience[14]

Duck would surely have protested at Cowper's 'chearful days and nights without a groan' (he graphically describes the opposite of both), but he would perhaps appreciate Clare's version of postlapsarian labour. We shall see that Duck and Thomson both make attempts, very similar to Cowper's, to draw the attention of 'ye that press your beds of down', to the pain of threshing, the tremendous hardship of producing food and comfort for others. As for threshing itself, we may conclude with George Ewart Evans's succinct quotation from an old Suffolk farm worker who 'had no two thoughts about it: "Threshing was real, downright slavery"'.[15]

Charring

Like Duck's threshing, Mary Collier's charring work is both the occupation of winter, and as she says, 'The hardest of our Toil' (p. 20). I have noted that it differs from Duck's work in that it is piece-work rather than guaranteed employment. Given the economic pressure to conform, to appear a 'good employee', that this would suggest, it is perhaps surprising that Collier is, as E. P. Thompson notes, significantly less deferential to her employer than Duck is to his.[16] She is also, as Thompson says, 'sharper'; and there are indications in her description of charring of a clear social and a political consciousness.

In her description of the work itself Mary Collier focuses especially on the 'Mistress', her employer. Stephen Duck's 'Master' in *The Thresher's Labour* is a sort of cartoon tyrant, always spying, ranting at his workers, or scraping at the stubble, determined not to waste good corn on the gleaners. But he seems to have only one concern (greed) and one mood (wrath), whereas Mary Collier's 'Mistress' manifests a range of bad qualities. First, she is idle. The women have been working several hours when:

> At length bright *Sol* illuminates the skies,
> And summons drowsy Mortals to arise.
> Then comes our Mistress to us without fail,
> And in her hand, *perhaps*, a mug of Ale
> To cheer our Hearts, and also to inform
> Herself, what Work is done that very Morn. (p. 21)

Collier seems to have the precise measure of the Mistress here, noting the meagre bribe of a mug of beer in her hand: the italicised word 'perhaps' shows the transparency of the ploy, and how poorly it disguises her real purpose, which is to spy. There is a suggestion in this that like Stephen Duck, Mary Collier does not like being overseen in her work. Close supervision is the sign of wage-labour rather than independent work, and Eric Kerridge notes its significance in relation to the role of out-workers in the eighteenth-century textile industry: 'In short, everything we learn [about skilled and unskilled, farmed-out and on-site textile work] reinforces and confirms Miss J. de L. Mann's perception: what mattered was whether or not the work had to be done under the master's eye.'[17]

Along with idleness goes luxury. Describing the range of fabrics the women have to wash, Collier notes their elaborateness:

> Cambricks and Muslins, which our Ladies wear,
> Laces and Edgings, costly, fine, and rare,
> Which must be wash'd with utmost Skill and Care.
> With Holland Shirts, Ruffles and Fringes too,
> Fashions which our Forefathers never knew.   (p. 20)

Clothes are for Mary Collier functional, their purpose to keep you warm. An awareness of cold permeates this poem, even in the summer fields, where: 'Our tender Babes into the Field we bear, / And wrap them in our cloaths to keep them warm.' So it is not surprising Collier has little time for the delicate, fancy fabrics whose increasing presence in eighteenth-century middle-class households signalled the arrival of modern consumer-capitalism.[18] There may also be an element of national chauvinism in Collier's hostility to 'fashions which our forefathers never knew'. The woollen industry and the government fought a fiercely protectionist battle against 'foreign' textiles and clothing throughout this period, and the cultural resonances would have been sufficiently pervasive for Collier to feel them. She lists 'Holland shirts' and 'Cambricks and Muslins', the latter terms of Dutch and Iraqi etymologies, respectively.[19] Elsewhere Collier is chauvinistic about the 'Turks' whom Duck emulates, in her view, by wanting the women to work in silence. In more practical terms, of course, the fiddly impracticality of 'Laces and Edgings' and 'Ruffles and Fringes', made the work of cleaning them very much harder: the Mistress instructs the washerwomen to 'take care / we don't her Cambricks or her Ruffles tear' (p. 21).

With idleness and luxury goes meanness. The Mistress 'most strictly' insists the washerwomen are to 'save her Soap, and sparing be of Fire', for she:

> Tells us her Charge is great, nay, furthermore,
> Her Cloaths are fewer than the time before.   (p. 21)

This final shot from the Mistress is clearly not believed, and serves only to add dishonesty to her character, and complete the quartet of vices.

Collier's attack on her employer, as with so many other things in the poem, has more than one function. It echoes Duck, providing a suitable character to match his 'Master'. It is part of the 'complaint' about the difficulty of the work. And the Mistress is also the representative of what Collier sees as social parasitism. This is overtly stated in the last lines of the poem:

> So the industrious Bees do hourly strive
> To bring their Loads of Honey to the Hive;
> Their sordid Owners always reap the Gains,
> And poorly recompense their Toil and Pains.   (p. 24)

This is syntactically separate from the rest of the poem, beginning a new sentence and a new (final) verse-paragraph. It is a simile without a grammatical subject, implying that it summarises all that has come before, the 'So' meaning 'In the Way I have just been describing'. Collier is saying, effectively, that in all the parts of her life she has described – the summer farm work, the winter charring, the additional work of looking after children and keeping house – she is being exploited. This is more than a complaint, an 'out-doing' of Duck, it is a complete analysis of her working life (which is to say her whole life, by her own account), and the lives of women like her.

The image of bees is an interesting one. E. P. Thompson suggests Collier may be alluding to Mandeville's influential work, *The Fable of the Bees* (1714), or at least may be showing an awareness of the so-called 'Luxury Debate' the book fuelled. This seems likely, as there are verbal similarities.[20] Collier also had some knowledge of the classics (as her clever uses of the Danae and the Danaus stories, pp. 16 and 23, show), so it is possible she was aware of Virgil's allegorical and didactic material on bees, in the *Georgics* (IV, line 21 ff.) Virgil mixes elements of folklore and political-social allegory with his georgic advice, as is his wont. Collier's simile makes it clear that if she had read Virgil these layers of meaning would certainly be accessible.[21]

Bees have always been of great significance in English folk culture. Both George Ewart Evans and Flora Thompson record the human duty of 'telling the bees' when someone had died (because of their role as psycho-pomps); Evans records the folk version of the belief, known to Virgil, that bees originated in Heaven; and both Evans and Thompson record the practice of 'tanging' the bees when they swarmed, to claim them. Bees were considered to be an intelligent and highly ordered community, and were treated with very great respect. Opie and Tatem record widespread traditions that one could not buy or sell them for money; and that they would not put up with owners who behaved badly. These traditions add ironic significance to Collier's simile. As a good feminist Mary Collier would perhaps also be aware that apiculture in general, and 'talking to the bees' in particular, was especially a female tradition.[22]

As for the charring work Collier describes, it is clearly very hard indeed. Its 'hardness' is emphasised when the Mistress gives the women pewter to clean. The description that follows gives a list of 'hard' kitchenware ('Pots, kettles, sauce-pans, skillets', p. 22) and 'hard' metals ('brass and iron', p. 23): untender objects against which 'Our tender hands and fingers scratch and tear' (pp. 22-3, 'tender hands' from all the washing).

Collier easily finds examples from her working conditions with which to parody and out-do Duck's descriptions of work. When he threshes peas the 'sweat, and dust, and suffocating smoke' begrimes the workers' faces (p. 4); whereas after Collier's cleaning work:

> Colour'd with Dirt and Filth we now appear;
> Your threshing sooty Peas will not come near.
> All the Perfections Woman once could boast
> Are quite obscur'd, and altogether lost.   (p. 23)

Her allusion to the idea of female beauty gives a twist to the subject. It may be that Collier means it is an extra burden of a woman's life that she is expected to look beautiful; or perhaps she means to strike another elegiac chord, in memory of a lost matriarchal golden age, a time when women could be 'beautiful'. Either way, the conditions of work undermine self-image.

Collier also finds in her brewing work a parallel with the way Duck has to keep threshing for fear the Master might notice a silence:

> Like you when threshing, we a Watch must keep;
> Our Wort boils over if we dare to sleep.   (p. 23)

Having been 'perhaps' offered a 'mug of Ale', the women now have to replenish the supply (wort is the brewing mixture). The impression is given that the very physical materials of consumption (pots and pans, boiling 'Wort') torment those who must supply the consumer culture.

Her work is extraordinarily harsh, too, in terms of time. Moira Ferguson quotes in this context Dorothy George's comment that 'Among the longest hours of outworkers were those of the wretched women who went out to wash by the day.' George goes on to write:

We find them arriving at their employer's house overnight in order to work all night and all next day. 'Women who go out a-washing for their livelihood' . . . had to be at work by one in the morning, but as a matter of fact they often went earlier. Ann Nichols, who washed and scoured for a master-builder at Hackney in 1753, arrived about 12 at night – 'that is what we call a day and a half's work', her master said. In 1765 a woman who went monthly to the house of an attorney, said (in connexion with a robbery): 'I went that night a little before dark, time enough to have filled my tubs and copper.'[23]

This explains why Mary Collier's description of her charring is constantly dominated by time. When she writes of 'rising early':

> When bright *Orion* glitters in the skies
> In Winter nights, then early we must rise   (p. 20)

she actually means 'in the middle of the night we must rise'. If Stephen Duck sees the year as a wheel which drives him endlessly on from one tedious task to the next, for Mary Collier and her washerwomen every day brings a fearful race with the clock:

> With heavy hearts we often view the Sun,
> Fearing he'll set before our Work is done;
> For either in the Morning, or at Night,
> We piece the Summer's day with Candle-light.   (p. 22)

Critics of *Macbeth* like to dwell on the 'hideous murder of sleep' in the play. For Mary Collier and her washerwomen, sleep seems to have been hideously murdered on a regular basis.

A later eighteenth-century poet, Anna Laetitia Barbauld, though she treats 'Washing-Day' (1797) in a more overtly humorous way, and from a perspective closer to that of Collier's Mistress, confirms that it starts with the murder of sleep, and an atmosphere of gloom from which 'the very cat' retreats:

> Come, Muse, and sing the dreaded Washing-Day.
> Ye who beneath the yoke of wedlock bend,
> With bowed soul, full well ye ken the day
> Which week, smooth sliding after week, brings on
> Too soon; – for to that day nor peace belongs
> Nor comfort; – ere the first grey streak of dawn,
> The red-armed washers come and chase repose.
> Nor pleasant smile, nor quaint device of mirth,
> E'er visited that day: the very cat,
> From the wet kitchen scared, and reeking hearth,
> Visits the parlour, – an unwonted guest.[24]

While one recognises much of this (having read Collier), one's sympathy remains strongly with the 'red-armed washers' who cannot so easily retreat to the parlour.

What is most surprising in Collier's work description, perhaps, is the deftness with which she deploys her evidence of what is clearly an extraordinarily difficult working life. Moira Ferguson's comment that the poem responds 'angrily' to Duck, and Donna Landry's statement that Collier 'hurls Duck's jibes at his fellow female workers back in his face' do not match the tone of the poem; E. P. Thompson's characterisation of it as 'witty rather than hostile' is much closer.[25] Dorothy George's evidence, as well as Collier's own, suggest that unimaginable hardship and exhaustion lie behind the statement that 'we have hardly ever Time to Dream' (p. 20), yet it is framed as a merely witty riposte to Duck. In describing her work Collier has moved beyond the 'complaint' of Duck: for as she says 'to rehearse all Labour is in vain / Of which we very justly might complain' (p. 23). She deploys her literary skills to testify to the hardship of her working life, and to present a clear social analysis of this; but the manner in which she does so indicates a defiant refusal to accept either the cultural poverty or the resigned demeanour that is her prescribed 'lot' in life. Her poem insistently brings allusiveness and wit to the description of her life not, for sure, because her life suggests either culture or humour, but in determined pursuit of poetry itself, with all its double-edged ability to speak both of what is, and what could be.

Shearing

If the threshing and the charring scenes form the essential element in the work description of Duck and Collier, Thomson offers his scene of sheep-shearing as a model of labour, and as evidence and example of his patriotic national vision:

> A simple Scene! yet hence Britannia sees
> Her solid Grandeur rise.   ('Summer', lines 423–4)[26]

What kind of a model is it? We have noted a range of approaches to different kinds of labour in *The Seasons*. Where hard work is involved, Thomson invokes a concentrated social effort, whereas his nutting scene is characterised by an easy, pastoral approach, and his shepherd also appears to commence his day's work simply, as part of the natural coming-to-life of dawn.

In no respect does sheep-shearing represent the kind of unremitting toil of threshing or charring, or even the pain of bringing in the hay and the corn harvests. John Dyer, who admittedly has a fairly robust attitude to labour, makes it the central scene of pastoral idyll, in *The Fleece* (discussed in Part II, below) in which his swains celebrate the 'harvest of [their] cares'. Thomson finds time for an idyllic scene of pastoral triumph in his description ('Summer', lines 400–5), though it is economically slotted into the respite between sheep-washing and sheep-shearing, reflecting the poet's extreme repugnance to any sort of idleness. Its placing, as we shall see, creates some problems.

Energy and movement are the key elements of his opening portrayal of

sheep-washing (lines 371–96). Thomson carefully builds a scene of controlled confusion, in which swains become 'impatient' and hurl the sheep
into the water, much clamour is in evidence, the fish are 'banish'd' and the
'harmless race' of sheep express their confusion loudly. Thomson, as we
have noted more than once, achieves his effects theatrically, and in
theatrical terms this is the lively overture to the idyll and the shearing
which follow it. The idyll itself is brief:

> The Housewife waits to roll her fleecy Stores,
> With all her gay-drest Maids attending round.
> One, chief, in gracious Dignity inthron'd,
> Shines o'er the Rest, the pastoral Queen, and rays
> Her Smiles, sweet-beaming, on her Shepherd-King;
> While the glad Circle round them yield their Souls
> To festive Mirth, and Wit that knows no Gall.
>
> ('Summer', lines 398–404)

Elsewhere we have seen how Thomson, using his privileged viewpoint,
intervenes to 'jolly along' the various activities his unified vision requires.
He is not as successful at doing so here. In the scenes of ploughing,
haymaking and harvest the workers are bound into their roles by a sense of
united purpose on whose significance the poet can expatiate, and busy
activity whose energy he can appropriate. Here he has neither resource.
This is, in agricultural terms, a scene of waiting, slotted between two parts
of a task: it lacks any intrinsic sense of energy or purpose; but on the other
hand it is not a suitable moment for the kind of pastoral festivity associated
with the completion of peak-time activities, as the task is not yet complete.

As if in compensation for the mistiming and misplacing of this idyll,
Thomson over-orchestrates it, and as at other weak spots in the poem, a
subtext of unease appears. Thus the creation of a pastoral 'King' and
'Queen' does not fit with the traditional practice among sheep-shearers of
electing a 'captain'; but neither is the harvest ritual of pastoral 'Kings' and
'Queens' appropriate to this moment of work.[27] There is a clash between a
vision of men and women as labourers, and another vision of them as a
miniature 'court' (one is reminded of Duck being made 'Warden of Duck
Island' by Queen Caroline). The effect is sanitised and patronising.

One can see this, for example, in the creation of the 'Queen', where the
sickliness again raises the spectre of Thomson's stultified and stultifying
attitude to women.[28] The unreality of this 'queen' also reflects a clash
between georgic and pastoral modes, because the real 'queen' in this work
situation, the farmer's wife or 'Housewife', has already been introduced
with 'all her gay-drest Maids', is presiding over the scene and must
necessarily eclipse this powerless mock-queen.

One senses restriction as well as anxiety in the portrayal of the 'glad
Circle' who surround the 'King' and 'Queen', and who exercise 'Festive

Mirth' and 'Wit that knows no Gall'. Readers of Swift, or *Private Eye*, will confirm that allowing 'no Gall' puts a severely limiting restriction on 'wit'. The scene is also artificially over-immaculate, from the 'snowy white' sheep to the 'gracious Dignity' of the artificial queen. This pastoral moment seems contrived, false and at odds with the passages that surround it. The effect of keeping up this idealising manner through the sheep-shearing passage that follows is increasingly bizarre, and ultimately, I think, overwhelms the poet:

> Meantime, their joyous Task goes on apace:
> Some mingling stir the melted Tar, and Some,
> Deep on the new-shorn Vagrant's heaving Side,
> To stamp his Master's Cipher ready stand;
> Others th'unwilling Wether drag along,
> And, glorying in his Might, the sturdy Boy
> Holds by the twisted Horns th'indignant Ram.
> Behold where bound, and of its Robe bereft,
> By needy Man, that all-depending Lord,
> How meek, how patient, the mild Creature lies!
> What Softness in its melancholy Face,
> What dumb complaining Innocence appears!
> Fear not, ye gentle Tribes, 'tis not the Knife
> Of horrid Slaughter that is o'er you wav'd;
> No, 'tis the tender Swain's well-guided Shears,
> Who having now, to pay his annual Care,
> Borrow'd your Fleece, to you a cumbrous Load,
> Will send you bounding to your Hills again.
>
> ('Summer', lines 405–22)

Good intentions and embarrassment stumble through this passage hand-in-hand. The appearance of the work is as of violence, for the sheep-shearers must wrestle the sheep into a position where it can be shorn, stamp the 'Master's Cipher' on its side and bring a sharp metal implement into close proximity with it. These facts, which Thomson's intense sense of realism will not hide, clash disastrously with the over-wrought idealism the poet has already brought to the scene and is endeavouring to maintain. The result is farcical. The poet's interventions become increasingly stressful, as his highly developed sense of concern for animals takes alarm at the implications of what is happening. Thus he resorts to apologising to the sheep for the depredations of 'needy man'; assures it, aghast, that the shears are not the 'Knife / Of horrid Slaughter' (always a tactless subject to raise with a sheep); and concludes by giving the beast an account of the 'borrowing' of its fleece that is, to say the least, economical with the truth.

Unseemly realities bulge uglily out. The true dynamics of power and interest are revealed by the 'Master's Cipher', the authoritative 'stamp' of the man who is really king in this situation; the poverty of the ersatz 'King' and his 'courtiers' is suggested in the reference to 'needy Man'. And the nursery-rhyme-like explanation given to the sheep serves only to enhance the vividness with which the gory death Man ultimately has in mind for it becomes suddenly, appallingly, clear.

In the midst of all this, Pandora's box again springs open. The sheep, as has been noted, must be wrestled to the ground, and thus it is that Thomson finds himself describing an earthy wrestling match between the two most potent male figures on the farm, in a scene heavily laden with the signifiers of rampant male sexuality: 'And, glorying in his Might, the sturdy Boy / Holds by the twisted Horns th'indignant Ram' (lines 410–11). The problem here is not so much that male sexuality is inappropriate; harvests, be they of hay, corn, or wool, are occasions in which sexuality, symbolic and literal, is appropriate, as we have seen. The problem is that there are conflicting forces at work. On the one hand Thomson's intense imaginative engagement with the 'peak periods' of harvests clearly sees and delineates their sexual element; on the other a set of preconceptions as to the socially allowable limits of sexual behaviour and self-expression fosters a coyness, which we see in Thomson's tone and language in his passage. It is the presence of this coyness in the scene that makes the appearance of male sexuality seem contrastingly bizarre.

This central scene of rural labour attempts and fails to reconcile forces which in the 'real world' are in conflict, using poetry to try and harmonise them. In the 'real world' conflict exists between social classes, between humans and animals, between social proprieties and sexual expression, and between official and counter-cultural views of the limits of rustic festivity. The conflict between humans and animals seems particularly to upset Thomson's harmony here. His other scenes of rural labour for the most part stick to the processes of arable farming. Where he deals with animal husbandry, his concern is with simple pastoral tasks which do not involve the kind of exploitation that the shearing scene hints at. In his treatment of blood sports in 'Autumn' no contradiction is present, because he feels able to express his hearty condemnation of them, exempting only the fox, whose status as 'vermin' excludes it from compassion.[29] Here he is in a quandary, and his anxiety leads him to expose potential sources of conflict he would perhaps sooner keep hidden: between the interests of the real 'queen' of the farm and her puppet-rival; between the interests of the man whose brand is indelibly stamped on the sheep and the 'needy' swain, who needs to 'borrow' (a suggestive and duplicitous word) the fleece; between the decorous straitjacket of 'Wit that knows no gall' and the alarming opposite its anxious mention conjures up: that there might be an unkind propensity among the labourers to laugh at their 'betters'. As well they might, if this 'simple scene', sinking inexorably into bathos, is to represent their lives and aspirations.[30]

4

Compensations

Respites

At the margins of the portrayal of labour in Thomson, Duck and Collier, in the moments of beginning and ending and in the seams that become apparent when different kinds of portrayal come into conflict, much can be determined. Another useful indicator of ideological intention is the way in which the poets describe or offer what I shall call 'compensations', meaning positive experiences or explanations which seem to alleviate or counterbalance the hardship of rural labour. We have seen a rather bizarre example in Thomson's attempt to explain to the sheep why it is being grappled to the ground, held down and fleeced by a man with a pair of shears; and we may opportunely take this as a graphic, if somewhat crude, model for the kind of compensatory material I have in mind, though my concern is with those who may feel fleeced of their labour rather than their coats.

We have also seen some of Thomson's more successful compensations: the enjoyment of Nature the poet offers for rising early on a summer morning (and, conversely, the terrible fate that awaits sleepers-in); and the sense of communal enjoyment in the labour of harvest and haytime. Compensations may also arise apparently spontaneously from the subject: thus in 'Autumn' Thomson sets his swains a-nutting. Although this is work of a kind, the passage is pure pastoral. I think Thomson recognises that this work is self-evidently pleasurable, and the passage presents no need for social or aesthetic intervention. The excitement of discovering the 'glossy shower' of hazelnuts, with their faintly sexual connotations, seems a natural compensation.[1] The more meagre compensations of Duck's vision have also been apparent: the brief period when each task is new; the pride in skilled work; the momentarily pleasurable registering of a new season or a new day. We have seen too how Mary Collier's women sustain themselves by their heroic determination and their sense of communality. I want to examine now a more oblique compensation that Thomson seems to offer.

There is a range of specified and unspecified addressees in the poem, and the uncertainty in some areas about who is being addressed is instructive. This can be seen in 'Summer', which is carefully structured to follow the progress of a summer day. Thus we have, between the digressions, the dawn and the shepherd's emergence (lines 43–66), the sun's rise (lines 81–96), the shepherd's second morning task (lines 220–4), the haymaking and sheep-shearing (lines 352–422), the mower's retreat from the sun (lines 432–50), the animals bothered by insects (lines 485–515), evening (lines 1371–6), sunset (lines 1620–9), the shepherds' homecoming (lines 1664–5) and night (lines 1684–5). Interspersed are the digressions, including three more rehearsals of the theme of idleness (lines 67–80, 342–51, 1630–40). If we place these in their context among the various passages of useful labour, we can see a pattern of antithesis: labouring is happy, useful, good, satisfying, sustaining; idleness is wretched, useless, false, unsatisfying, wasteful.

But who do these codes address? I raise this issue because Thomson also appears to license a quite different sort of behaviour, based on an effortless pastoral enjoyment. At the height of noon, for example, occurs the following passage:

> Resounds the living Surface of the Ground:
> Nor undelightful is the ceaseless Hum,
> To him who muses thro' the Woods at Noon;
> Or drowsy Shepherd, as he lies reclin'd,
> With half-shut Eyes, beneath the floating Shade
> Of Willows grey, close-crouding o'er the Brook.
>
> ('Summer', lines 281–6)

And again, in a second passage about 'raging Noon':

> Echo no more returns the chearful Sound
> Of sharpening Scythe: the Mower sinking heaps
> O'er him the humid Hay, with Flowers perfum'd.   (lines 443–5)

A third passage of leisure, the swimming episode (lines 1244–68) may be discounted in this context, as a digression with no immediate location in the diurnal pattern. But there remains an ambiguity in the two passages quoted: why are these workers lying in the shade, apparently with the poet's approval, after all he has said about idleness? It is noticeable that Thomson gives himself a privileged role in 'Summer', as one who can wander in and out of the action, now observing scenes of labour, now meditating in the woods. The figure who 'muses thro' the Woods at Noon' may be identified with the poet-narrator (note the first person of 'In vain I sigh / And restless turn, and look around for Night', lines 455–6). But the shepherd, the very model of industriousness, is also apparently being allowed to sleep under a tree at 'raging Noon'.

One simple explanation is that this is a reward for his early conscien-
tiousness, a kind of siesta or break. But that does not tally with any detail
the poet gives us. For the shepherd, getting up in the morning is seen as its
own reward, while sleeping during the day is for Thomson a terrible vice,
and considerable moral force is focused on its condemnation. The mower
is similarly indulging something that ought to be abhorrent within
Thomson's ideological framework. A distinction may possibly be made
between unacceptable 'lying in' in the morning, and an acceptable 'sleeping over' or 'sheltering from' the hottest part of the day. Thomson does not
make this distinction in his georgic advice or in his commentary, and I can
find evidence of no such tradition in the English or (for Thomson) the
lowland Scottish countryside. Where we do find this is in the Mediterranean siesta. Mediterranean rural traditions are by no means rare in
English rural poetry, but their presence invariably indicates the influence
of a non-naturalistic, neo-classical pastoral, rooted in the Theocritean
tradition. Theocritus himself gives advice on siestas in Idyll X, 'Milon's
Song', described by one translator as 'a string of popular maxims':

> They that thresh corn should shun the noonday sleep.
> > When the sun's high,
> Then is the time that chaff from straw will part most easily.
> But reapers should start toiling when the lark leaves his nest,
> And cease work when he sleeps; but in the noonday heat should rest.

(Milon concludes: 'It's songs like that, that men should sing who labour in
the sun.')[2] This is the pastoral tradition in which Thomson's mower
clearly acts.

I think that what may have happened, indeed, is a seepage between two
kinds of rural world. That Thomson's attack on idleness is concerned with
the activities of rural labourers is apparent by its context: it appears to be
addressed to mankind in general, but only the third and least powerful
passage has any general context. The two main attacks are very directly
linked to the shepherd's rise and to the haymaking. On the other hand the
poet, or indeed any lay wanderer, is not bound by these moral strictures.
Thomson moves easily between genres in *The Seasons*. Here, I think, some
of the characters from his industrious georgic have wandered off with him
into the territory of his idyllic pastoral. It is perhaps not surprising that
this kind of thing should happen, since the distinction between pastoral
and georgic, and especially between the description of ideal nature in
pastoral, and what Addison calls the 'beauties and embellishments' with
which farming advice is 'set off' in georgic is not so clear that we can
always separate the two.[3]

We might see this as a kind of accidental cross-pollination, the literary
equivalent of what happens when a gardener puts fennel and dill too close

together. But it may be that Thomson would see no such accident here. He weaves, as many of the authors of long poems in the eighteenth century do, many genres together, and is perhaps creating a hybrid deliberately. The advantage, if this is indeed purposeful, is that he can have his cake and eat it; he can give carrot-and-stick lectures on industry and idleness, and at the same time appear to admit the industrious labourer into the essentially idle territory of pastoral. A literary compromise is thus effected, in which stern labour provides the poem with credibility, while the pastoral ease of wandering at will amongst 'Nature' makes the poetry, and by implication the work, seem pleasurable.

In literary terms, Thomson's two summer 'rests' seem closest in spirit to the pastorals of Andrew Marvell, whose 'Damon the Mower' (stanza 4) pleads for a retreat from the midday sun, and whose narrative persona retreats to the woods in a very Thomsonian manner in 'Upon Appleton House' (stanza 61); and to the Keatsian pastoral of 'To Autumn', in which, by a miraculously compressed version of Thomson's georgic-pastoral sleight of hand, the rich harvests of September are won without anyone apparently moving a muscle. The only figure in Keats's landscape is the personified figure of Autumn, who is in a condition of advanced narcosis, 'on a half-reaped furrow sound asleep, / Drowsed with the fume of poppies' (lines 16–17). 'Autumn' does then briefly give the appearance of carrying gleaned corn across the brook, but in the very next line is again immobile, watching the apple juice drip 'hours by hours' (line 22). We do not usually question the lack of labour in this pastoral poem: indeed it seems slightly absurd for us to do so, probably because Keats does not offer the didactic material on labour and its importance that Thomson does. The illusion seems to the modern reader less successful in Thomson, where it sits awkwardly among passages of exhortations to avoid idleness.[4]

Duck cannot create such an illusion at all: as far as he is concerned, the shepherds are out in the fresh air, singing and story-telling to their hearts' content, while he sweats his life away in a dusty barn; and when he is mowing, there is no retreat from the relentless sun. His compensations must be worked more directly and painstakingly from the intractable seam of rural labour. Similarly Mary Collier can envisage no seepage of this sort. Time is for her relentless, sleep a rare luxury, and 'little rest is found' (p. 23) in any circumstances. Her consciousness of hardship is based solidly on being aware that for her, there is no pastoral idyll, leisure, or indeed genuine compensation of any sort.

Gleaning

Even if Thomson is purposeful in his generic mixing, it is a rather literary sleight-of-hand. A more practically sustaining compensation might be a plea for charity towards the rural worker. Both Thomson and Duck make such appeals in their poems formally, and I shall discuss and compare them presently. But first I want to look at a form of 'compensation' which is related to charity, and which occurs in all three poems: this is gleaning, and we get a range of approaches to it in the poems. Thomson opts for an exclamatory appeal:

> Behind the Master walks, builds up the Shocks;
> And, conscious, glancing oft on every Side
> His sated Eye, feels his Heart heave with Joy.
> The Gleaners spread around, and here and there,
> Spike after Spike, their sparing Harvest pick.
> Be not too narrow, Husbandmen! but fling
> From the full Sheaf, with charitable Stealth,
> The liberal Handful. Think, oh grateful think!
> How good the God of Harvest is to you;
> Who pours Abundance o'er your flowing Fields;
> While these unhappy Partners of your Kind
> Wide-hover round you, like the Fowls of Heaven,
> And ask their humble Dole. The various Turns
> Of Fortune ponder; that your Sons may want
> What now, with hard Reluctance, faint, ye give.
>
> ('Autumn', lines 162–76)

Duck gives us two entirely different versions of gleaning, and for once the later version seems more graphic and eagle-eyed than the earlier. The beginning of both versions is identical. The theme is the adversities the reapers encounter in the cornfield:

> The Morning past, we sweat beneath the Sun,
> And but uneasily our Work goes on.
> Before us we perplexing Thistles find,
> And Corn blown adverse with the ruffling Wind.
>
> (1730 version, p. 10; 1736 version, p. 24)

After this, the first version has the gleaners as a threat from the rear, to match the thistles and the badly aligned corn ahead:

> Behind our backs the Female Gleaners wait,
> Who sometimes stoop, and sometimes hold a Chat.   (1730, p. 10)

This is the 'double-fencing' of thistles and women which Collier parodies; and by doing so, as Thompson and Sugden point out, she demonstrates that she is responding to the 1730, not the 1736 version of the poem.[5] In the second version the women have gone, and in their place is the old enemy:

> Behind our Master waits; and if he spies
> One charitable Ear, he grudging cries,
> "Ye scatter half your Wages o'er the Land."
> Then scrapes the Stubble with his greedy Hand. (1736, pp. 24–5)

This is a major change, and if both versions are put alongside the Thomson passage some interesting questions about influence suggest themselves: all three passages begin with the same verbal formulation, and address the same subject. There is, as James Sambrook has noted, a later passage in 'Autumn' that seems to have been influenced by the ending of *The Thresher's Labour* (discussed below). Here we may well be seeing a two-way influence, in which Thomson borrows an image from the 1730 version of the poem, and Duck in turn recognises this borrowing, and decides to amend his own text for the 1736 version.[6]

Thompson and Sugden make an important point about Duck's first version: 'Gleaners would not have been following behind the backs of the reapers, since it was normally the custom not to permit gleaning until the harvest had been carried. In 1730 Duck had been eliding two labour processes: first, the women's labour of gathering the sheaves into stooks, ready for carrying, and secondly the gleaning'.[7] The implication of this inaccuracy (remembering Duck's haytime chauvinism) seems to be that he does not much care what the women are doing – chattering or gleaning or gathering – to him they are just a nuisance; and his marginalising their work (by not appearing to care what it is) seems purposely reinforced by this apparently casual error. There is also a second possible purpose to the mistake: if the women are gathering, then they are doing useful work. But that is not the impression Duck wants to give. Gleaners by contrast are a ritualised Other in the harvest process: where reapers and gatherers have to give to the harvest, they take. They are seen as a kind of licensed beggar – a tolerated nuisance. Here again the women's superfluousness is subtly nuanced.

Thomson, too, compresses the processes of harvesting and gleaning. This may also be purposeful, in that it enables him to provide a contrast between the farmer's pleasure in his situation and the gleaners' 'unhappy' demeanour in theirs, which I think is intentional. Thomson is concerned with a moral imperative here, and the contrast prepares it well. If Duck is indeed the influence, Thomson has used his compressed reaping-gleaning scene as a stepping stone to a larger (and different) idea.

Six years after the publication of 'Autumn', and a year after Duck had written a poem which praised Thomson, the 'official' version of *The Thresher's Labour* was published, with the old remark about gleaning abandoned, and the new quatrain about the greedy master in place. What had happened in the meantime? All other evidence points to Duck's rapid absorption by a culture that cared not a jot about the veracity of rustic poetry. Yet here he carefully increases his veracity, abandoning the poem's second attack on women workers, in favour of what is one of the most vivid and successful images in the poem, that of the stubble-scraping master. It seems to me highly probably that Duck had read 'Autumn';

recognised in Thomson's gleaning passage an echo of his own poem; noted how it built something he had passed briefly over into a matter of significance (while repeating his own careless mistake); and decided to think again about the harvest field, and rewrite gleaning in the light of 'Autumn'.[8] We shall see later that in the 1736 version of his poem Duck similarly tagged on to his gleaning a charitable appeal which echoes a similar appeal in 'Autumn'. In what follows I shall be looking at this revised 1736 passage on gleaning rather than the 1730 passage.

The moral imperative Thomson invokes is a very ancient one. It is likely that the practice of leaving a remnant of corn in the field stems from prehistoric propitiation rites. For Thomson and for Duck, however, the moral significance and ancient authority behind gleaning would be founded in the Old Testament. The Bible lists gleaning as a command of God, given twice among his instructions to Moses, and reiterated by Moses to the people of Israel. The story of Ruth illustrates its practice: she is a widow, and Moses had translated God's instruction that the gleanings be left 'unto the poor, and to the stranger' (Leviticus, 23, 22) into 'for the stranger, for the fatherless, and for the widow' (Deuteronomy, 24, 19). Behind the Thomson and Duck passages lies a characteristically inflexible command:

9 And when ye reap the harvest of your land, thou shalt not wholly reap the corners of thy field, neither shalt thou gather the gleanings of thy harvest.
10 And thou shalt not glean thy vineyard, neither shalt thou gather every grape of thy vineyard; thou shalt leave them for the poor and stranger: I am the Lord your God.   (Leviticus 19, 9–10)

Malcolmson notes the conflict in the eighteenth century, part of a larger struggle in the rural world, between gleaning as a right and gleaning as a favour, which the latter view increasingly won.[9] For both Thomson and Duck, writing in the 1720s, gleaning is already a favour, or at least something which is strongly begrudged. The exact nature of Thomson's appeal in 'Autumn', lines 162–76, is problematical. I think we can deduce that as with 'Spring', the separate identification of a 'Master' means that by husbandmen Thomson again means employees, or harvesters.[10] If this is so, Thomson is effectively inviting them (to put it in a legalistic way) to defraud the farmer of some of his corn. In this context the phrase 'charitable Stealth' ('Autumn', line 168) is revealing, suggesting that they should do this unobserved (and not get caught by the corn's owner), and that the justification for this bit of petty crime is charity. They are to steal from the rich to give to the poor.

However, the appeal is augmented into apostrophe (in the later lines quoted), in which Thomson declaims that the 'God of Harvest' has filled 'your flowing Fields'. This makes no sense if the addressee is still the husbandmen, who own no fields; and the rest of the speech is similarly addressed as if to someone of means. Unless (as seems unlikely) Thomson means to change his addressee in mid-stream, he is either blurring the differences between employer and employees, or else he considers there to be no difference in function or interest between the two. Either way it is clear that Thomson is not interested in delineating class roles within the peak-time activities: he will allow no conflict of interests, no hint of disharmony, into his harvest scene.

Having thus blended the workers and the farmer into a unified commu-nality of interest, he can acknowledge the existence of difference in status and interest in rural work by channelling it to the gleaners; that is, he can allow the rural poor to be distinctly separate from the harmonious unity of the harvest by rendering them harmless through the various euphemisms of patronage, pity and piety he uses to describe them (especially the Biblical 'Fowls of Heaven', from Psalm 104, 12); and by giving them a removed form of participation in the harvest, via gleaning. Thomson's moral argument for gleaning invokes the idea of the 'Wheel of Fortune': the privileged farmer might be in the gleaners' position one day, and should share the bounty of harvest. The unspoken link between the two ideas is that one represents a moral insurance policy against the other, put much more directly by Moses when he instructs the People of Israel to leave gleanings 'that the Lord thy God may bless thee in all the work of thine hands' (Deuteronomy, 24, 19): if the gleanings were not left, by implication, the Lord's blessing would be removed (and presumably given to someone else). Thus two achievements are neatly dovetailed: the rural poor are maintained, in both senses of the word, in their role as recipients of charity, reinforcing the privileged position of the harvest's winners; and the continuity of the winners' success is assured. The reference to 'your Sons' (line 175) lengthens this perspective, seeming to suggest that a small investment of corn (and morality) in the gleaning market is likely to pay good long-term dividends.

Duck's careful opening echo of Thomson's 'Behind the Master walks' ('Behind our Master waits', 1736, p. 24) responds to 'Autumn' politely enough; but Duck's concern is in fact to cut through the web of moral posturing Thomson has set up; to puncture the high ideals with a memory from his own field work. Duck shows here he has a good nose for mystification: his approach to the subject is plain and direct, like that of Cobbett, who later recorded that 'We left these poor fellows, after having given them, not "religious Tracts," which would, if they could, make the labourer content with half starvation, but, something to get them some bread and cheese and beer, being firmly convinced, that it is the body that wants filling, and not the mind.'[11] Duck's field workers seem to have precisely this kind of straightforwardness: to leave a bit of corn ('one charitable Ear', 1736, p. 24) for the gleaners seems an uncomplicated matter, an automatic act not worthy of elaboration, much less the kind of moralising we find in Thomson. Duck's Master, however, will not allow good grain to go to waste. His farmer – like those Cobbett often portrays – has a head full of the price of corn. Thomson's farmer is also counting ('glancing oft on every Side', 'Autumn', line 163), but there the resemblance stops. Duck's farmer is angry and unhappy, whereas Thomson's enjoys the success of the harvest. Duck's is a pleasing if predictable caricature: his farmer is greedy as well as angry, and as a result is inappropriate in his behaviour; scraping the stubble was the prerogative of the gleaners, even to the extent of cutting their hands. But this farmer would rather cut his own hands than lose any profit. As usual, his tone is one of thinly-veiled threat: he is essentially an absurd, comic figure.

It is in both cases the farmers for whom gleaning is a difficult issue, whether its rationale must be carefully explained to one, in 'Autumn', or the other is descending on its practitioners with grasping fury, in *The Thresher's Labour*. One gains an interesting composite picture here, which we might see in terms of an ancient, almost instinctive tradition coming into conflict with the new passion for profit and farming productivity. The two accounts, though very different, mesh together well.

I have left Mary Collier's gleaning until last, because she brings to her description of gleaning a perspective that differs fundamentally from the picture we get from Thomson and Duck. For both of them, whatever their sympathies, gleaning is outside the field work: gleaners are Other; whereas Collier is herself a gleaner, and not ashamed of it either. The first thing she does is to reintegrate it with the other tasks of harvest:

> When Harvest comes, into the Field we go,
> And help to reap the Wheat as well as you,
> Or else we go the ears of Corn to glean,
> No Labour scorning, be it e'er so mean,
> But in the Work we freely bear a part,
> And what we can, perform with all our Heart. (p. 17)

There are two hints of defensiveness here: the reference to 'mean' labour, and the pride in performing 'with all our Heart'. Both suggest that gleaning has a disparaged reputation; but Collier's defence is a good one: she deflects gleaning's meanness, refusing to accept that it is useless labour, and demarginalising the work by listing it alongside the productive labour of reaping. This is reinforced at the end of the gleaning passage, where, similarly, she puts alongside it both gathering and cutting peas (p. 20).

Collier's central scene of gleaning has been discussed; it is one of the most impressive moments in the poem, and it reverses Thomson's separation of the gleaners as the poor-relations of the harvest. Collier's gleaners have a low-key sense of communality: they must carry home at night 'Our Corn . . . and our Infant too' (p. 19), which does not leave much energy for sociability. Nevertheless the sense of community is as strong as anything Thomson offers, and it reinstates the ancient and honourable practice of gleaning as effectively as the more emphatic insistence Collier gives at the beginning and end of her gleaning section.

Charity

Though it begins as an echo of it, Duck's 1736 reference to gleaning undercuts Thomson's exclamatory didacticism. The two poets' appeals for charity have more in common, though their differences are also instructive. Thomson follows his gleaning passage with the exemplum of Palemon and Lavinia ('Autumn', lines 177–310), based appropriately on the Book of Ruth. He then introduces an autumn storm (lines 311–50). Thomson loves a storm, of course, and this one has its moments of dramatic excitement. Its purpose, though, is slightly different from those of 'Summer' (lines 1103–68) and 'Winter' (line 66 ff.). Their function is to invoke the sublime, and thus dramatise the essence of the two 'extreme' seasons. The 'Autumn' storm is a dramatic sequel to the warning Thomson has given in the gleaning scene. The storm's purpose is directly to reverse fortune, by destroying the husbandman's food and cattle. I use the word 'husbandman' here uneasily aware that the usual problem of terminology exists: the victim of the storm is again described as a husbandman, but the evidence of his status is contradictory. The landlord is asked not to demand the rent (implying a tenant farmer), while the husbandman is portrayed as a man whose physical labour keeps the landlord in luxury (implying a labourer, or possibly a small farmer). But in any case the occupation of tenant-farmer is itself, as John Barrell says, 'too capacious to be generalised about with any confidence'.[12] What we can say here is that Thomson is considering someone who carries out physical labour for a living. I cannot resolve this example of what is a fairly intractable problem in the poem further, so I refer to a 'husbandman', as Thomson does.

I have considered some of the many ways in which the poet intervenes *in propria persona* in the scenes he creates, seeing in this a need, sometimes anxious, to ensure that they always seem socially harmonious, that there is no source of conflict in the human part of his equation (especially when it comes to scenes in which, for Duck or Collier, there is a great deal of conflict). Thomson's daring use of the storm here again invites such a reading, but also marks the poet's intervention on a higher level of his world-picture: he asks the landlord to intervene on behalf of the husbandman against a disharmony caused by Nature itself. This is a new phenomenon in the poem. Nature's predations have hitherto demanded only a minimum of authorial tweaking: a counsel of patience here so that the ploughman can emerge at the seasonally appropriate time, a literary sleight-of-hand there to remove the farm workers from the midday sun. He now makes Nature do its worst, and then offers the human figures a way out.

A dramatic human intervention is needed if the husbandman is to survive. The appeal made (though it is euphemistically put) is for a suspension of rent. A forthright, ur-Marxist analysis of economic relationships is the principal argument:

> Comes Winter unprovided, and a Train
> Of clamant Children dear. Ye Masters, then,
> Be mindful of the rough laborious Hand,
> That sinks you soft in Elegance and Ease;
> Be mindful of those Limbs in Russet clad,
> Whose Toil to yours is Warmth, and graceful Pride;
> And oh be mindful of that sparing Board,
> Which covers yours with Luxury profuse,
> Makes your Glass sparkle, and your Sense rejoice!
> Nor cruelly demand what the deep Rains,
> And all-involving Winds have swept away.
>
> ('Autumn', lines 349–59)

This appeal takes us into territory more familiar to students of Gray's *Elegy*, in that its sense implies a criticism of the husbandman's position in society, while its aesthetics imply an acceptance of that position. A similar set of contradictory impulses haunts the potential aspirations and limitations of Gray's 'hoary-headed swain', as many critics have noted. The explanation, I think, is that Thomson wishes to invoke both feeling and intellect: he wants his landlord to feel pity for this unfortunate creature (and hence we have the aesthetics of sentimental acceptance), and at the same time to recognise a moral obligation to him (hence the harsh economic analysis). The husbandman must seem to pose, potentially, a moral threat, while remaining harmlessly pathetic. This I think he does. The first quality is a dangerous one if Thomson is to maintain his vision of perfect harmony. He risks this, I think, in order to attempt to prove the larger meaning that even the greatest upset cannot destroy the balanced forces of nature and society so long as moral obligation informs the economy of the latter.

Duck's charitable appeal risks less, but has something in common with Thomson's appeal:

> LET those who feast at Ease on dainty Fare,
> Pity the Reapers, who their Feasts prepare:
> For Toils scarce ever ceasing press us now;

Rest never does, but on the Sabbath, show;
And barely that our Masters will allow.
Think what a painful Life we daily lead;
Each Morning early rise, go late to Bed:
Nor, when asleep, are we secure from Pain;
We then perform our Labours o'er again:
Our mimic Fancy ever restless seems;
And what we act awake, she acts in Dreams.
Hard Fate! Our Labours ev'n in Sleep don't cease;
Scarce HERCULES e'er felt such Toils as these!   (1736, p. 25)[13]

The first thing to note is that Duck is not actually asking for anything material or financial. All that he asks is contained in the first couplet, 'Pity' – recognition by the consumers of what the winning of their food costs the labourers in toil. I have suggested that this couplet, which was added in 1736, was influenced by 'Autumn', and there are clearly similarities: to 'pity' (Duck) and to 'be mindful' (Thomson) are akin to each other. The economic analysis is also closely matched; Duck's characterisation of the reapers as those who 'prepare' the feasts is less euphemistic than Thomson's rather periphrastic lines, but they are saying essentially the same thing. Duck also manages without Thomson's sentimental metonymy for the reapers as 'Limbs in russet clad'. In the place of these literary tropes is an alarming sense of things getting worse, as 'Toils scarce ever ceasing press us now'; of barely stopping for the sabbath (we are in the middle of the corn harvest). Not only does the labour voraciously eat more and more time, but, as the passage on sleep conveys, the labourers have no place to retreat: the toil follows them to bed and haunts their dreams. This last passage epitomises Duck's poetic temper, in its combination of sincere complaint, consciousness of imaginative implications ('mimic Fancy'), and ambiguously underplayed humour. A good modern parallel, I think, is Charles Chaplin, especially the Chaplin of *Modern Times* (1936), playing a harried worker, whose mind-numbing work monstrously invades the poor remnant of his life, with the same mixture of humour and profound distress Duck registers. Chaplin's relentless machine is the 'Electro Steel Corporation', whose production line also allows (in Duckian terms) 'no intermission', driving the worker to nervous breakdown. Pastoralism – for Duck the lucky singing, story-telling shepherds, for Chaplin the worker's dream of suburban bliss with a real cow to milk – is a bitter joke for both. Duck's mowers 'but faintly eat', while Chaplin's boss tests on the worker a feeding machine that 'requires no energy' and so eliminates the need for a meal-break altogether. Duck's workers are counted off for their tasks by numbers, while Chaplin's opening shot is of a herd of sheep, dissolving into an image of workers rushing to work.

Mary Collier, equally harried by labour, asks for no charity. Her nature is not of a kind which will accept the humble demeanour a charitable appeal would require. Her equivalent address is to Duck himself, whose failure of solidarity as a fellow-worker she aims to expose and correct. Where she comes closest to asking for something, what starts as a question ends as a statement. The addressee is Duck: 'What you would have of us we do not know' (p. 20). Ten low words express her frustration plainly enough; but her major appeal is saved for the ending of the poem (discussed above, chapter 3). An economic analysis more clear than those of Thomson and Duck ends the song; and in the place of the suppliant demeanour of the charity ethic there is righteous anger and brave defiance. As E. P. Thompson suggests, this posture may have helped deprive Collier of a Duckian translation; but there were also advantages in avoiding the psychological morass of eighteenth-century patronage. Like the painter George Morland, Mary Collier is not prepared to sacrifice her art to the needs of social obligation, or patronage.[14]

5

Homecomings

The cottage door

Duck's haunted dreams, though he allows his sense of the absurd to modulate them, are disturbing. His apostrophe to:

> Hard Fate! Our Labours ev'n in Sleep don't cease;
> Scarce *Hercules* e'er felt such Toils as these!
>
> (p. 11)

is informed by the idea that something is very wrong, which he expresses in indignation, and translates with Duckian decorum into classical allusion. What is 'wrong', in cultural terms, is that in eighteenth-century portrayals of labour, home is the ultimate compensation, the symbol of warmth, food, safety, comfort, nurture and the 'miniature kingdom' of family. 'Coming home' is a tradition that stretches back through Western literature: to *The Odyssey* (whose hero conquers all enemies, braves all seductions and turns down at least one utopia in order to get home); and to Sappho, whose pastoral lyric addressed to the evening star encapsulates this pervasive theme exquisitely:

> Hesperus, you bring everything that
> the light-tinged dawn has scattered;
> You bring the sheep, you bring the goat, you bring
> the child back to its mother[1]

In Duck's world no place is sacred: not his home, nor even his bed: his mind itself is invaded by his labour. (Orwell's *1984* makes the modern reader especially sensitive to this ultimate horror.) The 'wrongness' of this is informed by Duck's understanding that a major cultural icon is being upturned by his work; and I shall complete this examination of the way the three poets portray rural labour by looking at their approaches to homecoming scenes, to see how they reflect their ideas and feelings about rural labour, and rural life.

If the homecoming scene is a universal western ideal, the eighteenth century adopted as a favourite depiction of it the 'cottage door' scene. John Barrell has charted some of the meanings such a scene could be made

71

to carry: 'a contentment that arises directly from the sense of labour honestly performed', a 'properly conducted family life', 'a balanced life in which repose is properly only the reward of industry', and so on. Barrell's reading of the image in later eighteenth-century poetry and painting leads him to conclude that the portrayal was a neutralising one, whose dissemination in art and literature had the function of keeping the labourer's energies within the microcosm of family life, and thus away from the kinds of consciousness-raising E. P. Thompson charts in *The Making of the English Working Class*.[2]

Barrell's model is a useful one to have in mind when considering portrayals of rural life in the period. However, we need to make some adjustments to it when looking at the poems under discussion. Firstly, in the paintings and poems Barrell examines, the rural labourer has the role of subject, and possibly addressee, but not that of creator; whereas two of our poets, as we have seen, are themselves labourers. Secondly, none of Barrell's poets and artists are women, a matter which cannot but be of importance in considering a *topos* in which women figure so centrally. In their homecoming scenes the obvious class and gender differences between Thomson, Duck and Collier would therefore seem to be of great potential significance: we may expect to see the cottage door from three different angles, as indeed we do; though the homecoming scenes in these poems also produce some surprises.

Thomson's two homecomings in 'Summer' may be regarded as the norm, the standard version of the cottage-door scene which conforms to Barrell's characterisation, and against which we may measure other such scenes. The first of these comes early in the poem:

> Home, from his morning Task, the Swain retreats;
> His Flock before him stepping to the Fold:
> While the full-udder'd Mother lows around
> The chearful Cottage, then expecting Food,
> The Food of Innocence, and Health!   (lines 220–4)

In fact this is a non-standard homecoming in two ways, though Thomson normalises both. Firstly, the shepherd has not been out all day. It is still morning, and the homecoming scene is typically an evening scene, associated with the contented musing appropriate to the period after one's work is complete. Thomson normalises this by making it a reward for the shepherd's early rising, a special morning idyll which conforms to Barrell's 'contentment that arises directly from the sense of labour honestly performed'. By getting up early, and getting the first task of taking the sheep to pasture done so soon, he has earned a reward already, though his day's work will continue later. Secondly, the shepherd is a bachelor, and thus the welcoming wife and children are missing. Again, this is no matter.

Thomson piles on the language of nurture and reassurance, and transfers to the shepherd's cow (the 'full-udder'd Mother') the maternal qualities conventionally ascribed to the woman in the scene. For the other qualities the scene requires, Thomson relies on the pleasant or positive associations of certain words: 'chearful Cottage', 'Food', 'Innocence' and 'Health'.

No labour behind the scenes, no sense of georgic engagement, is allowed to mar the vision. The shepherd, with his maternally reassuring cow, and surrounded by his sheep (for children), basks in the warmth of pastoral domesticity; and despite its abnormality, this is a cottage-door motif of a kind that suggests the miniature world of hearth and home: the power of the cottage-door scene is such that even a bachelor, with a little artifice, may be seen to receive a share of its benevolence. Thomson's second homecoming ('Summer', lines 1664–81) is equally conventional, and again concerns the shepherd. His homecoming comforts here take the form of chivalric flirtation with the milkmaid on the way; and his return to what is presumably an empty house is avoided by means of moving the description on to a folksy, reassuring passage about the evening culture of the village: 'Fairy People', 'Village-Stories', and so on.

There is only one other affirmation of the myth of the cottage door in the three poems under discussion, and it is a stringently qualified one. Stephen Duck has finished his first day's hay mowing:

> Homewards we move, but so much spent with Toil,
> We walk but slow, and rest at every Stile.
> Our good expecting Wives, who think we stay,
> Got to the door, soon eye us in the way.
> Then from the pot the dumpling's catch'd in haste,
> And homely by its side the bacon's plac'd.
> Supper and sleep by Morn new strength supply;
> And out we set again our works to try.   (p. 7)[3]

There is little sentiment here. The slow lines, with their combination of dragging 'w' sounds and sibilants, signal exhaustion. Its pleasure is centred on the basic human needs of 'Supper and sleep', with a conventional recognition of reassurance in 'Our good expecting Wives'. There are no children in the scene, nor any other detail of comfort or homeliness that is not strictly utilitarian. It is sandwiched between a painfully slow return, and the imperative to go out and do another day's work. In so far as there are compensations in Duck's homecoming, 'good' and 'homely' are their meagre verbal indications.

It is, nevertheless, clearly a cottage-door scene; and it is equally clearly written by a labourer. Is the cottage-door scene therefore a real compensation, a genuine reward? Three things warn us against believing so. The first we have seen. Duck is notably low-key, the compensations are very basic and the scene is fenced in, surrounded on both sides by more hard work. Secondly, Duck brings strong wishful thinking to the scene. The day which began in the heroic pride and warlike postures of a 'sportive race' has ended in utter exhaustion; and the 'good expecting Wives' must now provide comfort. This is to be Duck's only reward for his exhaustion, and the vested interest he has in it makes him a partial witness. Finally, as we shall see, Duck has already thoroughly subverted the conventions of the cottage-door welcome, in an earlier passage; Collier carefully exposes its assumptions; and even Thomson, the prophet of harmony, describes a scene (discussed below) which reverses its expectations. Although his intention in this is actually to reinforce the ethic of the cottage door, his sentimental rendering in 'Winter' of the 'lost swain', the labourer who never comes home, brings into question the nature and purpose of the cottage door *topos*, and perhaps his whole system of pastoral compensations.

Behind the cottage door

If the cottage door is a compensation, who compensates the compensators? This is the question Mary Collier's two descriptions of the evening homecoming imply. They carefully expose, point by point, the realities behind Duck's homecoming expectations, and the 'double-shift' of the labouring woman's life:

> When Evening does approach we homeward hie
> And our domestic Toils incessant ply:
> Against your coming home prepare to get
> Our Work all done, our House in order set.
> Bacon and Dumpling in the pot we boil,
> Our Beds we make, our Swine we feed the while,
> Then wait at Door to see you coming home,
> And set the Table out against you come.
> Early next morning we on you attend;
> Our Children dress and feed, their cloaths we mend,
> And in the Field our daily Task renew,
> Soon as the rising Sun has dry'd the Dew.   (p. 17)

> When Night comes on, unto our home we go,
> Our Corn we carry, and our Infant too;
> Weary, alas! but 'tis not worth our while
> Once to complain, or *rest at ev'ry Stile*.
> We must make haste, for when we Home are come,
> Alas! we find our Work but just begun;
> So many things for our Attendance call,
> Had we ten hands, we could employ them all.
> Our Children put to bed, with greatest care,
> We all things for your coming Home prepare:

You sup, and go to bed without delay,
And rest yourself till the ensuing Day,
While we, alas! but little Sleep can have,
Because our froward Children cry and rave.
Yet without fail, soon as Daylight doth spring,
We in the Field again our Work begin,
And there with all our Strength our Toil renew,
Till *Titan*'s golden rays have dry'd the Dew.   (p. 19)[4]

The endings of these two passages are strikingly similar, but also
significantly different. The similarity reinforces the idea of repetition; the
difference raises interesting questions about the nature of the work. In
both cases labour begins again in the morning; but in the hayfield (p. 17)
the women begin work *as soon as* the dew on the hay has dried out; whereas
in the gleaning field (p. 19) they work from daylight *until* the dew has
dried. This is unusual in that gleaning was normally restricted to between
eight in the morning and six or seven at night. What is suggested, I think,
is a special arrangement. Hennell writes: 'People who were known to be
honest and respectable had sometimes, by favour of the farmer, the
privilege of gleaning between the thraves [stooks].'[5] I suspect that in the
second passage Collier is suggesting she has been given a sun-up till
dew-dry gleaning right by the farmer. If so, then it is another point scored
against Duck, for it shows she is a trusted, privileged harvester. Collier's
claimed reason for the farmer's trust has already been declared:

You of Hay-making speak a word or two,
As if our Sex but little Work could do:
This makes the honest Farmer smiling say
He'll seek for Women still to make his Hay.   (p. 16)

This may well be true; the women workers were also cheaper to hire,
which doubtless reinforced the employing farmers' enthusiasm.[6]

As for the homecoming scene itself, two descriptions are needed to
identify and refute every cottage-door illusion, and although for the 1762
printing she altered little else in the poem, Collier took the trouble to
revise the second of these homecoming scenes, removing two of her three
uses of the word 'alas' (perhaps in the light of her view that all complaint is
'in vain').

The cottage-door scene, then, like the swan, appears to glide serenely
along, but beneath the water has to paddle like mad. The scene of
cottage-door welcome is shown as a male privilege, and the litany of
necessary activities behind the scenes provides the corrective needed even
for Duck's modestly orchestrated version of the cottage-door scene. Indeed
the implications of the two passages go further. Collier's exposure of the
reality behind the homecoming prefigures a radical idea more familiar in

the twentieth than the eighteenth century. As Sheila Rowbotham puts it: 'The irony behind the idyllic happy family as a place of repose is the consumption of female labour power . . . If it were admitted that the family is maintained at the expense of women, capitalism would have to devise some other way of getting the work done.'[7]

Collier also shows that there is simply no compensation to be had. Exhausted, and by now finding the act of walking a problem, Duck had written:

> Homewards we move, but so much spent with toil,
> We walk but slow, and rest at every Stile.   (p. 7)

Collier's reply is uncompromising:

> Weary, alas! but 'tis not worth our while
> Once to complain, or *rest at ev'ry Stile*.   (p. 19)

In her world of endless work, there is not the glimmer of a compensation, and she shows that even the slightest advantage, the smallest compensation Duck can seek, can only be taken at her expense: while he rests on a stile, she is cooking, making beds, feeding the pigs, cleaning the house, putting the children to bed.

As with Collier's gleaning description, one notices her particular emphasis on the children, and the attention and care they are given. By contrast neither Thomson nor Duck mention children in their positive renderings of the homecoming scene. Thomson's shepherd is, as we have seen, a bachelor; and in Duck's case his homecoming is deliberately minimal in its evocation of hearth and family. We may also, of course, see in the two male writers a view of the world in which the 'woman's labour' of childminding is marginal. But both poets do have scenes in which children are present: they are in fact saving the image of children for their reversals of the cottage-door scene. For them children are not part of the work but part of the compensation: the most powerful, most emotional ingredient of the cottage-door scene, to be invoked only to make more poignant the moment when the compensation fails.

Of the two, Duck's reversal of the cottage-door scene is more subversive to the integrity of its totemic value. It arises easily from his description of threshing:

> When sooty Pease we thresh, you scarce can know
> Our native Colour, as from Work we go;
> The sweat, and dust, and suffocating smoke,
> Make us so much like *Ethiopians* look,
> We scare our Wives, when Evening brings us home,
> And frighted Infants think the Bug-bear come.   (p. 4)[8]

The presentation is partly comic and partly threatening: the images of 'Ethiopians' and 'Bug-bear' are part of a wider network of images used to portray the excesses of work in the poem, some of which we have seen. The image of 'Ethiopians' would create for the eighteenth-century reader a complex of meanings, some threatening, some comic, all Other. David Dabydeen's essay, 'Blacks in Eighteenth Century English Art and Society' illustrates these well. In the visual art of the period black people are often rendered innocuous as visual accoutrements to images of the aristocracy; elsewhere they are either bizarrely comic, as in Rowlandson's *Broad Grins*, or shown exhibiting 'wit and quick thinking', as in *The Rabbits* (1792). This last example shows something of the kind of image Duck may be invoking. The black rabbit-seller's wit renders safe the inappropriate, outsiderly, vagabond qualities he shows, as he plies his trade at the door of a 'respectable' house. The impression one gets from these kinds of illustration is that 'Ethiopians' would be regarded as bizarre intruders to a sentimental cottage-door scene.[9]

Duck intends this as grotesquely comic, but there is a serious point. This would normally be a scene of recognition and reassurance, in which the children would, in Thomas Gray's phrase, 'run to lisp their sire's return', while Duck's 'good expecting Wives' would offer nurture. Here, both recoil in horror, and the reassuring motif of the cottage-door scene is instantly reversed.

Duck has placed this between the central threshing scene I discussed earlier, and the Master's 'Cursing' of the threshers:

> He counts the Bushels, counts how much a day,
> Then swears we've idled half our Time away.
> Why look ye, Rogues! D'ye think that this will do?
> Your Neighbours thresh as much again as you.
> Now in our Hands we wish our noisy Tools,
> To drown the hated Names of Rogues and Fools;
> But wanting those, we just like School-boys look,
> When th'angry Master views their blotted Book:
> They cry their Ink was faulty, and their Pen;
> We, the Corn threshes bad, 'twas cut too green.   (p. 4)[10]

The comparison with schoolboys being ticked off by angry schoolmasters is apt. The Master is humiliating the workers here, and they cannot reply. Their only utterance in the situation can be the noise-making of threshing; and their wish to 'drown' the curse shows both their frustration and their lack of possible redress: incapable of verbally confronting the master, they have no other means of dealing with his scolding.

Thus Duck's reversal of the cottage-door scene provides the essential central image in a three-part picture of the labourer frustrated and deprived of solace in his work, alienated from his compensatory home-

coming, and finally humiliated like a schoolboy by his Master. It is a
carefully constructed and dramatised piece of descriptive poetry, and
although it lacks the keener practical insights we find in Collier's
homecoming scenes, it conveys Duck's feelings about the effect of his work
on his life with great skill.

'The cheat'

Before we look at Thomson's final dramatic reversal of cottage door
expectations, it would be useful to consider briefly a related kind of
reversal in compensatory expectations, one which is both literary and
documentary. The great moment in the farming year, the moment most
laden with ritual and positive expectation, is of course the completion of
the harvest – the corn harvest, particularly, but also other summer
harvests. It is accordingly placed at the climax of Duck's poem. First we
have the triumph of the final wagon being brought in, to the sound of
cheering harvesters:

> In noisy Triumph the last load moves on.
> And loud Huzzas proclaim the Harvest's done.   (p. 11)

Then we have the celebratory harvest feast:

> Our Master joyful at the welcome sight,
> Invites us all to feast with him at Night.
> A Table plentifully spread we find,
> And jugs of humming Beer to cheer the Mind,
> Which he, too generous, pushes on so fast,
> We think no toils to come, nor mind the past.   (p. 11)

Despite the general tone of gladness and relief, there is a note of warning
here. The Master is being 'too generous' with the beer, and both 'toils to
come' and 'the past' – the next and the previous cycles in the story of
eternal toil which is Duck's central theme – are being rapidly forgotten.
But not for long: both the reader and the labourers are being set up here
for a 'Cheat', a bathetic final reversal which will lead Duck to an
irredeemably gloomy conclusion. The poem continues:

> But the next Morning soon reveals the Cheat,
> When the same toils we must again repeat,
> To the same Barns again must back return,
> To Labour there for room for next year's Corn.   (p. 11)

And Duck concludes:

> Thus as the Year's revolving course goes round,
> No respite from our Labour can be found.
> Like *Sysiphus*, our Work is never done;

> Continually rolls back the restless Stone.
> Now growing Labours still succeed the past,
> And growing always new, must always last. (p. 12)

The farming cycle of course goes on forever: but the literary rendering of it has to end. Pope had followed Virgil in concluding the poem of his georgic phase, *Windsor Forest*, with the first line of his earlier *Pastorals*, thus cleverly containing the infinite cycle of the rural world within the finite cycle of his rural poetry. This literary sleight-of-hand allows the reader a satisfying sense of completion, while acknowledging that the subject is infinite. Duck's ending owes something to this technique: in the dedicatory first verse-paragraph he wrote of 'endless toils which always grow anew', which he now echoes. But the positive spirit of the Virgilian-Popean ending, the sense of a kind of closure which can look back with satisfaction and forward with optimism, is entirely absent. The poet and his companions have had their sense of past and future suppressed by drink, and when they come to, in the morning, they have to confront a terrifying sense of work never finished, and the knowledge that it has all been a 'Cheat'.

This is an effective and dramatic ending to the poem, and it reverses compensatory expectations in a very radical way. The harvest supper, the traditional end-of-cycle compensation, is portrayed as a kind of crude anaesthetic, an ineffectual river of forgetfulness into which the labourers are annually tossed, only to emerge the next day even more painfully aware of the Sisyphean nature of their task (I shall discuss Duck's Sisyphus reference shortly). By continuing on into the scene 'the next Morning', Duck confounds the reader's expectation of a Virgilian cyclic closure; and takes us *beyond* the compensatory experience, to see what lies ahead of it. The effect, as with Mary Collier's glimpses behind the cottage door, is salutory.

Neither Thomson nor Collier could ignore this powerful conclusion. James Sambrook notes its similarity to a passage from Thomson's harvest celebration in 'Autumn':

> Age too shines out; and garrulous, recounts
> The Feats of Youth. Thus they rejoice; nor think
> That, with tomorrow's Sun, their annual Toil
> Begins again the never-ceasing Round. (lines 1231–4)[11]

The seasonal context and the idea are essentially the same, and there are significant linguistic similarities (Thomson's phrase 'never-ceasing' echoes Duck's description of harvest: 'Toils, scarce ever ceasing, press us now', p. 11). Unless a common ancestor has been overlooked, the possibility of influence looks strong.

Although both poems were published in the same year, it is very much more likely that Duck influenced Thomson than the reverse. Before the end of 1729 Duck had completed his poem, achieved some local fame, and was becoming, as E. P. Thompson puts it, 'a theme of genteel conversation and a target for competitive patronage'.[12] He was being commissioned to write poems, and although he was also being given improving things to read (a process which culminated in his intellectual 'grooming' for Court by Alured Clarke in the summer of 1730) it is hard to believe they would have included the manuscript of 'Autumn'. On the other hand Joseph Spence, who had befriended Thomson in 1729, had a week-long meeting with Duck in 1730; and Thomson's patron Frances Thynne, Countess of Hertford, also visited Duck at this time. Though we cannot precisely date these visits (Spence's came first), they almost certainly took place before Duck's grooming for Court began in the summer. So Spence, Hertford, or one of Duck's other visitors, could (and, knowing what Thomson was then writing, surely would) have communicated *The Thresher's Labour* to him in some form before 'Autumn' finally went to press in the 1730 subscription quarto of *The Seasons* (subscribers had their copies by 8 June).[13]

In taking up Duck's 'Cheat' (assuming that my reasoning is correct), Thomson slightly softens it by making simple garrulousness its cause, rather than the doling out of strong drink, and by moving directly from the lines quoted, into a rendering of that reassuringly familiar theme from Virgil's *Georgics*, the 'happy swain' speech. But it is a measure of the imaginative force of Duck's conclusion, that Thomson seems to feel the need to include its central image in what is otherwise a mellow and celebratory moment in his poem.

Mary Collier's response to Duck's concluding summary of his work is at once more direct, more sophisticated and more central to her own project. Indeed the felicitous way she uses classical mythology to rival Duck is an impressive example of her insistence on the value of poetry and allusion. Duck has made several classical comparisons: in his threshing his comparison is with legendary smiths: 'Cyclops' and 'Vulcan' (p. 3); the harvesting is compared to the labours of 'Hercules' (p. 11); and finally he compares the unending nature of his work to the labours of Sisyphus. Collier selects the last of these as the best one to represent him; and then finds her own comparison:

> While you to *Sysiphus* yourselves compare,
> With *Danaus*' daughters we may claim a share;
> For while *he* labours hard against the Hill,
> Bottomless Tubs of Water *they* must fill.   (p. 23)

Both allusions relate to punishments in hell, and both are apt. Sisyphus, in punishment for his crimes on earth, is condemned in Hades to push a massive block of stone over a hill. As Robert Graves, paraphrasing

Odysseus' account of his visit to the underworld in Book IX of the *Odyssey*, tells the story: 'As soon as he has almost reached the summit, he is forced back by the weight of the shameless stone, which bounces to the very bottom once more; where he wearily retrieves it, and must begin all over again, though sweat bathes his limbs, and a cloud of dust rises above his head'. This, it seems to me, is Stephen Duck to the life: the sweat, the dust, the never-ending cycle of tedious, backbreaking labour. Furthermore, Graves finds the origin of the story in the idea of pushing the 'sun-disc' up the vault of Heaven, which again makes this highly appropriate for Duck's sun-ruled temporal scheme. Mary Collier is indeed perceptive to choose this as his most appropriate self-image.[14]

Yet in the story of the fifty daughters of Danaus, the Danaids, Collier sets up an even more subtly ironic allusiveness. Caught in a family feud, all but one of the Danaids faithfully follow their father's instructions to marry then murder their fifty male cousins. In punishment, they are condemned in Hades, as Graves puts it, to the 'endless task of carrying water in jars perforated like sieves'. This is even closer to the work of Collier's washer-women than the stone-rolling is to Duck's. The allusion to the Danaids also nicely evokes Collier's 'Strong propensity to call an Army of Amazons to vindicate the injured Sex' (from the preface to the 1762 edition of her works, discussed in chapter 1). Although the Danaids were not Amazons, they were, like the Amazons, priestesses of the matriarchal moon-goddess, and were credited with having brought the Mysteries of Demeter from Egypt to Greece. Their punishment represents, according to Graves, the sympathetic magic of rain-making; the leaking pot remaining 'a distinguishing mark of the wise woman many centuries after the abolition of the Danaid colleges'.[15]

These two powerful classical images of unremitting toil prepare the way well for Collier's strongly politicised finale, with its central image (discussed above, chapter 3) of 'industrious bees' whose 'sordid Owners always reap the Gains'. That image itself nicely suggests Collier's mixture of classicism/conservatism (Virgil), and modernism/radicalism (Mandeville). Again, the result is a powerfully conceived ending.

The homecoming reversed

Thomson's reversal of the homecoming scene is very different from those of Collier and Duck. Collier deconstructs the motif with cold facts and irony; Duck subverts the scene's sentiment with humour, the anecdotal and bizarre. Thomson by contrast is serious, exemplary and sentimental. 'Winter' has been characterised by Donna Landry as indulging in 'self-regarding sympathetic pastoralism'. She attacks the support for the *status quo* implied by its 'religio-political "consolation"', and finds in it a justificatory attitude to class inequality. Her quotation is from the summarising passage at the end of the poem, but her comments are also pertinent to the passage I have in mind, and what I have to say benefits from the example and commentary made in her essay and book.[16]

Thomson offers two main categories of images in 'Winter'. The first and most predominant is the imagery of the season's harshness. The major examples of this are the description of the storm (lines 41–208) and the 'excursions' to various remote winter scenes (lines 389–423, 765–78, 794–949). The second is the imagery of consolation in winter. The cosy indoor 'Village' scene (lines 617–29), and the scene of winter sports (lines 760–78) are the principal examples. Both offer reassuring images of the season either shut out or rendered safely enjoyable. Between these two extremes of danger and safety lies a third category, which feeds off both, creating a characteristic uncertainty between reassurance and alarm. The three passages I would put in this category are consecutive, so that their effect is cumulative; and like the progression of events in 'Spring' their movement is upwards through the Thomsonian hierarchy. The episodes are the robin's visit (lines 245–64); the advice to the shepherd (lines 265–75); and the lost swain episode (lines 276–321), with its moral (lines 322–58).

My concern is with the last of these, but some attention to the others will be useful. The movement in the first two seems to be from danger to safety. Thus the robin moves from the fields to the 'warm Hearth' (line 252); the shepherd is advised to be 'kind' to his 'helpless' sheep (line 265), to 'lodge them below the Storm' (line 267). Because a tension exists in both of these passages between safety and danger, nurture and exclusion, a hybrid aesthetic quality begins to emerge in them. While the tension is unresolved, it can form itself into neither pity and indignation on the one hand, nor relief and pleasure on the other. Both the robin and the shepherd passages (though one is descriptive and the other prescriptive) seem to resolve in the direction of safety and nurture. Or do they? Keith Thomas locates the robin as a privileged, semi-domestic creature in the eighteenth century, but there is also an extensive folkloric tradition, recorded by Opie and Tatem, that the robin was believed to be an omen of death, especially if it entered a house.[17] Thomson's robin may not be as reassuring a presence as it seems, and may indeed warn us of the impending death of the swain. But whether the robin leads us to safety or to danger, the lost swain episode is certainly resolved in the latter direction. Before it is, however, the hybrid mood I have noted is developed at some length. The scene moves from safety to danger as the swain becomes lost in increasingly threatening, inhospitable and alien landscapes. Then the opposite possibility is suddenly raised, and the reversal of cottage-door expectations portrayed as part of his dying thoughts:

In vain for him th'officious Wife prepares
The Fire fair-blazing, and the Vestment warm;
In vain his little Children, peeping out
Into the mingling Storm, demand their Sire,
With Tears of artless Innocence. Alas!
Nor Wife, nor Children, more shall he behold,
Nor Friends, nor sacred Home.   ('Winter', lines 311–17)

It seems to me insufficient merely to slot this into its place in terms of
literary parallels, to take the image back to Lucretius or forward to Gray's
Elegy. As Raymond Williams writes, attacking the practice of giving
literary antecedents as if they were adequate explanation of a pastoral
motif (his example is a Horatian *Beatus ille* passage), 'All traditions are
selective.'[18] Thomson chooses to heighten the pathos of the death by
tormenting the swain with visions of what he has lost here, and we may
hold him (not Lucretius or Gray) responsible.

I use the word 'tormenting' purposely: the first problem in our reception of the 'lost swain' scene is that Thomson appears to be showing it in
primarily aesthetic terms: he seems, in fact, to be enjoying it too much.
One expects a predominance of moral over aesthetic considerations
because of the patterns Thomson has set up throughout the poem, and we
are disturbed to find him, in the build-up to the death of the swain,
apparently wrapped up with the aesthetics of the situation. Cottage-door
images, like Thomson's other consolatory images, are deployed elsewhere
in a way that suggests a concern for the quality of experience of the rural
labourer. Here the image seems to be indulged, as a pleasingly poignant
scene. The labourer's role in it is pathetically to die, excluded from the
consolation, the aesthetics, the poignancy: he is here expendable.[19]

Why does Thomson let him die? The poet empties a storm over the
hapless husbandman of 'Autumn', but then provides a socially organised
means of relief, thus apparently proving the human part of his pattern of
harmony. Here, to the dismay of the sensitive reader, he allows 'nature' to
kill off his swain, a course from which there can be no back-tracking. R. S.
White, beginning a book on poetic injustice in Shakespearean tragedy
makes the simple but important point that 'Although death is inevitable,
nobody *deserves* to die', and his book therefore seeks (and finds) moral
significance beneath the apparently meaningless deaths of Shakespeare's
various 'innocent victims'.[20] Were such significance not available, he
writes, 'how could we justify the poets' claims to "teach and delight",
using a hypothetical world to instruct us in the virtues and vices by which
we may choose to live our own lives?'

But the eighteenth-century didactic poets give us less room to
manoeuvre than Shakespeare. Their habit is to make what they consider
to be the moral or practical lessons of the poem apparent as they go along.

While the dialogue and stage directions of a Shakespearean tragedy may let a thousand interpretations bloom, a poet like Thomson directs his reader far more closely. Thus the moral of the swain's death is given in the passage which follows it, clearly marked off as a separate verse-paragraph, and signalled by its opening exclamation ('Ah little think the gay licentious Proud', 'Winter', line 322). This, it is made clear, is where our search for significance must begin; here, if anywhere, will Thomson's wallowing in the pathos of the swain's death be vindicated.

However the modern reader is likely to work through the moral with mounting frustration. It consists of an extended exclamation on the theme of man's inhumanity to man. The fact that we can locate its theme so easily by this well-known phrase of Burns gives some indication of how predictable and familiar it is. Thomson's sincerity need not be doubted; there is feeling in some of its social indignation:

> How many pine in Want, and Dungeon Glooms;
> Shut from the common Air, and common Use
> Of their own Limbs. How many drink the Cup
> Of baleful Grief, or eat the bitter Bread
> Of Misery. Sore pierc'd by wintry Winds,
> How many shrink into the sordid Hut
> Of chearless Poverty.   ('Winter', lines 332–8)

But the passage as a whole merely reiterates and enlarges on, rather than offers explanation or compensation for the death of the swain. It is a great speech, but it offers no real solution, or analogy, or moral to the scene. Its real weakness can best be seen at its moments of transition, firstly its beginning, following on from the image of the dead swain:

> . . . a stiffen'd Corse,
> Stretch'd out, and bleaching in the northern Blast.

> Ah little think the gay licentious Proud,
> Whom Pleasure, Power, and Affluence surround;
> They, who their thoughtless Hours in giddy Mirth,
> And wanton, often cruel, Riot waste;
> Ah little think they, while they dance along,
> How many feel, this very Moment, Death
> And all the sad Variety of Pain.   ('Winter', lines 320–8)

As in the sheep-shearing episode, stylistic and intellectual weaknesses coincide. The opening to this new verse-paragraph is flaccid, its anaphora ineffectual, its antithesis unfocused, its movement uneven and faltering. These may seem like trivial criticisms, but the most talented poets of the eighteenth century, Thomson among them, were especially skilled in these techniques, and in this kind of moralising speech. Here are three well-known examples:

> A little Rule, a little Sway,
> A Sun-beam in a Winter's Day,
> Is all the Proud and Mighty have,
> Between the Cradle and the Grave.
> > (John Dyer, 'Grongar Hill', 1726, lines 89–92)

> The boast of heraldry, the pomp of power,
> And all that beauty, all that wealth e'er gave,
> Awaits alike the inevitable hour.
> The paths of glory lead but to the grave.
> > (Gray, *Elegy Written in a Country Churchyard*, 1751, lines 33–6)

> Condemn'd to hope's delusive mine,
>   As on we toil from day to day,
> By sudden blasts, or slow decline,
>   Our social comforts drop away.
> (Samuel Johnson, 'On the Death of Dr Robert Levet', 1783, lines 1–4)

The modern tendency has been to undervalue these kinds of poetic statement, to see them as being inherently conventional or derivative. But in each of these examples one can hear an individual voice, a particular poet using familiar ideas to say something that is nevertheless his own, and is appropriate to the context he and his poem confront. Thomson's approach puts one in mind of those smooth clergymen who flawlessly deliver their funeral eulogies over the remains of someone they knew nothing about: if one listens carefully it is possible to detect the join where the name of the deceased is grafted into the pre-set speech.

Of the three poets quoted above, each has a specific context for his comments: the first distils a general idea from the view of a ruined castle, the second finds in the 'obscure' destiny of past villagers a meaningful pattern, and the third seeks to acknowledge the wider truth with which the death of a friend has confronted him. The morals may be conventional, and fairly similar, but there is no disparity, no marriage of convenience, between context and content.

Thomson's moral seems inadequate and alien to its context: it huffs and it puffs, but it does not deal with what has just occurred. The moral is placed as if in conclusion to the death of the swain, but then uses its own examples, which are not related to the death of the swain. We are not told where the cause of the death lies, or what its meaning might be. Is it, as its context implies, simply a function of the 'cogenial horrors' of the season (which hitherto the poet has been rather enjoying) or is it the result of a social injustice of the kind the moral is concerned with? It lies between the two, on the page, but no syntactical connection is made with either. In particular Thomson fails to make the connection with social wrongs, and his failure to do so increases our feeling that the death is an excuse for, rather than the subject of, the 'moral'.

The other moment of transition, the ending of the moral, is equally unsatisfactory. The argument is essentially circular. If 'fond' Man 'thought' of the injustices Thomson lists, he would be a better person. No amount of personified abstract nouns ('Charity', 'Benevolence' and so on) can conceal the banality of the message that if man were not so bad he would be good; and the exit door from this increasingly inadequate speech is marked 'diversion':

> And into clear Perfection, gradual Bliss,
> Refining still, the social Passions work.
>   And here can I forget the generous Band,
> Who, touch'd with human Woe, redressive search'd
> Into the Horrors of the gloomy Jail?   ('Winter', lines 357–61)

'And here can I forget' is the eighteenth-century georgic-writer's way of saying 'And that reminds me'. Thomson's new concern is with the architects of a concrete social reform, an improvement for one group of people (prisoners) he has used as an example. But it takes us even further away from the 'swain', and when Thomson returns to the subject of winter (line 389) he reverts to the old subject of winter's 'cogenial horrors': the death of the swain is now forgotten.

I read in all this a kind of reluctance. All previous reference to the rural labourer has ultimately offered an optimistically harmonious and rational view of cause and effect. Each problem, whether between Man and Nature or between Man and Man, has been resolved. The most illuminating element of Thomson's vision of rural labour has been its focus on co-operative effort; the most admired feature of the poem as a whole a presentation of Nature which may be seen as simultaneously truthful and conciliatory. Man may find harmony with Nature by the exercise of moral qualities, patience, industry, charity and so on: mimetic and didactic truth have gone hand in hand. With the death of the swain, Thomson's imaginative truth and his moral truth become dislocated. He must portray at its harshest the force of winter, his imaginative and his aesthetic faculties unite to demand this. The movement that results leads him inevitably towards the pitiful spectacle of humanity destroyed by Nature, which his aesthetic sense fills out into a fully blown scene of sentimental pathos. But the moral imperative that then cuts in is incapable of rescuing the situation. He can, as it were, neither revive nor decently bury his swain, and in this dilemma may be glimpsed the terrestrial limits to Thomson's vision of harmony. Ultimately the poem, as we have seen, ends in a generalised religious consolation for all hardship, but the poet keeps the details of the hardships (whose victims might prefer a sublunary compensation he can no longer guarantee), syntactically separate from the superlunary consolation he suggests is the only redress on offer. The poet's optimistic view of the rural world has here failed to cope with that world's most extreme moment of crisis, and his vision of a harmonious rural world pays a heavy price.

In a sense we can expect no more from Thomson than we get: he has not offered, like Crabbe, a 'real picture' of rural labour and the labouring poor, but a celebration of the 'varied God' of the seasons, and we have to some extent to read against him or between his lines to find more.[21] The point I made at the beginning about extracting only one theme or strand from a greater whole is perhaps significant here.

Yet Thomson claims consideration as an observer of the natural and the rural world. He is, or was for a long time, a revered poet of nature, and there is much in the work that validates that characterisation. His poem also seeks to represent credibly the oppressed generally, be they animals, or the poor, or a ruined farmer. His abandonment of the swain in 'Winter' casts a shadow over this, suggesting that his concern for rural labourers may be a limited one that is primarily concerned with their exemplary value, their usefulness in making credible his version of rural life, his vision of harmony in nature. Seen in this light, his system of compensations, however much it may be informed by a desire for rural life to be pleasurable for the labourer as well as the poet, seems particularly slippery; his championing of the ideal of communal work at best double-edged. His haymaking, for example, seems to embody positive values very similar to those ascribed to haymaking in William Morris's utopian novel *News from Nowhere* (1891); but at the same time its prescription and description appear to be sited in the real, the non-utopian eighteenth-century countryside; and there, Duck's 'Bitter mingled with the Sweet' (p. 5), Collier's 'many Hardships daily' (p. 20), were considerable understatements.

One is inevitably brought back by these issues to Barrell's reading of the cottage-door scene as a diversion, both in the descriptive terms of idealising reality, and the prescriptive terms of diverting attention from the raising of political and social awareness. Thomson's poem ultimately conforms and contributes to this anaesthetising tradition, despite its passages of sympathy and concern for the oppressed, and however fervently the poet wishes for what he calls 'happy Labour, Love, and social Glee' ('Summer', line 370).

Stephen Duck, by contrast, finds little harmony or love in the countryside. His poem, far less ambitious in its scope, sings a sadder song of continuous hardship and disappointment, interrupted only by pleasures which are briefly felt or inadequately grasped. Duck was self-effacing about his poetry; 'I have indeed but a poor Defence to make of the Things I have wrote,' he said. 'I don't think them good, and better Judges will doubtless think worse of them than I do'.[22] There has never been a great shortage of such judges, of course, but his major poem nevertheless survived, and remains important. *The Thresher's Labour* inspired a tradition of workplace poetry which survives to the present day: one need go no further than Fred Voss's factory poems, collected in *Goodstone* (1991), to see that this is a living tradition: the realistic descriptive style, the grimly comic view of the bosses, the rueful and ironic self-deprecation of the worker-poet, are all palpably Duckian. Duck initiated a genre which could express the hardship of labour, and which, with the example of his success, gave those who were voiceless precious resources to draw on.[23]

Mary Collier used these resources well. We learn from her poem how thoroughly the 'double shift' dominated the life of a labouring woman; how limited were the sources of strength she could hope for; how much resilience it took for a woman of her class to survive, let alone gain entry into the well-guarded sanctuary of literature and poetry. 'We who write', says Tillie Olsen, 'are survivors'; and she notes the implications of this 'survival': 'For myself "survivor" contains all its other meanings: one who must bear witness for those who foundered; try to tell how and why it was that they, also worthy of life, did not survive. And pass on ways of surviving; and tell our chancy luck, our special circumstances.'[24] *The Woman's Labour* is just such a survivor's testimony, bearing witness to the lives of women who did not survive, both literally and physically (the mortality rates in the early eighteenth century were horrific), and in the sense of not themselves speaking, bearing witness, 'passing on' their lives.[25] Susan Griffin observes 'how little of women's daily lives is reflected in literature, how little of our real daily lives'.[26] To this plain truth Collier's poem is a rare and valuable exception.

PART II

'A pastoral convention and a ruminative mind': agricultural prescription in *The Fleece*, I

6

Sheep and poetry

Rereading *The Fleece*

In the first part of this book it was suggested that caution needed to be exercised in extrapolating social history from literature, especially from that most mystifying of literary forms, poetry. The search for information about the conditions of labour led some critics into an over-simplified division between the 'poetry' of Thomson and the 'truth' of Duck or of Collier, but there is some basis for this division. One feels in the poetry of Duck and Collier, more strongly than in *The Seasons*, something of the sweat and dust of the threshing floor, the wash house, and the harvest field. At the same time all three poets show signs of engagement with work-related folkloric traditions; and there are revealing ways in which Thomson's poem attempts to resolve some of the practical and ideological problems of rural labour; while Duck, and especially Collier, insist on the values of poetry as well as those of realistic documentation. Pleasure and pain are present in all the poems; as are a range of implicit and explicit 'compensations' for the hardship of rural labour. A nuanced reading reveals many areas in which eighteenth-century rural poetry can describe and express the experience of labour, and can tell us much about the ideologies that inform the construction of labour.

I want to turn now to a poem which places more emphasis on 'prescribing' than 'describing', though the techniques it uses to do so, which are based on Addison's interpretation of Virgil's *Georgics*, involve an artful blending of the two tasks, and we shall continue to measure descriptive as well as didactic and ideological meanings as we examine it. This is John Dyer's ambitious poem on shepherding and the woollen industry, *The Fleece*, published in 1757 after a long genesis.

Dyer offered his readers a three-part theme:

> The care of sheep, the labours of the loom,
> And arts of trade, I sing.
> (lines 1–2)

I shall be looking here at the first of these themes, 'the care of sheep'; at the agricultural and ideological principles which inform its presentation; and at the literary and historical meanings it offers. (My citations are to Book I unless otherwise stated.)

The critical history of *The Fleece*, up until fairly recently, makes sorry reading. The poem has routinely been dismissed, ridiculed, damned with faint praise, summarised unread ('a poem in three books') and indeed declared (by Sir Leslie Stephen) 'unreadable'.[1] Its defenders have accordingly seemed uneasy, and have usually been in a minority. The poem still lacks textual stability and has no critical edition.[2] Dyer's manuscripts have disappeared from sight (mostly over the last century).[3] Biographical misconceptions about the poet continue to proliferate. To give a couple of examples, the recent (1989) reprint of Edward Thomas's 1903 edition of Dyer bears a portrait, not of John Dyer but of Samuel Dyer, a member of Johnson's Literary Club, and no relation. This mistake was first made over 200 years ago, and was corrected in 1855: to see it reappear is disheartening.[4] Most reference books, including recent ones, give Dyer's death date as 1758. In fact, as Williams and Humfrey both record, the poet died of consumption in December 1757, and was buried on the 15th, at Coningsby, Lincolnshire.[5]

The impression one gets, indeed, is that – as was wittily predicted to Dodsley, and unkindly repeated by Johnson in his 'Life' of Dyer – the poet and his poem have been 'buried in woollen'. There is hope, however. In recent years *The Fleece* has begun to receive serious attention for the first time since its first reviews, and there have been major essays on the poem by Laurence Goldstein (1977), Richard Feingold (1978) and John Barrell (1983).[6] We may take these three readings of an otherwise generally unannotated and unloved text as our starting point. The great advance they represent in Dyer Studies is their tendency towards the ideological interpretation of what had hitherto been seen as purely 'aesthetic' procedures in the poem.

All three critics locate a central dilemma, though they characterise it in different ways. For Goldstein, whose theme is ruins and empire, Dyer's dilemma was that of his society: how to avoid the 'entropy' (p. 53) which destroyed earlier societies; how to 'relocate the moral centre of civilisation' (p. 46) to accommodate the momentous socio-economic changes of eighteenth-century society, and especially the ongoing shift in land ownership to a 'new bourgeoisie' (p. 49). Dyer's response, as Goldstein encapsulates it, was to recommend an 'elevated pastoralism as a cure for social no less than spiritual ills' (p. 25). The familiar eighteenth-century theme of the use of riches (pp. 53–5), and the 'Whig concern [with] the proper stewardship of England' (p. 47) are the twin intellectual challenges the poet must address; and his 'pastoral' response to them throws up a series of contradictions: between 'luxury' and mercantile motivation (p. 56);

between 'the timeless joy of shepherds [and the] grim details of country life' (p. 56); between the ideal of a 'mighty brotherhood' of trade, and the 'mailed fist' of imperial power which Dyer seems to accept as a means to achieving it (p. 57). Like James Thomson, whose *Britannia* (1729) Goldstein locates as the 'chief influence on *The Fleece*' (p. 52), Dyer inevitably finds himself 'loyal to irreconcilable myths: that of the pastoral Golden Age and that of the progress of empire' (p. 55).

Surveying Dyer's achievement, between readings of the equally contradictory pastoral visions of Spenser and Wordsworth, Goldstein admits that history was soon to make Dyer's 'epic attempt to revitalize the pastoral' appear 'evasive of bedrock realities' (p. 57). He nevertheless advises a generous acknowledgement of the poet's heroic struggle to harmonise his song and his society, in the face of the undermining 'mockery of his own muse' (p. 58).[7]

Richard Feingold (1978) is less sympathetic to the idea that Dyer may be aware of the paradoxical nature of his vision. He locates this in the contradiction between the formal conservatism of the Virgilian genre and the 'striking' originality of the poem and its themes (p. 7). Dyer describes 'two worlds of work', the 'real and the mythical' (p. 106). But they do not sit easily together, because *The Fleece* lacks the 'limits' (p. 115) and the 'tragic sense' (p. 118) of the *Georgics*, and because the new experience cannot be successfully accommodated within old, pastoral literary conventions. Dyer's procedures set up contradictions between the 'placidity' of pastoral and the 'power' of commerce (p. 110), and between the 'divine' and the 'secular celebration of secular energies' (pp. 110–11), as Dyer attempts to 'link the domains of God and the market' (p. 115). Feingold finds Dyer to have had 'no clear sense that the forces he was celebrating were inevitably part of a new order, very different from that sense of things which sustains the pastoral vision' (pp. 116–17). The poet is 'naive' (p. 118); and the result is that his 'enthusiasm', like Goldsmith's 'despair' in *The Deserted Village* (1770), creates 'an imaginative result which is inadequate to the historical moment' (p. 117).

Feingold's points are generally well made, though a rather high level of hindsight is imposed on the poet (one can think of few works of literature which with hindsight seem 'adequate' to their 'historical moment'). John Barrell (1983), by contrast, is not puzzled by Dyer's generic choice. The georgic, which he describes as 'a genre officially committed to the fairly detailed description of, in particular, rural labours, and a view of modern society as progressive by its labour' (p. 90), was the 'only genre' which could encapsulate Dyer's views of the social function of labour. This does not free Dyer's text from contradictions, but like Goldstein, Barrell allows the poet some consciousness of the disunities his text attempts to unite. Indeed he goes further than Goldstein, and considers that 'Of all the poets writing in mid eighteenth-century England, Dyer is the one most willing to acknowledge divisions in society: *The Fleece* sets out to demonstrate a unity of interest among the practitioners of different occupations whose attitudes to work and whose styles of life seem utterly opposed' (p. 91). The major strand of Barrell's reading is thus concerned with Dyer's purposeful 'play[ing] off against each other' (p. 95) of pastoral and georgic styles, to represent differing levels of commitment to labour, and different degrees of pleasure in labour. The poet makes the transitions between the two modes with 'ease' and 'sang-froid'. He seems 'assured' that the contradictions of his approach can be resolved (p. 95), and that society can indeed be shown as capable of unity through the positive communal effects of individual motivation and individual labour.

There is of course a price to be paid for such 'assurance'. Barrell's reading is a comparative one which puts *The Fleece* alongside Thomson's *The Seasons* and *The Castle of Indolence* (1748); and where he is critical of Dyer's engagement with his subject, his criticism occurs within this comparison between the poets:

> If, in the attempts he makes to argue that the society of Britain is harmonious and unified, Thomson, and especially in *The Seasons*, appears to fail where Dyer seems to succeed, it is because he is only too aware, that the conflict between industry and idleness is not primarily a conflict of concepts, or of different productive occupations, but of classes ... What looked to be, in the context of Thomson's work considered in isolation, a willing agnosticism, becomes in a comparison with *The Fleece*, an awareness of problems of social organization in England Dyer never approaches.   (p. 106)

If I read him correctly Barrell is suggesting that Dyer exercises a kind of substitutionism, in which real patterns of division (that perhaps cannot be resolved), are disguised as, or imitated by, artificial divisions which *can* appear to be resolved, at least within the poem. It is a subtle, tentative reading of Dyer's dilemma (and of course of the dilemmas I have discussed in relation to labour in *The Seasons*); though it is also, as Barrell says of Thomson's awareness of class-conflict, p. 106, 'not something that can easily be avowed'.

With these three essays, it seems to me, the study of *The Fleece* has finally come of age. It is simply no longer adequate, as it apparently was as recently as the fifties, to declare that *The Fleece* 'sings the wool-trade with honest observation and amiably rotund diction' – as though Dyer were rather dim-witted, and wrote verse only in the sense that Molière's *Bourgeois Gentilhomme* spoke prose.[8] However we read the poet's particular strategies for finding harmony in the contradictions and conflicts of his society, the intensity, seriousness and care with which his poem engages with major social issues should no longer be in serious doubt. Goldstein, tackling the old aesthetic question of high style/low theme in the poem from a new perspective, notes that:

The didactic poets of the century descended the hierarchy of poetic subjects because they possessed information the country urgently needed for its survival. Verse was a popular medium in which the spiritual dimension of commercial subjects might be fruitfully explored. Poems like *Cyder*, *The Fleece*, *The Sugar Cane*, and *The Hop-Garden* assume an ignorance of practical matters in the English public; contemporary accounts suggest that poets were not wrong in such assumptions.
(p. 48)

The 'intellectual rot' – as Pope had also understood – 'began at the top', with the 'narrow vision' and 'low tastes' of King George II. It blighted the ability of both old and new landowners to meet the socio-economic challenges of a rapidly changing society, and percolated through all levels of that society.

Dyer's response was radical and thorough. What Barrell (p. 107) describes as 'the most comprehensive and well-informed Georgic in English' is emphatically addressed to everybody:

> Ye rural Nymphs!
> Ye Swains, and princely Merchants! aid the verse.
> And ye, high-trusted Guardians of our Isle
> Whom public voice approves, or lot of birth,
> To the great charge assigns! ye Good of all
> Degrees, all sects! be present to my song.   (lines 2–7)[9]

and, taking the bull by the horns, to the King himself:

> But chiefly Thou,
> The people's Shepherd, eminently plac'd
> Over the numerous swains of every vale,
> With well-permitted power and watchful eye
> On each gay field to shed beneficence,
> Celestial office! Thou protect the song.   (lines 12–17)

Goldstein (p. 46) reads this last element of the invocation well: 'When Dyer apostrophizes the king as a shepherd, in a poem devoted to the manufacture of wool, and asks that he keep watch over rural occupations, the wit and point of the suggestion must be distinguished from similar compliments in the conventional idyll. Dyer does not allegorize entirely; he means what he says.' Certainly Dyer would not have had a mercenary motive for apostrophising the King; poets found little enough favour from 'Dunce the Second', and in any case Dyer had already achieved pre-ferment and established his patrons. The King is invoked, with an intense consciousness of the implications of the word 'shepherd', because all classes of society must be recruited for Dyer's vision of a harmonious society to be able to work.

The model for the rhetoric of this opening invocation, signalled especially by its adjectives ('princely', 'numerous', 'watchful', 'Celestial'), is *Paradise Lost*, and particularly the opening addresses of Satan's four speeches in Hell (I, lines 315, 622; II, lines 11, 430). Its 'high' Miltonic manner is entirely characteristic of Dyer's style. This style has been criticised more than any other feature of the poem, usually being dismissed as absurdly inappropriate to the 'low' themes of the poem. But the new readings I have briefly discussed here, and particularly those of Goldstein and Barrell, may begin to suggest that the nature of Dyer's task was such that it could only be attempted in the high, epic manner. To lend credibility to his definitive apologia for the Christian cosmology and the age of revolutions he had lived through, John Milton had, as it were, gathered his bardic robes imposingly around himself, and declaimed *ex cathedra*. If in the eighteenth century, as may fairly be argued, the ability of the nation to survive and flourish depended to a great extent on the ability of landowners and farmers to supply large amounts of inexpensive mutton to the capital, and large amounts of wool to the textile industry and thence to the world, then 'The care of sheep' might indeed become an epic theme. And, similarly, if the poet felt that these processes were in danger of being stifled by widespread intellectual and economic dissipation, then the language with which Satan rallies his demoralised troops in hell could be an appropriate model for an epic attempt to alert the nation to the dangers it faced, and to rally it to a new sense of economic and philosophical purpose.

Engagement and disengagement in mid eighteenth-century poetry

This intense sense of purpose, the serious and practical engagement the new readings of *The Fleece* imply and the rationale I have suggested for Dyer's use of epic language and form, seem at first sight surprising. We tend to think of mid eighteenth-century poetry in terms of a group of poets whose major concerns were very far from the current socio-economic demands of their society. The only kind of nation they seem to rally is the mythical thirteenth-century Wales for which Gray's doomed 'Bard' performs his heroic suicide; and the classic location for their poetry is not the textile factory, the trading exchange, or even the sheep pastures of England, but the country churchyard. Our usual reading of the poetry of the 1740s and 1750s tracks a retreat from the social and historical engagement of the Queen Anne poets.

The position has been eloquently put by John Sitter.[10] He finds the poets in the 1740s moving sharply away from the sense both Dryden and Pope had, of 'the poet's role as historian of his own times' (p. 83). For the new generation of poets contemporary history is a 'crushing presence' (p. 84), from which to escape into the 'politics of melancholy' (p. 85). Considering the changes in terms of the Horatian ideal of retirement, Sitter writes: 'By the mid-century, retirement has hardened into retreat. The poet characteristically longs to be not only far from the madding crowd, which Pope had wanted as much as Gray, but far from everybody' (p. 85). Yet Dyer's feelings in *The Fleece* are exactly the opposite of this. His most intensely felt poetic moments are social ones: the communal idyll of the shepherd's feast (lines 698–720), the Bishop Blaize procession (II, lines 539–56) and even the communal labour of the factory-workhouse (III, lines 259–302). His most emphatically expressed theme is the unifying social virtues of labour and of trade.

It would not be especially productive to pursue here the whys and wherefores of this divide: one could argue endlessly over what the characteristic literature of a period is, to little appreciable effect. The essential point, I think, is that literary history, like other kinds of history, tends to be written from the point of view of the winners, and the winners in this context have been the 'solitary' poets, whose sensibilities coincide with, and indeed prefigure, the modern view of poetry, as Sitter notes in his Preface:

One major shock of recognition for the modern observer is the discovery, made in the 1740s, that poetry, if it is to be 'pure poetry,' should be about a lonely poet surrounded by 'nature' – an idea hardly pure or natural but inherited today by almost any beginning writer of verse. It is primarily this new assumption and its variants in the particular consciousness mid-eighteenth-century authors had of themselves as solitary writers for solitary readers that I have tried to characterise as 'literary loneliness.'

(p. 9)

One result of the modern understanding of poetry as the product of a 'lonely poet surrounded by "nature"' has been the exclusion from the canon of mid eighteenth-century poetry of the georgic poem, whose stance is primarily social and sociable. As well as *The Fleece*, other poems of this sort, such as John Armstrong's *The Art of Preserving Health* (1744), Christopher Smart's *The Hop Garden* (1752), Robert Dodsley's *Agriculture* (1753) and James Grainger's *The Sugar-Cane* (1764) also tend to be ignored.

The problem this raises is not primarily one of how to reinstate the genre, but of how to 'read' it. Recent work on eighteenth-century poetry, particularly Roger Lonsdale's two anthologies (published in 1984 and 1989) has led to the rediscovery of many new genres and works from the period, and to a much more open-minded approach to what is significant than has ever been the case before.

But the receptive implications of a renewed critical engagement with *The Fleece*, and poems like it, need some attention. Sitter uses the phrase 'pure poetry', albeit in cautious quotation marks. Is the kind of poetry represented by *The Fleece* therefore perhaps 'impure poetry', by modern standards? What kind of information can we expect to find in it? Should we treat it as being primarily of historical and documentary interest, or can it also maintain its status as poetry? And if it is poetry, does it have a relationship with the personal, solitary, intuitive kind of utterance which to the modern mind is poetry, or are its poetic qualities mortgaged to rational and practical requirements, to its public and social responsibilities?

The reading which follows of one of *The Fleece*'s three themes attempts, as I think Goldstein, Feingold and Barrell have attempted, to 'outgrow' these problems, drawing on interdisciplinary information to measure the historical and documentary value the poem holds, and at the same time treating it as a poem, in the sense of a discourse which involves imaginative and volitional and well as cognitive processes, and draws on the rhythmic, harmonious and connotative as well denotative values of language. The important question in this is not so much whether the poet found inspiration in a twilit churchyard or in a clothing factory, as how effectively and credibly s/he uses the force of poetry to express and to find the meaning of the subject, whatever it may happen to be.

It is not at all clear, of course, that poetry can satisfy both rational and imaginative criteria. Shelley, for example, was to make a clear distinction: 'Ethical science arranges the elements which poetry has created, and propounds schemes and proposes examples of civil and domestic life ... But poetry acts in another and diviner manner. It awakens and enlarges the mind itself by rendering it the receptacle of a thousand unapprehended combinations of thought'.[11] The poets of a slightly earlier period (as we saw in Thomson's 'Winter') attempted to incorporate what Shelley calls 'ethical science' within poetry; so that *The Fleece* itself 'propounds schemes and proposes examples of civil and domestic life'. The dilemma of the poem lies within this combination of tasks, and the major critical issue is how, and to what effect, they are combined. We may now attempt to unravel this issue, beginning with a look at the historical and theoretical situation in which Dyer's agricultural theme was constructed.

The agricultural revolution

To the modern mind, the combination of 'beauty' and 'truth' belongs typically in a Keats poem, and therefore within the discipline of English literature. It is not a theme we would expect to find, for example, within the discipline of agrarian history. Keith Thomas has noted that it was the early modern period (the era of Dyer and Keats) which 'engendered that split sensibility from which we still suffer. What was useful and productive was most likely to be ugly and distasteful.'[12] Dyer fought spiritedly against this psychological split. *The Fleece* is a poem that attempts to contribute to historical progress by giving practical advice on the new industrial and farming methods; and it is also a didactic treatise that attempts to encompass poetic ideals of beauty, and an idealised, 'poetic' view of past history. So far as agriculture is concerned, this attempt to combine 'beauty and truth', from which our modern 'split sensibility' recoils, has another historical analogue, one which is particularly relevant to Dyer's poem.

The idea that in the eighteenth century an agricultural revolution took place has undergone much revision in the last twenty-five years.[13] One element of it, however, has held its position and status as a major mid eighteenth-century event. This is the animal-breeding revolution, associated particularly with the pioneering work of Robert Bakewell (1725–95). This revolution was of major significance in the economic development of modern society, and established new methods of animal husbandry not only in Britain, but in areas such as Australia, South America and Africa, where the new British breeds became the basis for large-scale livestock agriculture. So far as sheep husbandry is concerned, the breeding revolution had two major and interlocking features. Firstly, it was the central event in a general change of priorities in the national utilisation of sheep, from wool to mutton. It signalled, effectively, the end of the woollen industry's hegemony within national economic life, after some six centuries of central significance. The wool clip in fact increased in the eighteenth century, though not sufficiently to keep pace with national demand. By 1776 two million tons of wool had to be imported to supply the indigenous clothing industry, and by 1800 the figure was eight and a half million tons. But while the breeding experiments may have actually helped increase the quantity of the clip in some cases, it decreased the quality, and helped put the decline of the high quality combing and carding wools beyond retrieval.[14]

Secondly, the purpose and result of the breeding experiments were to turn the free-ranging, slow-maturing, unprolific, boney English sheep into a closely monitored, fast-maturing and prolific slab of 'mutton on the hoof'; an animal which could answer significantly the demands of the rapidly expanding cities, particularly London, for large amounts of cheap protein.[15] In Bakewell's home county of Leicestershire the great droving-routes from the North, Scotland and Wales converged in the rich pasture land of the Soar valley. It was naturally a nursery for English mutton and beef, and a remedial centre for the drovers' cattle and sheep. Locally bred animals were fattened; and drovers' animals regained there the weight and condition they had lost on the long migration south and east. The new turnpike roads made the final journey to Smithfield a fairly easy one; and the area was well situated for sending cattle and sheep in other directions too.[16]

In the Middle Ages, mutton had been a relatively insignificant product. Sheep were bred for two main purposes: to manure the land, via folding and cotting, and to grow wool. Mutton was a side-product, no more significant than other fringe benefits like milk or parchment. By contrast the economic role of wool was central, enabling the very rise of England as a major economic power. It might not have been apparent in the mid eighteenth century that the most glorious days of the wool industry were over, but the growing significance of mutton as a staple diet for the city masses could be perceived by the more far-sighted, and the Leicestershire graziers were well placed to possess such insights. Even before Bakewell's time the area, as one commentator noted in 1790, had 'for many years abounded with intelligent and spirited breeders'.[17]

The new, mutton-producing sheep husbandry, then, was born in Leicestershire. We may note at this point that John Dyer owned farms and worked glebe lands in Leicestershire between 1738 and 1755; that he conducted much of his hard research on agriculture there; that he lived in Nuneaton briefly, and from 1742–51 was vicar of Catthorpe, eight miles south-east of Nuneaton. Between Catthorpe and Nuneaton the rivers Avon and Soar, and the ancient routes of Watling Street and the Fosse Way all intersect, in the area of the three-way boundary between Leicestershire, Northamptonshire and Warwickshire. He could hardly have had a better place from which to view the breeding revolution and gain an understanding of its significance than this fertile meeting-point, which he calls in his poem 'Tripontian fields', from the Latin 'Tripontium', meaning a place where there are three bridges, or where there is a bridge with three arches.[18]

The old, wool-oriented sheep husbandry and its associated woollen industries were more widespread, being strong, for example, in the West of England, much of the South East, Lincolnshire, Oxfordshire and the Southern chalk-belt. There were as many uses for wool as there were grades and qualities of it; and the uniquely wide range of sheep and wool-types the British landscape and climate had helped to evolve fostered a rich diversity in the woollen industry.[19] Its greatest glory, however, and the area in which it reigned virtually supreme in the early modern period, was its fine quality wools: its lustrous combing long-wools and its fine carding short-wools. These types were most strongly associated with two adjacent areas and two kinds of sheep. For high quality, lustrous combing wools the Cotswold sheep was for a long time unmatched; while the fine carding wool produced by the Ryelands sheep had acquired an almost mythical status. The Cotswold sheep was most concentrated in Gloucestershire, and the Ryelands sheep in Herefordshire.[20] Again, we may note that from 1730 to 1734 Dyer toured the West of England and Wales (especially the Welsh Marches) as an itinerant painter; and that he managed a farm at Bromyard near Leominster as a working farmer from 1734 to 1737.[21] Ryelands wool was known in the late medieval and early modern period as 'Lemster Ore', from its main wholesaling centre, Leominster, and the enduring belief that its best grades were worth their weight in gold. As with the time he spent in 'Tripontium', Dyer could not have found a better way to learn the history and traditions of British fine wool production than by travelling and farming in these areas, which he calls in his poem 'Siluria'.[22]

Here we see, then, two elements in eighteenth-century sheep husbandry: the golden legacy of a highly successful woollen industry stretching back to the Cistercian monks; and the new agri-business of mass mutton-production, still at an early stage in its development, but of enormous future potential and significance. Only hindsight allows us to see that the latter would eclipse the former, and we cannot expect the poet to know this; but we have seen that he was in a position to engage with both subjects. His main concern, of course, is the fleece, but it is also 'the care of sheep', which must relate to mutton as well as wool production.

We may note here a number of potential contrasts suggested by this preliminary survey. The first is between wool and mutton production. All shepherding practice aims to produce both, but the new breeding programmes, in concentrating on mutton production, were to destroy fairly swiftly the fine quality of Ryelands and Cotswold wool, which depended on sparse feeding. There is perhaps also a tension here between history as legacy (or, as we would now say, history as 'heritage'), represented by the achievements of the woollen industry; and history as progress, innovation and change, represented by the mutton-orientated breeding revolution. There is thus a sense of potential conflict between the past and the future, a familiar theme in georgic.

A conflict between the aesthetic and the practical manifests itself within the poem; and we shall find that it also manifests itself within the discourse of the breeding revolution. Was the scraggy English sheep transformed in the eighteenth century into an object of austere utilitarian beauty, as many contemporaries felt it was? Or had its diverse natural beauty been sacrificed to produce an ugly, unnatural machine for producing mountains of watery, grainy, low-grade mutton, as those who savoured the legacy of 'Lemster ore', the ancient 'Cotswold Lion', and the sweetness of pre-improvement English mutton would have argued? It will become increasingly apparent as our reading proceeds that these two points of view, the two major concerns of eighteenth-century sheep husbandry, and the two locations I have associated them with, are at the heart of the conflicts and contrasts in *The Fleece*, and particularly of Dyer's attempt to encompass what I have called 'truth' and 'beauty'.

7

'Soil and clime'

Pastoral landscapes

Dyer's shepherding advice fills most of the first book of the poem, and overlaps a little into Books II and III. Although he tends to work backwards and forwards over a few key ideas – the value of improvement and labour, the appropriate response to environment and the need for a modulation between human intervention and natural development – Dyer is fairly systematic, and we may read his advice in a sequential way. Firstly he treats the two variables of terrain (lines 18–124) and weather (lines 125–84), before considering the kinds of sheep suitable to different environments (lines 185–250). There follows a section of veterinary advice (lines 251–320), and a 'calendar' of information on different concerns in the shepherd's year (lines 321–554), which ends triumphantly in a pastoral rendering of the shearing festival (lines 555–720). We may examine each of these areas of advice in turn.

Dyer's first task, then, is to establish and comment on the basic variables of farming: terrain and weather. As soon as the invocation to the people and the 'people's Shepherd' is completed, the poet launches very positively into the subject of terrain:

> On spacious airy downs and gentle hills,
> With grass and thyme o'erspread, and clover wild,
> Where smiling Phoebus tempers ev'ry breeze,
> The fairest flocks rejoice: they nor of halt,
> Hydropic tumours, nor of rot, complain,
> Evils deform'd and foul: nor with hoarse cough
> Disturb the music of the past'ral pipe;
> But, crowding to the note, with silence soft
> The close-woven carpet graze, where Nature blends
> Flow'rets and herbage of minutest size,
> Innoxious luxury. Wide airy downs
> Are Health's gay walks to shepherd and to sheep.
>   All arid soils, with sand or chalky flint,
> Or shells deluvian mingled, and the turf
> That mantles over rocks of brittle stone,

> Be thy regard; and where low-tufted broom,
> Or box, or berry'd juniper, arise;
> Or the tall growth of glossy-rinded beech;
> And where the burrowing rabbit turns the dust;
> And where the dappled deer delights to bound.   (lines 18–37)

This is Dyer at his most effective. The idyllic pastoral imagery gains strength from, and in turn supports, the georgic prescriptivism to which it is tied. For example Dyer uses sound, contrasting 'coughing' with 'the pastoral pipe'. In prescriptive or agricultural terms, shepherding is an observational art, but Dyer here picks up the chief way in which it is also an art of listening: coughing meant trouble, as Dyer shows later, when he describes how 'The coughing pest / From their green pasture sweeps whole flocks away' (lines 264–5). This reference is probably to either brucellosis or tuberculosis: both are now eradicated, but in Dyer's time both were quite capable of wiping out a flock; and the intelligent shepherd who is the poem's implied reader would recognise the danger signals of the word 'coughing'. In case they do not, Dyer reminds them of some of the diseases sheep can get on less perfect ground. 'Halt' is foot-rot; 'rot' is liver-rot or liver fluke; 'hydropic tumours' are literally dropsical or watery swellings. Though no specific disease is suggested, Dyer later refers to 'pleurisies and dropsies' (line 294), caused by over-rich or over-wet pasture; and I think he is generally concerned with the range of dropsical diseases such as redwater and the various forms of enterotoxaemia.[1]

In descriptive, or literary terms, the harsh sound of coughing, evoking the often grim realities of shepherding, is contrasted with the literary idea of the 'pastoral pipe', the sweet music of an ideal rural world; and here its idyllic overtones are credible and appropriate. The terrain Dyer describes is indeed ideal for sheep. He emphasises several aspects of this. It is naturally dry ('all arid soils'). On such sandy and light soils, especially chalk, water drains away or is absorbed; and thus a number of digestive and infectious diseases associated with wet pasture and stagnant water are avoided. The hilly terrain Dyer describes would also help make this pasture free-draining. The 'airiness' and 'spaciousness' he describes is also an important element of his picture of health. Dyer seems to be following Galen's theories that 'atmospheric corruption' was the cause of epidemic disease. Brown and Beecham fairly condemn the way that veterinary practices based on these ideas survived into the nineteenth century; nevertheless space and airiness made good general sense as health-giving qualities.[2]

A particular kind of pasture is then evoked which contains, as well as grass, 'thyme' and 'clover wild'; and is also described in fine detail as: 'The close-woven carpet ... where Nature blends / Flow'rets and herbage of minutest size, / Innoxious luxury' (lines 26–8). The sense of vibrant healthiness which this carries has several sources. Both the range of 'Flow'rets and herbage', and the fact that it is 'close-woven', suggest well-established sheep pasture, whose structural qualities and variety of grasses have developed over a long period, and which (as the phrase 'close-woven' secondarily suggests) has been maintained as good pasture through constant grazing by sheep. The variety of grasses is itself a good sign, suggesting that the pasture will provide a range of 'bites', which also (as grasses come up at different times) make the pasture of use for a longer part of the year.

The traditional pastoral words 'thyme' and 'flow'rets' are deployed to suggest agricultural richness, but also work in an accurate descriptive-prescriptive way: 'thyme' is exactly the kind of creeping plant which would have strengthened and enhanced the quality of this kind of pasture; and 'flow'rets' indicates the healthy range of flowers and grasses. As Defoe (vol. I, p. 211) wrote of the land around Dorchester (which is one of Dyer's 'examples' of this kind of pasture): 'The Grass, or Herbage of these Downs is full of the sweetest, and the most Aromatick Plants, such as Nourish the Sheep to a strange degree.' Dyer's pastoral and georgic materials are exactly matched and interdependent in this powerful opening section. His task is to describe the best kind of land for sheep, and he does so in a rationally and poetically ordered sequence of different ways. First he describes the shape of the land and the nature of its pasture (lines 18–29). Then he gives the soil descriptions: dry soils in general, and sandy, chalky or marly ('shells deluvian mingled') soil in particular, and preferably with a shallow tilth over 'brittle' rock, that is, absorbent lime-stone, chalk, sandstone, etc. (lines 30–3). This is all excellent descriptive work and is agriculturally correct. Dyer then further indicates the right sort of terrain by describing its most visible features, its characteristic shrubs and trees. They are broom, box, juniper and beech, and together they signal the kind of free-draining, light soils he has in mind.[3] This again works well in practical terms, (it is a good way of identifying the right kind of land), and as poetry, in which the listing of things, especially living species, is a well-established rhetorical technique. The last two lines of the verse-paragraph, following this, are: 'And where the burrowing rabbit turns the dust; / And where the dappled deer delights to bound' (lines 36–7). Dyer frequently uses anaphora, with varying degrees of success. Here I think it works well. It is a consciously idyllic 'pastoral' ending to the paragraph, yet it maintains something of the sense of prescriptive functionalism of the rest of the passage, for of course herbivores such as the rabbit and the deer are indeed likely to thrive in the same areas as the sheep, and thus it is another good piece of observational advice.

Dyer completes and particularises this opening advice in a second verse-paragraph (lines 38–66), which gives a kind of directory of good pastures and appropriate locations:

> Such are the downs of Banstead, edg'd with woods
> And towery villas; such Dorcestrian fields,
> Whose flocks innumerous whiten all the land:
> Such those slow-climbing wilds that lead the step
> Insensibly to Dover's windy cliff,
> Tremendous height! and such the clover'd lawns,
> And sunny mounts of beauteous Normanton,
> Health's cheerful haunt, and the selected walk
> Of Heathcote's leisure: such the spacious plain
> Of Sarum, spread like Ocean's boundless round,
> Where solitary Stonehenge, gray with moss,
> Ruin of ages! nods: such, too, the leas
> And ruddy tilth which spiry Ross beholds,
> From a green hillock, o'er her lofty elms;
> And Lemster's brooky tract and airy Croft;
> And such Harleian Eywood's swelling turf,
> Wav'd as the billows of a rolling sea;
> And Shobden, for its lofty terrace fam'd,
> Which from a mountain's ridge, elate o'er woods,
> And girt with all Siluria, sees around
> Regions on regions blended in the clouds.
> Pleasant Siluria! land of various views,
> Hills, rivers, woods, and lawns, and purple groves
> Pomaceous, mingled with the curling growth
> Of tendril hops, that flaunt upon their poles.   (lines 38–62)[4]

The primary focus of the locations named is on good sheep pastures. Banstead (line 38) was, as Lord Ernle says, 'especially famous for the quality of its mutton'; a point also alluded to by Pope: 'and Bansted-down, / Thence comes your mutton'. Banstead Downs, outside Epsom on the North Downs in Surrey, were famous both as sheep downs and as a place of healthy retreat from the city, being conveniently situated near Epsom Spa (in Book II, line 375 Dyer links Banstead wool with 'Gay Epsom's too'). Defoe had been impressed by the quality of land on the Downs: 'the Ground smooth, soft, level and dry; (even in but a few Hours after Rain) they conspire to make the most delightful Spot of Ground, of that kind in all this Part of Britain'.[5]

Of Dyer's 'Dorcestrian fields' (line 39), the area round Dorchester, Defoe had conjured an impressive statistic: 'They who would make any practicable Guess at the Number of Sheep usually fed on these Downs, may take it from a Calculation made, as I was told, at Dorchester, that there were 600000 Sheep fed within 6 Miles of that Town, measuring every Way round, and the Town in the Center.' We do not have to take those figures too literally to see that this was one of the most successful sheep-grazing areas in the land. Camden had also noted Dorset's 'great flocks of sheep'; while Drayton's phrase 'Dorsetian fields' may have influenced Dyer.[6]

The Dover area (line 42) is famously chalkland, and hence good grazing country. Defoe notes the 'pleasant Champaign Country' of the downs on his way to Dover (vol. I, p. 122); while Drayton (Song XVIII, lines 763–4) follows Shakespeare (*King Lear*, IV, vi, 15), in noting the samphire grown on the chalk cliffs. Dyer's lines 41–3 suggest other Shakespearean resonances, too; compare, for example, his 'tremendous height' with Edgar's description of the ground as 'Horrible steep', *King Lear*, IV, vi, 3.[7]

'Sarum' (line 47) is the old or poetic name for Salisbury. Defoe's description of Salisbury Plain (vol. I, pp. 187–8) aptly illustrates Dyer's main interest in the area:

From Winchester, is about 25 Miles, and over the most charming Plains that can any where be seen, (far in my Opinion) excelling the Plains of Mecca, we come to Salisbury; the vast Flocks of Sheep, which one every where sees upon these Downs, and the great Number of those Flocks, is a Sight truly worth Observation; 'tis ordinary for these Flocks to contain from 3 to 5000 in a Flock; and several private Farmers hereabouts have two or three such Flocks.

The area was simply the best sheep pasture in the country. Camden characterised southern Wiltshire as 'a large champagne fruitful Country' which 'feeds innumerable flocks of sheep' (p. 85). Defoe shows that by the eighteenth century it had been made even more agriculturally productive.

These areas were all renowned for their qualities as sheep pasture. However Dyer's topographical references also evoke other sorts of information, to create a vivid tapestry of geographical, historical and literary allusion. Dover cliff, like a number of other places Dyer names, is the site of a castle, and a place which gives a 'prospect'. Apart from its Shakespearean resonances it is traditionally a focus of patriotic feeling. Banstead Down was a health-giving recreational area. Dorchester and Salisbury have historical associations; and Dyer makes the latter explicit by his mention of Stonehenge, a familiar subject for poets in the early modern period.[8]

Interwoven with these well-known locations are a more personal set of topographical references. All but one are 'Silurian', and the exception, Normanton Hall in Rutlandshire, is 'Tripontian'. Dyer is building his own mythology here, to suggest the agricultural richness of the two major areas, and to incorporate references to patrons and other levels of meaning. Examining these references in sequence, we come first to Normanton (line 44). Dyer's note describes it as 'A seat of Sir John Heathcote in Rutlandshire'. Normanton Hall had become the seat of the

Mackworth family in the reign of Henry VI; they were later heavily involved on the Parliamentary side in the Civil War. The seat was purchased in about 1729 by Sir Gilbert Heathcote (1652–1733), father to Sir John. Knighted by the Queen in 1702, Sir Gilbert was a long-serving MP, a founder of the Bank of England, and Lord Mayor of London in 1710, awarded a baronetcy in 1732–3. He was unpopular, and Pope's two attacks on him are revealing:

> The grave Sir Gilbert holds it for a rule,
> That 'every man in want is knave or fool'

> Heathcote himself, and such large-acred Men,
> Lords of fat E'sham, or of Lincoln Fen,
> Buy every stick of Wood that lends them heat,
> Buy every Pullet they afford to eat.
> Yet these are Wights, who fondly call their own
> Half that the Dev'l o'erlooks from Lincoln Town.[9]

Dyer is making a reference to his patron Sir John Heathcote (b. 1689), MP for Grantham (1715–22) and Bodmin (1733–41).[10] He addresses him again in Book III:

> So thou, the friend of every virtuous deed
> And aim, tho' feeble, shalt these rural lays
> Approve, O Heathcote! whose benevolence
> Visits our vallies, where the pasture spreads,
> And where the bramble; and would justly act
> True charity, by teaching idle Want
> And Vice the inclination to do good;
> Good to themselves, and in themselves to all,
> Thro' grateful toil.   (III, lines 14–22)

The word 'benevolence' expresses Dyer's gratitude to Sir John for his patronage of the poet, to whom he presented the livings of Coningsby (1751–7), and Kirkby-on-Bane (1755–7). The phrase 'would justly act' seems to express a more general belief in Heathcote's benevolence. But 'bramble' is a word that marks the emergence of the agricultural improver in Dyer, and it seems Sir John's 'benevolence' is specifically associated with agricultural developments: Heathcote was an enthusiastic enclosurist. G. E. Mingay gives a dramatic picture of Sir John's attempts to enclose a common pasture on his estate being 'frustrated by a mob who peremptorily threw down his fences'. This perhaps suggests something closer to Pope's hard-headed view of the older Heathcote than to Dyer's benevolent view of the younger. Sir John also showed some interest in crop developments. Pevsner records that the 'great Palladian house' at Normanton was demolished after the war, but that the estate still had stables, farm buildings and houses 'in a sound and pleasant classical style'.[11]

The 'leas / And ruddy tilth which spiry Ross beholds / From a green hillock, o'er her lofty elms' (lines 49–51), introduces an important cluster of Silurian references. This is Ross-on-Wye, and both the 'leas' (water meadows) and 'ruddy tilth' (ploughed fields of red earth) it 'beholds' may still be seen from the A40/M50 motorway, which runs through much of southern 'Siluria'. The moment is as typically eighteenth-century as my motorist's view is twentieth-century. To characterise a landscape the eighteenth-century poet sought the vantage point, climbing a hill as Dyer himself does in 'Grongar Hill' (1726). Here he uses the town of Ross as his hill, the 'overseer' of the area. The town is set on an eminence ('a green hillock') and looks down on both the water meadows at its feet, and (seen over the tops of the elms beneath it) the ploughed lands beyond. Its prominence was later noted by Gilpin, who wrote that it 'commands many distant views'. Dyer thus makes it an important central focus for the southern part of his 'Siluria'. He refers to it later as 'elmy Ross' (line 206), and in Book II he uses the old word for the area, in the epithet 'sandy Urchinfield' (II, line 37). This is both agriculturally and historically alert, for it is the old sandstone rock which gives the earth its rich red colouring, while 'Urchinfield' evokes important historical associations.[12]

Ross overlooks and focuses the agricultural richness of southern Siluria. It also had a contemporary significance as the location of Pope's exemplary 'Man of Ross' in the 'Epistle to Bathurst' (1733). The 'Man of Ross', as John Barrell notes in this context, is an archetypal georgic figure of 'simple, unobtrusive industry'. His philanthropy was typical of the values Dyer projects. Pope had mentioned Ross's 'heaven directed spire' (line 261) which Dyer makes into the town's essential characteristic as 'spiry Ross' (line 50). In 1782 another artist, William Gilpin, was to note that what was by now known as the Man-of-Ross's spire 'tapers beautifully'.[13]

Four more Silurian references follow, and lead directly into the passage of praise for 'Siluria'. The significance of Leominster as the trading centre of Ryelands wool, 'Lemster Ore', has been noted. Defoe (vol. II, p. 448) was suitably impressed: 'Indeed the Wool about Leominster, and in the Hundred of Wigmore observ'd above, and the Golden Vale as 'tis called, for its richness on the Banks of the River Dove (all in this County) is the finest without exception, of any in England, the South Down Wool not excepted.' He also found (vol. II, p. 447) that Leominster had 'a very great Trade for their Corn, Wool, and other Products of this Place, into the river Wye; and from the Wye, into the Severn, and so to Bristol'. Dyer uses Leominster to provide a focus for the northern part of 'Siluria', as Ross focuses the southern part; and the three seats Dyer now names in quick succession fan out in a line to the north and west of the town.[14]

The phrase 'airy Croft' is a punning reference (compare 'Lemster's crofts', II, line 200) to Croft Castle, the seat of Sir Archer Croft (1683–1753). Sir Archer was the brother-in-law of Dyer's brother Robert, and represented an old Silurian family which had been extensively involved in Herefordshire politics since the Middle Ages, intermarrying with the other two families in this group of references (Batemans and Harleys), not to mention Janet, daughter of 'the renowned Owen Glendower, Representative of the Princes of Powys' who married Sir John De Croft at the beginning of the fifteenth century.[15]

'Harleian Eywood's swelling turf' (line 53) is one of three 'Harleian' seats in the area. As it happens Defoe (vol. II, p. 447) had visited the other two:

The Country on our right as we came from Ludlow is very fruitful and pleasant, and is call'd the Hundred of Wigmore, from which the late Earl of Oxford at his Creation, took the title of Baron of Wigmore: And here we saw two Antient Castles, (viz.) Brampton-Brian, and Wigmore-Castle, both belonging to the Earl's Father, Sir Edward Harley.

The rich historical and agricultural legacy of these seats would have greatly stimulated Dyer. We get an indication of the excitement of the former and the scale of the latter, from *Agrarian History* (V, ii, p. 133), which records that when the royalists attacked the estate of Brampton Bryan in 1643 Sir Robert Harley lost '800 sheep, besides cattle and a stud of 30 brood mares'.[16]

What interest Dyer may have had with the Harley family is not known: probably encouragement or patronage for his painting. The former Prime Minister, Robert Harley (1661–1724), first Earl of Oxford, was a patron of writers and collector of manuscripts who liked in his periods out of politics, 'to share the company of scholars and literary men'. He died rather early to have known Dyer, but his son Edward (1689–1741), the second Earl, was also an important literary patron, and a passionate collector of 'books, manuscripts, pictures, medals and miscellaneous curiosities, which he usually bought at prices much beyond their worth'.[17]

Dyer's use of the word 'Harleian' is enough to suggest the Wigmore and Brampton Bryan Harley associations, but Eywood itself is further south, beyond Croft Castle, at Titley. This was the seat of the first Earl's brother Edward ('Auditor') Harley (1664–1735), and his son, also Edward Harley (1699?–1755), the third Earl. Both father and son had literary and patronly interests, like the other branch of the family. The third Earl was also connected with Dyer's patrons the Yorkes, as Linda Colley, discussing his initiation of the Cocoa Tree coffee house 'Board' in 1727, notes: 'Unquestionably loyal to the Hanoverian dynasty and a close friend of the Attorney-General, Philip Yorke, Harley was a man distin-

guished by "cool good sense" as well as over-burdened by his own moral
rectitude.'[18]

At the time Dyer was a travelling painter and then a farmer in the area,
Auditor Harley was an old man, his son was MP for Herefordshire
(1727–41), and Prime Minister Harley's son was busying himself with
literature, gardening, building, collecting and spending too much money.
Dyer may have been known to any of the three, and I suspect he received
patronage, probably from Yorke's friend the third Earl, identified as the
current inhabitant of Eywood in Dyer's footnote.[19]

'Shobden for its lofty terrace fam'd' (line 55), is Shobden Court, the seat
of William Bateman, created Viscount Bateman in 1725, who died in
1744; and of his son and heir John Bateman (1721–1802), the Second
Viscount. Both were archetypes of Silurian good citizenship: the father
was Whig MP for Leominster in 1721–2 and 1727–34, and the son held the
same office in 1768–84, and was Lord Lieutenant of Herefordshire from
1747 until his death. Like the Harleys, William Bateman 'made a great
collection' (according to Gibbs), his interest being paintings and sculpture
rather than manuscripts. Dyer has a proven connection with Shobden, in
that his friend Lewis Crucius was chaplain there for a number of years,
and Dyer's biographer Williams thinks the poet may have visited Crucius
at Shobden.[20]

These three topographical references, grouped to the north and west of
Leominster, lead directly to the praise of 'Pleasant Siluria! land of various
views!', and like the passage about Ross they suggest the perspective of
views of the land. Defoe tells us that 'from the Windows of Brampton-
Castle, you have a fair Prospect into the County of Radnor, which is, as it
were, under its Walls' (vol. II, p. 448), and I think Dyer uses the other
seats to focus Siluria; both visually, and in historical terms through his
allusions to the ancient families of Croft, Harley and Bateman. His is a
painter's-eye view, but his prospects are evaluated in terms of historical
and agricultural richness. In his praise of Siluria (lines 59–63) he draws
together the two sides of this approach, to conclude a section which
succeeds both as a poetry of topographical allusion, and as a prescription
of good sheep pastures.

It would perhaps be hard to find another passage in the poem which
unites pastoral, topographic and georgic elements quite so felicitously as
this one. Its success is precisely based on the fact that Dyer is describing
perfect land for sheep; and we shall see that he describes an idealised
'Silurian' sheep later on, to go with this ideal terrain. But it is important to
notice that he does not make this section successful solely by traditional
pastoral means; that is, by the exclusion of any but the most nominal
indications of postlapsarian reality. In particular he has not feared that
the queasy subject of sheep diseases might damage his pastoral vision. As

this is ideal sheep pasture his characterisation of disease is made in a negative way, but it does not prevent it from being vividly unpleasant: 'they nor of halt, / Hydropic tumours, nor of rot, complain, / Evils deform'd and foul: nor with hoarse cough' (lines 20–22). This is the real as well as the pastoral world, and Dyer's poetry is faithful to both kinds of landscape in this section. Indeed his mention of these diseases gives warning that he will be describing and discussing disease, the sign and subject of a mortal, non-pastoral world, in what is to follow, alongside his pastoral material.

Georgic landscapes

But clearly Dyer cannot proceed in so triumphantly idyllic a manner. His didacticism must concern itself also with less obviously wonderful terrain, less perfect pasture. Hence he moves on to a second piece of advice on land, related to a specific kind of sheep husbandry:

> But if thy prudent care would cultivate
> Leicestrian Fleeces, what the sinewy arm
> Combs thro' the spiky steel in lengthen'd flakes;
> Rich saponaceous loam, that slowly drinks
> The blackening shower, and fattens with the draught;
> Or heavy marl's deep clay, be then thy choice,
> Of one consistence, one complexion, spread
> Thro' all thy glebe.   (lines 67–74)[21]

We are drawn here into a somewhat tougher world where the need to work ('the sinewy arm') seems more strongly present, and where the environment is more potentially hostile, with its 'deceitful veins / Of envious gravel'. Dyer's engagement with the subject here is simultaneously less pastoralised and more physical, more 'real'. The poet's attempts to describe the nature of soil and land types are invariably made in strongly sensuous ways. In the first of the two soil descriptions here (lines 70–1), the effect of the poetry is as if Dyer had picked up a handful of the soil and were squeezing it between his fingers: as a good farmer, and a good poet (one thinks of some of Seamus Heaney's work) would do. We ought not to be put off by polysyllabic Latinate words like 'saponaceous': Dyer is describing a peat-based loam characteristic of formerly forested areas, and he notes its particular qualities in the conditions in which it is most easily sensuously identifiable, i.e. when it gets wet. Moistened, peaty soil gradually absorbs ('slowly drinks') water; darkens ('blackening') and expands ('fattens'), holding the water, and showing 'saponaceous' (soapy or emulsifying) qualities. One could hardly describe peat-based soil better, in sensuous terms.

A potentially more difficult kind of terrain for sheep is suggested here. It is not enough just to choose the peaty or the marly clay soil Dyer describes, to grow heavy fleeces; one must also have consistency of soil, and one particular danger is described in conspiratorial terms:

> where no deceitful veins
> Of envious gravel lurk beneath the turf,
> To loose the creeping waters from their springs,
> Tainting the pasturage: and let thy fields
> In slopes descend and mount, that chilling rains
> May trickle off, and hasten to the brooks.   (lines 74–9)

For a man who, as we shall see, is intensely proud of England's rainy climate, Dyer seems strangely hydrophobic here, but his advice makes good sense. Standing water was a major source of sheep diseases in the eighteenth century; efficient under-field drainage systems were a nineteenth-century innovation. His poetic procedures here are rather different from those used in the opening advice on land. His aim is to foster in the landowner and the shepherd an alert awareness of soil and land conditions, so that standing water, springs, drainage, soil types and their qualities are more carefully observed and responded to. By characterising the water and the water-bearing strata as traitors who, 'envious' and 'deceitful', 'creep', and 'taint', Dyer again recruits Milton's Satan to the new heroic cause of good land-use. The landowner and the farmer are revealed as epic heroes; modern farming becomes the battlefield for a renewed war against evil; and the otherwise rather dull subjects of soil science and land drainage take on a new aura and a new significance.

This in itself might be in danger of seeming bathetic or banal, but Dyer's procedures carefully avoid these pitfalls. In the opening Miltonic invocation, as we saw, Dyer plays on his implied literalisation of the King's role as 'people's Shepherd', and one effect of this is to tie epic procedures to the sublunary subject of 'the care of sheep'. Here, he keeps his feet on the ground in other ways. The Miltonic allusion is a subtle one: we would need to search *Paradise Lost* fairly carefully to find clear echoes; yet at the same time the satanic significance of the words I have highlighted ('envious', 'creeping', etc.) would be easily imaginatively available, not only to a reader acquainted with Milton, but to anyone brought up to know the Old Testament, or merely used to hearing Sunday sermons (i.e. any of Dyer's contemporary readers). It is at once a subtle and a blunt, a 'high' and a 'low' instrument. Then, the passage moves swiftly on from the epic evocation of lurking threat (lines 74–7), into a transitional passage which combines the positive force of practical advice with the reassuring music of flowing water (lines 77–9). Dyer's use of the harmony and energies of moving water, here and elsewhere, reflects the influence of his friend Thomson: *The Seasons* is animated by moving water more than any other kind of natural image.[22] The fearful reader is soothed, the practical reader given ways to respond to the creeping menace. And finally, Dyer then proceeds to a moralising passage which puts the whole issue into a familiar universalised context. He characteristically acknowledges complexity and difficulty while turning it to rhetorical advantage, introducing a modulating hint of pathos, and an plea for 'social aid'. This in turn prepares for a new offering of advice and practical remedies, which moves naturally into the direct address of prescription:

> Yet some defect in all on earth appears:
> All seek for help, all press for social aid.
> Too cold the grassy mantle of the marle,
> In stormy winter's long and dreary nights,
> For cumbent sheep; from broken slumber oft
> They rise benumb'd, and vainly shift the couch;
> Their wasted sides their evil plight declare:
> Hence, tender in his care, the shepherd swain
> Seeks each contrivance. Here it would avail
> At a meet distance from the shelt'ring mound
> To sink a trench, and on the hedge-long bank
> Sow frequent sand, with lime, and dark manure,
> Which to the liquid element will yield
> A porous way, a passage to the foe.
> Plough not such pastures; deep in spongy grass
> The oldest carpet is the warmest lair,
> And soundest: in new herbage coughs are heard. (lines 80–96)[23]

Here a potentially bland moralising statement is brought to life by the close descriptive work within the advice it leads into. The discomfort sheep feel on cold damp ground, their moving around in the night to try and find a comfortable position, and the way in which loss of condition shows in 'wasted sides' are all accurate, and seem to be based on observation.[24] Having created this credible image, which evokes pity and concern, Dyer again offers a remedy, adopting a reassuring, practical tone of measurement and decision: 'Here it would avail / At a meet distance'. This is the poet as improving agriculturalist, providing new solutions to age-old problems.

Drainage is of course a good solution, in general terms, though the details of his advice raise one or two questions. In this and in the previous passage Dyer is suggesting some fairly radical environmental interventions. Though the instruction to 'let thy fields / In slopes descend and mount' (lines 77–8) appears to be part of the poet's advice on choosing the right sort of land for sheep, it also seems to suggest landscaping, and hence large-scale earthworks. The implied reader, here as elsewhere, appears to be the shepherd or farmer, but in this context is in fact more probably the large landowner, the only person who would be financially capable of landscaping fields (or indeed of choosing the best land for different agricultural purposes). It would perhaps be thought indecorous or tactless for the poet to seem to be telling the large landowners how to manage their land, so Dyer disguises the addressee as a simple shepherd, by means of the pastoral imagery of the caring 'shepherd swain', and the Virgilian 'careful swain' exemplum which completes this section (lines 108–24, discussed below). His *real* addressee can be deduced from the tactful, civil tones employed in the instruction ('thy prudent care', 'Here it would avail', and so on: one can almost hear in the tone of these phrases the address 'My Lord'); and the fact that both the 'shepherd swain' and the 'careful swain' are in the third person, and are not in fact directly addressed, though they seem to be. Choosing land, landscaping and especially large scale field drainage were not shepherdly but aristocratic tasks. Dyer was well aware of this, as his praise for 'Russel' (II, lines 165–76), the fen-draining fourth Earl of Bedford, shows. This is not quite the full picture, however. The invocation carefully recruited all the social classes into Dyer's labouring utopia, and if it is a patrician task to authorise the sinking of trenches and the landscaping of fields, it is certainly the 'swain' who gets to do the digging. He is thus not only a stalking-horse for an appeal to the mighty which might otherwise appear impertinent, but also a genuine addressee. He is not directly addressed, but the poet finds a tonal way of making him the addressee in the last part of the passage. Drainage of course represents 'improvement' and new ideas, as well as aristocratic concerns; but the warning Dyer gives to complete the paragraph reverts to an older style of shepherdly precept, signalling that the addressee is now in part the real 'swain', the shepherd, from whose culture the tone and shape of the advice is borrowed: 'Plough not such pastures; deep in spongy grass / The oldest carpet is the warmest lair, / And soundest: in new herbage coughs are heard' (lines 94–6). This is good advice, which follows up the earlier images of structural integrity in pasture (lines 26–7). It is also consciously proverb-like. The whole instruction, and especially the middle line, echoes the reassuring rhythm and phraseology of folk wisdom, a device often employed in pastoral, for instance by Theocritus in Idyll X (Milon's Song, also discussed above, chapter 4), which weaves together many maxims of this sort, to create a literary effect. Virgil also incorporates proverbial wisdom into the *Georgics*; and Tusser uses pithy, concise statements of this sort, especially in the 'abstracts', whose short couplets suit them well. Dyer uses the technique to balance the aristocratic-oriented tones and the new ideas we have seen, subtly readmitting the shepherd into areas of agricultural planning and administration from which he is more usually excluded.

The prescriptive side of the passage is less assuredly managed, but interesting in some ways. Professor Kerridge, who has found extensive evidence for most kinds of agricultural improvement before the mid eighteenth century, makes no great claims for early modern field drainage techniques, and Dyer cannot be expected to be as far-sighted here as he seems to be in other areas of agricultural development.[25] He advises a conventional hedge ('mound') and ditch construction along the field boundary, but his phrase 'meet distance' is vague; and I think he may be confusing two procedures, when he writes:

> and on the hedge-long bank
> Sow frequent sand, with lime, and dark manure,
> Which to the liquid element will yield
> A porous way, a passage to the foe.   (lines 90–3)

This seems to suggest that sand, lime and manure are appropriate drain-lining porous materials; in fact they are materials associated with hedge-planting. Sand was a medium to carry seeds, and lime and manure are fertilisers (in which role they tend to cancel each other out, though Dyer would not know this). The poet seems partly aware of procedures for planting hedges and for ditching, and it may be that he means to advise on both, and that his advice is simply not very well communicated, rather than accidentally conflated from two procedures.

But Dyer also has a second and more important idea about drainage. His advice on the 'deceitful veins' of gravel which 'loose the creeping waters from their springs' (lines 74–9) is simply to avoid them. However he does make a second attempt at advice on the subject slightly later, by example, in the 'careful swain' passage:

> And oft with labour-strengthen'd arm he delv'd
> The draining trench across his verdant slopes,
> To intercept the small meandering rills
> Of upper hamlets.   (lines 111–14)

In this passage we are returned from an aristocratic, selective approach to land use, to the self-help ethic of Dyer's exemplary swains. These labouring farmers, of course, cannot avoid the conditions of their land, and so Dyer has to try and show them how to change these conditions. He shows in both passages an awareness of the significance of springs; and his ideas of tailoring drainage systems to the progress of the water flow, being observationally aware of the subtle patterns of rilling, and intercepting the spring water, put him quite close to the major development in eighteenth-century field drainage. In 1764 James Elkington introduced a system of deep drainage. As Kerridge describes the process, 'he used an auger to locate the spring and then intercepted it by a drain at the highest point of the affected patch'. If Dyer's swain is not actually augering, he is certainly moving towards this kind of approach by digging deep drains, intercepting rills and so on.[26]

Dyer's characterisation of the qualities of 'old' pasture is a good one, and his warning against ploughing it up is well made. The modern reader, mindful that our traditional pasture and meadow lands are now almost entirely lost, will find the advice made poignant by the passage of time.

This warning is the first in a series of pieces of negatively constructed advice by which Dyer is leading to his exemplary positive. They continue in the next verse-paragraph:

> Nor love too frequent shelter, such as decks
> The vale of Severn, Nature's garden wide,
> By the blue steeps of distant Malvern wall'd,
> Solemnly vast. The trees of various shade,
> Scene behind scene, with fair delusive pomp
> Enrich the prospect, but they rob the lawns.
> Nor prickly brambles, white with woolly theft,
> Should tuft thy fields. Applaud not the remiss
> Dimetians, who along their mossy dales
> Consume, like grasshoppers, the summer hour,
> While round them stubborn thorns and furze increase,
> And creeping briars.
> (lines 97–108)

Dyer's often mixed motivations reach an interesting crossroads in this passage, because the landscape he chooses as a negative example is a 'Silurian' one, and the river Severn is, as we shall see, an especially important element in his vision of agricultural and commercial harmony. This is perhaps why, having used the example negatively (lines 97–9), he strings on a number of subordinate clauses in praise of the area (lines 99–101). Dyer is also challenging his own feeling for the picturesque, his sentiment pulling here in two directions. The 'scene behind scene' of the trees (a very eighteenth-century way of seeing prospect and landscape) is also a picture of 'fair delusive pomp'. Trees do indeed 'steal' from the ground, and tend to sour the grass around them for sheep, but Dyer finds no solution to this paradox of give and take, aesthetic enrichment and agricultural impoverishment. The 'prickly brambles' (lines 103–4) are less of a problem: they are not picturesque, and they are straightforwardly an 'enemy' to the fleece and to sheep, as Dyer's evocative characterisation of them 'white with woolly theft' reveals. His final sentence, however, (lines 104–8) represents a difficult decision in the choice between aesthetics and practicality, for the 'Dimetians' Dyer rounds on at this point are the West Wales farmers who inhabit the romantic landscape of the poet's youth, celebrated in 'Grongar Hill' and 'A Country Walk'.[27]

He is of course right that shrubbery, and especially brambles, hawthorn and other prickly bushes are a danger to sheep (they can entangle and kill sheep as well as just 'robbing' wool), and that neglected pasture swiftly becomes 'rough pasture' (as compared to the lawn-like ideal he has described earlier). Kerridge describes the pre-improvement Welsh system of ploughing up pasture from time to time – perhaps once every thirty years – to try and gain a corn crop from the poor soils. Several harvests might be achieved in this way, and when they were done, as Kerridge puts it:

Tillage abandoned, the land was simply thrown open to gain a sward as best it could ... what grass did come would soon be invaded by fern, heath and furze. Having degenerated into rough grazing, the land could not be ploughed up again until rested a long time, when its turn came to be folded or beat-burned. Cultivation was thus merely temporary, and since the soils were so fleet [thin], all ploughing was necessarily shallow, and the normal team of two shod oxen led by two ponies hardly more than scratched the surface.[28]

Kerridge accurately literalises the term 'scratched the surface', and could perhaps have done the same with the phrase 'scratching a living', though he in fact calls this system 'shifting cultivations'.

Dyer, who has just praised, and warned against digging up, the kind of pasture that takes decades or centuries to establish, is naturally hostile to this kind of farming, but his view is somewhat unrealistic. His attitude, as we saw in his enclosure speech, is that land should not be over-used (if it is, 'Nature frowns'). He does not see that the farmers are driven not by ignorance, but by the imperative of gaining a crop. 'Balance of Nature' is a luxury available only to those with rich soil, and the idea that Dimetian farmers laze around all day is an unjust imposition of moral terminology on to agricultural imperatives.

Yet there seems more to this rejection of 'Dimetian' farming practice than agricultural fastidiousness. Dyer's characterisation of the West Wales shepherds as 'grasshoppers' makes a cleverly appropriate biblical allusion which reveals a larger concern. The reference is to Nahum 3, 17–18:

17 Thy crowned are as the locusts, and thy captains as the great grasshoppers, which camp in the hedges in the cold day, but when the sun ariseth they flee away, and their place is not known where they are.
18 Thy shepherds slumber, O king of Assyria: thy nobles shall dwell in the dust: thy people is scattered upon the mountains, and no man gathereth them.

In the land of his fathers Dyer finds the very model of the kind of decay against which his poem aims to provide a bulwark. The Dimetians are indeed 'scattered upon the mountains'; and for Dyer their failure to get a grip on the rampant growth of unproductive vegetation means it will ultimately overwhelm them, until 'their place is not known where they are'. Dyer takes the role of Nahum, the prophet of destruction, and the allusion may also be read as a disguised warning to another 'king', the 'people's shepherd' of Dyer's invocation, that his land (or at least part of his land) is in agricultural decay, and opportunities are being dangerously squandered. The ultimate fear is the one Dyer had expressed more melodramatically in *The Ruins of Rome* (1740), in a passage which also owes something to Nahum's warning:

> Fall'n, fall'n, a silent heap! her heroes all
> Sunk in their urns; behold the pride of pomp,
> The throne of nations, fall'n! obscur'd in dust.   (lines 16–18)

In more personal terms, his rejection of 'Dimetia' represents an abandonment of his youthful view of the landscape (though that also, as 'Grongar Hill' famously expressed, was sensitive to decay and loss): he is now, as Humfrey puts it, 'not an artist, concerned with fine views, but a farmer'.[29]

However Dyer is not to be caught concluding any area of his agricultural advice in a negative way, and his 'remiss Dimetians' prepare us by contrast for the bramble-burning 'careful swain' who follows, and who completes the section of advice on land with a positive example:

> I knew a careful swain
> Who gave them to the crackling flames, and spread
> Their dust saline upon the deepening grass;
> And oft with labour-strengthen'd arm he delv'd
> The draining trench across his verdant slopes,
> To intercept the small meandering rills
> Of upper hamlets. Haughty trees, that sour
> The shaded grass, that weaken thorn-set mounds,
> And harbour villain crows, he rare allow'd;
> Only a slender tuft of useful ash,
> And mingled beech and elm, securely tall,
> The little smiling cottage warm embower'd.   (lines 108–19)

As has often been noted, this is a close imitation of the famous passage from Virgil's *Georgics* which begins:

> For where with stately Tow'rs *Tarentum* stands,
> And deep *Galesus* soaks the yellow Sands,
> I chanc'd an Old *Corycian* Swain to know,
> Lord of few Acres, and those barren too;
> Unfit for Sheep or Vines, and more unfit to sow:
> Yet lab'ring well his little Spot of Ground,
> Some scatt'ring Potherbs here and there he found:
> Which cultivated with his daily Care,
> And bruis'd with Vervain, were his frugal Fare.[30]

Virgil, however, makes his exemplum one of modest retirement and harmonious adaptation to the limitations of the environment, so that

Rosenmeyer can aptly characterise the Corycian swain as 'neither Stoic nor Epicurean but an unphilosophical embodiment of Roman peasant virtue'.[31] Dyer's swain is by contrast a heroic figure, physically exerting himself with 'labour-strengthen'd arm' to change the environment; battling with the robbing brambles, 'creeping briars', 'haughty trees' and 'villain crows'; single-handedly conquering the massed armies of the fleece's enemies, armed with trenching spade, axe, and fire.

Keith Thomas cites Dyer's hostility to trees in this passage (lines 114–16) as an example of a wider movement against them related to 'improvement' and the better utilisation of land. *OED* lists but does not define 'thorn-set' (line 115), quoting only the present example. However its definition of the verb 'thorn' is interesting in this context: 'Thorn, v. now rare. 1. trans. to make thorny, to furnish with thorns; esp. to protect (a newly planted quickset hedge or the like) with dead thorn-bushes'. Dyer seems to be saying that nearby trees will weaken the ability of newly planted hedges to grow. He uses 'mound' here, and in line 89 ('shelt'ring mound') to mean hedge. *OED* says this is a dialect word which is 'current only in Oxfordshire and the counties near its border'. The use may reflect Dyer's field research; on the other hand Dryden uses it in his translation of Virgil's *Eclogues*, which Dyer of course knew. The crows (line 116, also mentioned in line 421) are 'villains' because they prey on weak or sick sheep and on lambs, often pecking out the eyes of sheep which cannot protect themselves.[32]

One notices especially in this passage the Dyeresque motif of turning a problem to advantage: the brambles are burned and used to fertilise the soil – excellent advice, and showing Dyer again as an energetic improver.[33] The final image is one of reward, and the poet again uses a characteristic pattern of anaphora to fill this out:

> ... The little smiling cottage warm embower'd.
> The little smiling cottage! where at eve
> He meets his rosy children at the door,
> Prattling their welcomes, and his honest wife,
> With good brown cake and bacon slice, intent
> To cheer his hunger after labour hard.   (lines 119–24)

We have examined other examples of this kind of 'cottage-door' image elsewhere (see above, chapter 5). Little needs to be added here, except to notice the Duckian emphasis on food as an important element in the reward, which shows that Dyer remains alert to at least one reality of rural labour, the need for food, even in his most pastoralised moments. I think Dyer's 'good brown cake' is probably cake in the Scottish/Welsh sense of bread or oaten-bread, rather than the English sense of sweet or fancy cake. 'Bacon' is of course, with bread, the basic meat of the provident cottager in the eighteenth century, referred to by both Duck and Collier.[34]

Otherwise this is a fairly conventional conclusion to the poet's advice on types of land. We have seen that in this advice Dyer merges appeals to large landowners with hints on improvement to small farmers and shepherds; and that he manages to give the impression that each environment has its natural role, while advising the avoidance or alteration of certain adverse conditions. Idealised pastoral and tough georgic are intrepidly intermixed throughout, and Dyer's sense of topographic richness has been brought powerfully into play. The combination of techniques is characteristic of Dyer at his strongest.

Climate and national identity

The second major variable of farming is climate, which offers less sense of having to select or alter the environment. Specific shepherdly advice is not really needed in the general context (the advice on seasonal kinds of weather comes later). Thus Dyer swiftly moves from prescription into a piece of patriotic rhetoric, which interestingly reveals some of his structural concepts. He first compares the different nations as potential sites to 'nourish locks of price':

> Nor only soil, there also must be found
> Felicity of clime, and aspect bland,
> Where gentle sheep may nourish locks of price.
> In vain the silken Fleece on windy brows,
> And northern slopes of cloud-dividing hills,
> Is sought, tho' soft Iberia spreads her lap
> Beneath their rugged feet and names their heights
> Biscaian or Segovian. Bothnic realms,
> And dark Norwegian, with their choicest fields,
> Dingles, and dells, by lofty fir embower'd,
> In vain the bleaters court. Alike they shun
> Libya's hot plains. What taste have they for groves
> Of palm, or yellow dust of gold? no more
> Food to the flock than to the miser wealth,
> Who kneels upon the glittering heap and starves.
> Ev'n Gallic Abbeville the shining Fleece,
> That richly decorates her loom, acquires
> Basely from Albion, by th'ensnaring bribe,
> The bait of avarice, which with felon fraud
> For its own wanton mouth from thousands steals.   (lines 125–44)

We shall have more to say about 'windy brows' and 'northern slopes' later: Dyer is right to say that mountain sheep do not produce high-quality wool. His supplementary clause about Spain ('Iberia') by contrast does not seem to say much at all: I think what prompts it is the sudden thought that Spain is mountainous, and yet produces, as the poet would be keenly aware, the best quality wool in the world, from the Merino sheep. The Spanish system of transhumance, involving the movement of sheep between the mountainous north in summer, and the southern lowlands in winter, was to become a subject of intense interest and speculation to a slightly later generation of agricultural improvers, but Dyer gives little suggestion of that here.[35] Indeed what he says does not advance his argument, which is that England is perfectly placed in temperate conditions which 'nourish locks of price'. The north ('Bothnic' and 'Norwegian' Scandinavia) is too cold and mountainous, the tropics ('Libya') too hot and barren. And if Spain manages to produce superb wool despite being both hot and mountainous, the poet would sooner celebrate the poetical naming of its mountains than ponder the issue further. Despite his deep hostility to Britain's major wool-trade rivals, Dyer seems rather to admire Spain, and he gives it a brief but heroic place in his history of wool (in Book II, lines 368–9).

France is a very different matter. Dyer was wishing defeat on 'restless Gaul' (line 10) before he had finished his first verse-paragraph, and he returns contemptuously to the 'hairy wool of Gaul' in Book II (line 138). Here, his desert simile of the miser and his gold (lines 136–9) seems to inspire him to a torrent of chauvinism against France in general and the French woollen industry in particular. Spain grows good wool fairly: but France, according to Dyer, simply steals it. The major French woollen manufacturing centre of Abbeville, on the river Somme in north-east France, is singled out for its success, which is attributed to illegally-acquired British wool.

Behind Dyer's nationalistic fury lies a century of legislation against exporting wool to France, a thriving smuggling industry and a fierce ongoing national debate on the subject.[36] The resulting contrast is a disconcerting mixture of lyricism and venom:

> How erring oft the judgment in its hate
> Or fond desire! Those slow-descending showers,
> Those hovering fogs, that bathe our growing vales
> In deep November (loath'd by trifling Gaul,
> Effeminate), are gifts the Pleiads shed,
> Britannia's handmaids: as the beverage falls
> Her hills rejoice, her valleys laugh and sing.   (lines 145–51)

Dyer's almost Keatsian vision of autumn sits uneasily alongside the crude, gendered stereotyping of the French. The contrast seems bizarre, and one can understand why John Chalker, the historian of the English georgic, finds a 'saving element of self-mockery' in some of Dyer's effects, citing this passage as an example. Chalker considers that when Dyer invokes England in the formulation 'Hail noble Albion! ... Rich queen of Mists and Vapours!' he is 'either being accidentally bathetic or achieving a deliberate effect'. 'Accidental bathos', Chalker notes, 'would hardly have been expected, and it seems likely that Dyer is deliberately producing an air of comedy in these lines' (by discussing foggy English weather in his 'most elevated style'). Dyer's mockery of 'trifling Gaul, effeminate', though 'appropriately emphasized' by the 'burlesque Miltonic dress', rebounds on the poet. It is 'reasonable enough to dislike fogs', and this makes the Frenchman a 'sympathetic figure'.[37]

Chalker's reading rather assumes that the modern, city-dweller's view of the rainy, foggy English weather as a negative, humorous and low subject is an appropriate standard by which to judge an eighteenth-century epic poem on the care of sheep, which I question. Bathos and burlesque are the product of this clash of sensibilities, and the problem is at least as much that of the modern reader as the poet. I fear, indeed, that Dyer is entirely serious here. The caricaturing attacks on France, however unpleasant we may find them, are within a recognisable literary tradition; and similar attitudes may be found, for example, in Shakespeare, Dryden and the Scriblerian writers.[38] Dyer's praise of English weather, which his antigallicism is designed to bolster by contrast, has an equally serious purpose:

> Hail noble Albion! where no golden mines,
> No soft perfumes, nor oils, nor myrtle bowers,
> The vigorous frame and lofty heart of man
> Enervate: round whose stern cerulean brows
> White-winged snow, and cloud, and pearly rain,
> Frequent attend, with solemn majesty:
> Rich queen of Mists and Vapours! These thy sons
> With their cool arms compress; and twist their nerves
> For deeds of excellence and high renown.
> Thus form'd, our Edwards, Henries, Churchills, Blakes,
> Our Lockes, our Newtons, and our Miltons, rose.   (lines 152–62)

We are accustomed to dealing with the rainy, damp weather of England in rueful, humorous or stoical terms, and we need to understand why the poet is praising the climate in grandiose and heroic terms: it is not enough just to set our views against his, and find the latter ridiculous. Dyer's subject in Book I is 'the care of sheep', and he is especially concerned here with lionising the qualities of British wool. His successors in this task know, even better than Dyer, what this has to do with the rainy British climate, as we see, for example, in a catalogue of *British Sheep and Wool* issued by the British Wool Marketing Board a few years ago. 'British wool', says the Board, 'has a number of unique characteristics':

Most British fine and medium apparel wools ... have a much higher degree of crimp for a given diameter of fibre than wools from other parts of the world ...

Most of the major sheep growing areas of the United Kingdom have a relatively high rainfall, especially in the hill and mountain regions. To live and thrive there, our native breeds have developed a fleece which will shed rain instead of absorbing it. This makes their wool especially valuable for use in outdoor garments where the wearer needs a warm covering which will resist cold and wet weather.

And the Board concludes by declaring, in a manner that Dyer would surely approve: 'No doubt about it. British wool is one of the truly great fibres of the world.'[39] Dyer's progression is from fibre to *moral* fibre: if the secret of British wool lies in the conditioning effects of English rain, it is a short step for the poet to locate a wider national success in the invigorating effect of our climatic 'cold showers' on a number of British heroes. In the labour-based ethic of the eighteenth-century georgic, luxury and decadence, qualities routinely ascribed to France and other southern countries, are the enemy of progress. The weather may thus be seen as a natural indicator of a nation's success or failure.

We may find this kind of contentious moralising more than a little ridiculous; but, in agricultural terms at least, Dyer was essentially right. A recent historian of the animal-breeding revolution ascribes the 'immensely rich genetic pool' available to the British stock improvers to the 'extraordinary range of elevation, climate, soil type, and herbage' of the country. And a standard modern text-book on the subject tells us stirringly that 'England is one of the best farming countries in the world', giving a clear agricultural gloss to the emphasis on mildness and variety Dyer has made in the opening part of the poem: 'Its varied soils and its relatively mild extremes of temperature and rainfall make possible the practice of mixed agriculture, i.e. animal and arable husbandry in combination, in most parts of the country in most months of the year'.[40] Dyer is clearly aware of the agricultural potential of these conditions, which he celebrates with bravura in the next verse paragraph:

> See the sun gleams; the living pastures rise,
> After the nurture of the fallen shower,
> How beautiful! How blue th'ethereal vault!
> How verdurous the lawns! how clear the brooks!
> Such noble warlike steeds, such herds of kine,
> So sleek, so vast! such spacious flocks of sheep,
> Like flakes of gold illumining the green,
> What other paradise adorn but thine,
> Britannia?　　　　　　　　　　　　　　　(lines 163–71)

It seems paradoxical to us that a rainy, foggy climate can be the sign, and indeed the animating force, of an Other Eden. But nevertheless Dyer manages to make it so; and within the agricultural sphere on which his lyricism fixes here, it seems reasonable for him to do so.

8

Environment and heredity

Mountains

'Soil and clime', terrain and weather, are the major variables of farming, the given circumstances. Like Thomson's seasonal forces they are the parameters within which human activity must operate. We have some choice as to land: if we are rich we can be selective, or mould the landscape; if not we can clear it of brambles and dig drainage ditches. We can do little about the weather, of course; but as we have seen the rainy climate of the British Isles is portrayed as an entirely positive force. It nurtures not only fine, waterproof wool, but also the sturdy masculinity of God's Englishmen, 'our Edwards, Henries, Churchills, Blakes, / Our Lockes, our Newtons, and our Miltons' (lines 161–2). It makes us regal, heroic and war-like, nurtures our skills in philosophy and science, and fosters the stoical qualities required to write long poems in blank verse ('slavish work', according to Cowper).[1]

The third variable in sheep husbandry is the animal itself. Dyer's advice on this subject (lines 185–230) follows on from his advice on terrain and weather. It is perhaps the most important section of the poem, so far as our assessment of the agricultural theme is concerned and I shall be examining it in some detail. It begins clearly enough as a piece of agricultural advice. The first part of it (lines 185–91) tells the shepherd that having chosen (or improved) the right terrain, and avoided the poor climate Dyer has described as 'windy brows / And northern slopes of cloud dividing hills' (lines 128–9), he must 'procure a breed' which will match these two variables.

But there is also a kind of double viewpoint here. The first sentence implies that to succeed the shepherd must assign the animals:

> Ye Shepherds! if your labours hope success,
> Be first your purpose to procure a breed,
> To soil and clime adapted.   (lines 185–7)

However the second sentence moves to another perspective:

125

> Every soil
> And clime, ev'n every tree and herd, receives
> Its habitant peculiar: each to each,
> The Great Invisible, and each to all,
> Thro' earth, and seas, and air, harmonious suits. (lines 187–91)

By the end of this sentence God ('The Great Invisible'), rather than the shepherd, has become the force which locates the animals. There is a dual perspective, although the two views seem to be knitted harmoniously together. In *The Seasons* Thomson resolves a similar overlap of roles more clearly:

> Be gracious, Heaven! for now laborious Man
> Has done his Part. Ye fostering Breezes blow!
>
> ('Spring', lines 48–9)

This is conceived as a sort of bargain. Man ploughs, sows and harrows; and God (in Nature) is asked to do his part by kindly sending breezes, rain and sunshine. But Dyer does not make such a clear division of labour.

One aspect of this is the way the poet silently moves from instruction (lines 185–7) to a moralising explanation (lines 187–91). He will next give examples of the explanation he has given, but it is not made obvious that he has actually ceased to prescribe, and in fact does not continue giving advice until line 203. Dyer *seems* in this passage to tell the shepherd he must select the right sheep (lines 185–7), to offer a metaphysical explanation as to why he must do this (lines 187–91), to give three examples (lines 192–9; 200–13; 214–24) and to conclude by explaining that this correctly 'copies' nature (lines 225–30). What he *actually* does is to tell the shepherd to select the right sheep (lines 185–7), then to tell him that God does this (lines 187–91), giving an example of how God has placed one type of sheep on the mountains (lines 192–9). He then begins a second 'example' (lines 200–13) by saying that the 'hills of milder air ... boast' a fairer species: that is, such a species currently dwells in hills of this kind. But there is a subtle alteration in the sentence structure and meaning here. In the first example:

> Tempestuous regions, Darwent's naked Peaks,
> Snowden and blue Plynlymmon, and the wide
> Aerial sides of Cader-ydris huge;
> These are bestow'd on goat-horned sheep.   (lines 192–5)

The mountain areas are 'bestowed on' the goat-horned sheep. This is in the passive mood, with the mountains as subject, the sheep the object; but the 'bestower' in the implied active sentence is clearly God. In the second example, the land is the subject, and the 'fairer species' the object:

> But hills of milder air, that gently rise
> O'er dewy dales, a fairer species boast,
> Of shorter limb, and frontlet more ornate:
> Such the Silurian. (lines 200–3)

The land 'boasts' the sheep. But there is no implied 'bestower' behind the sentence, no hidden hand; although the way in which it follows on from the previous example does not alert one to this change. At this point, half-way through the example, Dyer reverts to instruction:

> If thy farm extends
> Near Cotswold Downs, or the delicious groves
> Of Symmonds, honour'd thro' the sandy soil
> Of elmy Ross, or Devon's myrtle vales,
> That drink clear rivers near the glassy sea,
> Regard this sort, and hence thy sire of lambs
> Select. (lines 203–9)

The shepherd must 'regard' – must (passively) attend to – this sort, but must (actively) select a ram. The example appears to look both ways – back to the mountains and God; and forward to the lowlands and Man.

In the third and final example, Man is clearly the selector:

> Yet should thy fertile glebe be marly clay,
> Like Melton pastures, or Tripontian fields,
> Where ever-gliding Avon's limpid wave
> Thwarts the long course of dusty Watling-street;
> That larger sort, of head defenceless, seek. (lines 214–18)

We are now back into purely prescriptive work, where the shepherd must select or locate the animals. The moral which follows seems to reconcile the two agents of change (God and Man):

> Thus to their kindred soil and air induc'd,
> Thy thriving herd will bless thy skilful care,
> That copies Nature, who, in every change,
> In each variety, with wisdom works,
> And powers diversifi'd of air and soil,
> Her rich materials. (lines 225–30)

The philosophical reasoning behind this seems to be that the shepherd's work is a continuation or a representation of God's work. God has placed animals on the earth in an environmentally appropriate way (Dyer gives many examples of this in the poem). Within limits the shepherd chooses his soil and clime, and then selects an appropriate breed for this kind of area, and in doing so continues or completes the natural process of environmental harmonisation.

But if the shepherd is continuing God's work, why is he only continuing part of it? The mountain sheep are already in place; he needs do nothing further in their selection. The sheep of the 'hills of milder air' are also in place, though here the shepherd needs to select a ram (but without much sense of urgency, to judge from the tone). And in the lowland area the shepherd must introduce the right sheep population, implicitly via a breeding programme involving the ram 'with head defenceless'. Why must the shepherd intervene in some areas and not in others, and with different degrees of urgency? Only one model can adequately explain this particular combination of quietist and interventionist approaches, and that is a model, not of ethics or piety, but of agricultural expedience. If we examine the three examples or descriptions Dyer gives, we shall see how this works; and we shall find as we do so a number of the poem's major alternatives and dualities: between environmental and hereditary ideas of sheep development; between different uses of sheep; and between aesthetic and practical, poetical and agricultural concerns.

Mountain sheep, then, are left to God, and require no shepherdly intervention. This is not just because for a mid eighteenth-century Christian poet mountains were awe-inspiring places in which to contemplate the deity while admiring the sublimity of his handiwork; but also because mountains were essentially beyond the reach of the new farming methods. Mountainsides, which are basically rough grazing land, could not support the new fodder crops, rotations or irrigation systems, and were unenclosable even for as enthusiastic an advocate of enclosure as Dyer. The traditional system of mountain sheep management did not really lend itself to 'improving', and has indeed survived until quite recently in one or two remote areas. Breeding programmes depended on the new techniques. And, apart from the possibility of artificial improvements to soil fertility, that fairly well exhausts the possibilities of the Agricultural Revolution.[2] Russell gives one further explanation for the neglect of mountains as sites for improvement, but it is one the stoical and hard-working Dyer would surely deny: 'Exposed hills and cold, early-morning Spring lambing pens could have had only limited appeal to civilised improvers, whose whole philosophy was based on the exertion of control over the environment and the physical comfort that such control produced.'[3]

Of course the improving breeders could and did draw on the gene pool of mountain sheep, with considerable success. Mountain sheep were prominent, for example, in crossings which attempted to breed back into the new sheep qualities which Bakewell's pursuit of fast maturation, prolificacy and good fattening qualities had sacrificed, such as hardiness and maternal qualities. So the new breeds were themselves interbred with mountain sheep, as they were with virtually all older breeds; and in this process something was often added to the old mountain types. But the mountains and mountain sheep were not of interest *per se* as sites for improvement.

One of the long-term results of this is that mountain sheep have to a considerable extent maintained the hardy characteristics Dyer describes. His characterisation of the 'goat-horned sheep',

> . . . of Fleece
> Hairy and coarse, of long and nimble shank,
> Who rove o'er bog or heath, and graze or brouze
> Alternate, to collect, with due dispatch,
> O'er the bleak wild, the thinly-scatter'd meal   (lines 195–9)

remains a good description of mountain sheep. They are wide-ranging foragers, always on the move, and able to survive, as Dyer says, on the 'thinly-scattered meal' of the mountainsides. Hartwell notes a characterisation of the Blackfaced Mountain or Heath sheep of the eighteenth century as 'the boldest, the hardiest, and the most active and industrious of all sheep species'.[4] Anecdotal information suggests it has not changed much: I have been told of Welsh mountain sheep conducting raids on the dustbins of Blaenau Ffestiniog and rolling over cattle-grids (being, as Dyer says, 'nimble'); and of a marauding band of Cumbrian mountain sheep stealing fell-walkers' sandwiches. They are to a great extent as beyond the reach of agribusiness as they were beyond the reach of Bakewellian improvement; and it is easy to see Dyer's leaving them to God as a calculated piece of utilitarian common-sense. The improver is effectively redundant here, and it may be left to the creator of mountain sheep to see they may safely graze.

The remaining issue is breed identification. There is a certain amount of interest in Dyer's description of the mountain sheep, and some appropriate characterising, but the sheep is not of significance to his advice in a way that requires close identification. His description therefore concentrates on the points which show the beast's hardy, independent, semi-feral qualities, and that it is appropriately matched to its environment. As a result, the best identification we can make here is that it is a 'mountain sheep', that is, by using Dyeresque terms of locational appropriateness. The 'hairy and coarse' fleece, nimbleness and hardiness are all generally characteristic of mountain sheep; and no other identifying feature is made, apart from the epithet 'goat-horned', which might apply to many heath, forest, or mountain sheep of the time. No colour indication is given, though as it happens the predominant horned type of the Peak District (Dyer's 'Darwent', line 192) was dark or black-faced; whereas the major variety of Welsh mountain sheep (Dyer's 'Plynlymmon'; 'Snowden' and 'Cader-ydris', lines 193–4) was tan or white-faced.[5]

Speculating, one would perhaps conclude that Dyer is thinking of the

Welsh mountain sheep, whose rams were goat-horned, and whose nimble wildness was well known. Dyer may have seen some similar sheep in the Peak District (the division of types and areas was by no means absolute); but more probably the word 'Darwent' is simply designed to strengthen the sublime and wild associations of the mountain sheep, which mention of the Peak District would at that time achieve. The reputation of the Peak District dates back at least to Charles Cotton's poem *The Wonders of the Peake* (1681): Drayton had also sung its 'Wonders', with extensive mytho-topographic explanations.[6] The significance of Dyer's 'Plynlymmon' will become more fully apparent when we consider the pastoral shearing festival at the end of Book I (discussed below). Snowdon is the highest, Cader Idris the most sublimely steep of the North Wales mountains. Francis Kilvert noted the glories of Plinlimmon and Cader Idris, in a diary entry for Tuesday, 22 February, 1870:

After luncheon went for a walk with Mr V. to the top of Drum du. When we got to the cairn Plynlimmon was quite visible, but only the ghost of Cader Idris to be seen. We went away disappointed but had not gone far before the clouds suddenly lifted and a sun burst lit up grandly the great snowslopes of round-backed Plynlimmon and the vast snowy precipices of the giant Cader Idris near 50 miles away.[7]

The most important point to note about Dyer's mountain sheep is that they show his descriptions are not necessarily close identifications, but do contain observed features. How specific and reliable Dyer is in his description depends on the particular purpose of a given example. It should also be noted that there is some uncertainty as to the exact characteristics and appearance of sheep types of the early modern period. The breeding revolution altered virtually all British sheep breeds extensively, and many breeds were altered further in the nineteenth and twentieth centuries. Because the initial phase of this revolution – from about 1780 to the 1830s – changed the character of most breeds fairly rapidly, it is difficult to see behind it and find out the nature of earlier (or 'pre-improvement') sheep. The experts differ as to how pre-improvement sheep may be classified. There were as many as twenty recognised pre-improvement 'breeds' (like the Cotswold and Ryelands breeds I have referred to); but many agricultural historians prefer to discuss the issue in terms of 'types', such as the four basic types described by Trow-Smith, or the seven types described by Russell. Caution is required in making specific identifications, especially from the fairly limited evidence offered by sources such as *The Fleece*.[8] Bearing this caution in mind, we may proceed.

Lowlands

I want to put Dyer's rather ambiguous middle sheep (the 'fairer species' which inhabits 'hills of milder air', lines 200–13) to one side for the

moment, and concentrate next on his third, lowland sheep, whose characteristics and location seem more straightforward:

> Yet should thy fertile glebe be marly clay,
> Like Melton pastures, or Tripontian fields,
> Where ever-gliding Avon's limpid wave
> Thwarts the long course of dusty Watling-street;
> That larger sort, of head defenceless, seek.   (lines 214–18)

We need to consider the locations named here. I have noted the significance of 'Tripontium' as a place where trade routes meet, and where
cattle and sheep are fattened. 'Melton' is modern Melton Mowbray,
another, less significant, point of confluence, of the Rivers Wreak and Eye;
and nowadays of the A606 road, which links the ancient textile centres of
Nottingham and Stamford, and the A607, which runs between Leicester
(another early textile centre) and Grantham, once a major centre of
agriculture.[9] Like 'Tripontium', it is the central focus of an area of lush
pasture (as Cobbett noted), an area of animal-fattening country. Monk
(1794) gives some pasture/arable ratios which illustrate well why Dyer
chooses 'Melton' and 'Tripontium' (bearing in mind Dyer's gloss for
'Tripontian fields' as 'the country between Rugby, in Warwickshire, and
Lutterworth in Leicestershire'): 'About Ashby-de-la-Zouch, and Lough-
borough, three parts in four are in pasture. Near Melton Mowbray, there
is very little arable, not more than one acre to thirty. Market Harborough
has also very little arable. The pasture near Lutterworth is in proportion
of eight to one. At Hinckley, five parts in six are in pasture.' This is a
selective survey, but the high pasture ratios of Lutterworth and Melton
Mowbray are interesting. A modern agricultural atlas shows that the
south Leicestershire area still has a high sheep density.[10]

However, Dyer's 'marly clay' is slightly more problematic. We need to
put two other pieces of text alongside the passage to see why this is so. This
is not the first time Dyer has mentioned 'marly clay' in the context of
Leicestershire. Earlier, as we saw, he gives the advice:

> But if thy prudent care would cultivate
> Leicestrian Fleeces, what the sinewy arm
> Combs thro' the spiky steel in lengthen'd flakes;
> Rich saponaceous loam, that slowly drinks
> The blackening shower, and fattens with the draught,
> Or heavy marl's deep clay, be then thy choice,
> Of one consistence, one complexion, spread
> Thro' all thy glebe.   (lines 67–74)

In the 'Commercial Map', (fo. 3a), Dyer had written:

ye soil <of y[e]> across y[e] Mid of Eng[land] from sea to sea – a deep stiff clay
or marl – at least 50 m[iles] broad & in some places much more – Query & [c.] --

('Mid' may mean either 'Middle' or 'Midlands'). There is a further reference to the 'marly' area of Leicestershire in Book II (lines 385–8):

> Need we the level greens of Lincoln note,
> Or rich Leicestria's marly plains, for length
> Of whitest locks and magnitude of Fleece
> Peculiar? envy of the neighbouring realms!

Putting these extracts together, we can see that Dyer makes a powerful association between a type of soil, 'marly clay', and a particular location. In the main extract under discussion (lines 214–18) he gives the two Leicestershire locations as examples of a soil type. In the earlier extract (lines 67–74) he recommends this soil type (together with the peaty soil type whose description we have discussed) for a 'Leicestrian' sheep. In the 'Commercial Map' note we see the source of both passages: Dyer has a distinct concept of an extended area of 'marly clay' in the Midlands. The three passages show that this concept is associated with a particular pasture area, and a particular type of sheep and wool associated by name and by historical location with the area; that is, the Leicester sheep.

We need to consider here what Dyer means by this fifty-mile band of marly clay. His word 'Query' warns of an uncertainty; and indeed there is no 'sea to sea' belt of 'marly clay' in the Midlands. There is, however, a belt of Lais clay (i.e. limestone-based, 'marly' clay) covering much of the part of Leicestershire east of the Soar. It is roughly fifty miles long; and the Rugby/Lutterworth and Melton Mowbray pasture areas Dyer mentions are sited in the area it covers. This seems to be the belt of 'marly clay' he means.[11]

The next issue is whether he is recommending his third, 'larger sort' of sheep to this kind of soil in general, or to the Leicestershire band of it in particular. On the face of it, both passages point to the soil type. But both also link it with Leicestershire and nowhere else, giving the impression that it is the place, and not just the soil which Dyer recommends for this sheep (there would of course be other areas of good pasture which had marl-clay soils). Thus he has it both ways. By focusing on the soil type Dyer extends the idea that there is a suitable environment for each kind of sheep. By associating this soil type with Leicestershire alone, the specific location of the breeding revolution, Dyer seems to be leading us towards newer agricultural ideas. He was anxious to get this soil-mapping right, and in a letter to Dodsley, following first publication, made it clear he was not happy with the way an earlier reference to marl/clay had been changed:

If the poem sh[oul]d come to a 2[n]d edition, be pleased, in particular, to make this necessary correction in line 72, B. i.

> Or marl with clay deep-mix'd

either by restoring the l[ine] of the copy,

     Or heavy marl's deep clay, &c.
or by this l[ine]
     Or depth of heavy marl, be then thy choice.
The absurdity of marl w[i]th clay deep mix'd is very glaring to us graziers.[12]

The recommendation for the lowland sheep also seems to go two ways. At the beginning of this section Dyer tells the shepherd to 'procure a breed / To soil and clime adapted' (lines 186–7). His advice concerning the second sheep (the 'fairer species', line 201, discussed below) is for the shepherd to 'Regard this sort, and hence thy sire of lambs / Select' (lines 208–9). In this third example, Dyer tells the shepherd to 'seek' the 'larger sort' of sheep; and he closely describes the ram. If the earlier ambiguity we noted was between a quietist and an interventionist approach to sheep management, then here it is between two kinds of intervention. The advice might simply mean the shepherd is to obtain suitable sheep, by buying them or moving them to the chosen area. Or it might mean he is to breed them. All three verbs in the advice, 'procure', 'select' and 'seek', might be used in either context. The choice is between environment and heredity as the major determinant in the qualities of animals; and Dyer's position on this matter is important in assessing his engagement with agricultural developments.

Both positions were available. Kerridge demonstrates that 'breeding' (and thus by implication awareness of heredity) was 'a point of husbandry much attended to' in the early seventeenth century, and possibly even earlier. On the other hand an environmental interpretation of animal characteristics continued to hold sway. Russell writes: 'Even after the changes wrought by Bakewell and Ellman had been widely diffused, the opinion that the sheep of any region were largely determined by the environment persisted', adding: 'In the early 19th century Luccock believed that wool quality was a consequence of breed but the geologist Robert Bakewell [another Bakewell, not the pioneer breeder] thought that the fleece form was completely under environmental control.'[13]

The fact that the environmental view survived most strongly in relation to the quality of wool is interesting, for Dyer seems at his most environmentalist whenever the subject turns to wool. We have seen that in an earlier passage (lines 67–74) he makes poetic connections between the sensuous qualities of combing wool ('lengthen'd flakes'), and the two soils, 'saponaceous' peaty soil and 'heavy marl's deep clay'. The passage on weather (lines 125–84) posits a view in which the climate forms the qualities of the wool. The modern sources I quoted on that subject saw climatic conditions as working gradually, through heredity. But Dyer may be read in terms of a direct effect of climate on each fleece:

> Nor only soil, there also must be found
> Felicity of clime, and aspect bland,
> Where gentle sheep may nourish locks of price.   (lines 125–7)

The verbs are noticeably in the present tense, suggesting the weather 'nourishes' the quality of each fleece, although the historical section on British heroes which follows perhaps implies a development over many generations, i.e. a hereditary view of environmental influence. Dyer is also enthusiastic about cotting, a practice which was dying out in the eighteenth century, and whose function was partly to promote the improvement of fleeces by protecting them from bad weather This is referred to later in Book I:

> Or, if your sheep are of Silurian breed,
> Nightly to house them dry on fern or straw,
> Silk'ning their Fleeces.   (lines 492–4)

There is a similar passage in the second book (II, lines 91–106). Russell notes that the 'plasticity of wool fibres in response to environmental change' is the reason wool tended to be the focus of the environmentalist view of animal development: it was one animal characteristic that could be seen to respond directly to environment, though its general character is determined genetically.[14]

As a wool enthusiast, then, Dyer tends towards the environmental view of animal determination. In the passage under consideration this is reflected in the suggestion of finding rather than breeding the right sheep. However there are also in the passage clear implications of selective breeding, and therefore heredity. The second example ('hills of milder air') specifically tells the shepherd to select a ram with particular qualities, for his 'sire of lambs'. The third, lowland example advises the shepherd to 'seek' a type of sheep, but the particular focus on the ram indicates the same pattern of advice. To select a ram is to start a breeding programme, though the suggestion of advice on moving sheep to the appropriate area may also be present. The emphasis on the ram is characteristic of eighteenth-century sheep breeding practice, a point Russell reveals in explaining a gap in Bakewell's ram records: 'The record is incomplete because of the habit of contemporary breeders of believing the sire record to be far more important than that of the ewe.'[15]

Dyer's implied advocacy of a breeding programme is very important. It suggests that despite his environmental ideas he is aware of the genetic interpretation of animal qualities, and is thus in touch with the most important new development in sheep husbandry. We shall be able to measure how close he is to this if we can establish the nature of the ram he recommends in this passage. The description is the most detailed in the poem:

That larger sort, of head defenceless, seek,
Whose Fleece is deep and clammy, close and plain:
The ram short-limbed, whose form compact describes
One level line along his spacious back;
Of full and ruddy eye, large ears, stretch'd head,
Nostrils dilated, breast and shoulders broad,
And spacious haunches, and a lofty dock.   (lines 218–24)

There is a little external evidence on identification. The prose 'Argument' to Book I lists the subject of 'the two common sorts of ram described'. The ram described in this passage would be the second of the two. We may assume that as Dyer does not mention the four 'arguments' in his letter to Dodsley of 12 May 1757, he did not object to them, and was probably their author.[16] On the other hand William Youatt, the nineteenth-century historian of the sheep, quotes all but the last phrase of this description, without comment, as an epigraph for his chapter on 'The New Leicester Sheep'. Later historians and literary critics have left the passage alone, apart from John Barrell, whose important comments on Dyer's language in it we shall be examining later.[17]

These are thin pickings, and there seems to be a contradiction between the 'Argument', which says this is one of two 'common sorts of ram'; and Youatt, who not only considers it to be a 'New Leicester', but chooses it as the best description of the breed to head his chapter on that subject. Which is it to be? A 'common sort of ram' is a fairly loose characterisation; but I do not find Dyer's description to tally with any of the known pre-improvement breeds, according to the major early and modern sources I have examined. What he seems to be describing is in fact, as Youatt had recognised, a New Leicester; or, to avoid the breed-naming fallacies Trow-Smith, Russell and others have warned against, an improved Midlands pasture sheep. The descriptive similarities are inescapable. The 'level line along his back' is the most striking visual clue. Dyer, with his training as an artist, would naturally notice it. The New Leicester is the only sheep illustrated by Youatt which has such a straight back. The illustration in Low also shows a ramrod-straight back. And the portrait of Bakewell's prize New Leicester ram 'Two-Pounder' repro-duced by Pawson, shows an exact straight line from ear-tip to rump. Other major features of Dyer's description, 'stretch'd head', 'short-limb'd', 'breast and shoulders broad', 'spacious haunches' are all equally clear in these illustrations. But even allowing for stylistic conventions in these illustrations, the early verbal descriptions of the New Leicester all tally with Dyer's.[18]

This interpretation raises one or two problems. The traditional view that Bakewell 'invented' the New Leicester has been reiterated in a major reference work as recently as 1989; and it is usually accepted that the new breed was made public in 1760, the year Bakewell first hired out rams.[19] This is not compatible with Dyer having described the sheep before 1757, and probably before 1750 (the year the poet took the manuscript of the first book to London).[20] The statement in the first 'Argument' about the 'two common sorts of rams described' must also be considered.

Although Bakewell's rams did indeed make their first official public appearance in 1760, he had been at work on them for many years. Bakewell took over the management of his father's farm in 1755, but he had been breeding sheep much longer than this. Russell, citing a wealth of contemporary and near-contemporary sources, considers that 'he appeared to have begun his sheep-breeding activities in the mid-1740's and to have developed his ideas during a long period of concentration on this species'. This takes us back at least fifteen years from the date often given, and into the major period of Dyer's research. As for the inventor, there were many earlier improving breeders, as Marshall notes; indeed, Bakewell's own father was one. Kerridge considers that 'selective breeding had long been employed in improving Midland pasture sheep'. Intense stock-moving and breeding was going on in the area in response to the wet seasons and 'great rot' around 1747, exactly at the time that Dyer was researching the first book of *The Fleece*.[21]

Why then does the 'Argument' refer to a 'common sort' of ram? One can only speculate; but the picture we get from Kerridge and from Russell may suggest that Dyer, living in Catthorpe in the 1740s, just twenty-five miles as the crow flies from Bakewell's Dishley, was in fact surrounded by ram breeders, experimenting shepherds, enthusiastic improvers and visionary graziers. That he had seen a prototype of the New Leicester is clear from the description; and it may even be the case that the shape and features of the new breed were already widespread enough to be regarded in that area of the country as characteristic of one of the 'common sorts of rams'. One should also note that the 'Argument' to Book I only tallies in general terms with the content of the poem: Dyer may possibly have intended to describe a 'common sort of ram', and gone on to describe something quite new. Elsewhere in the poem Dyer shows a general awareness of the 'common' Midlands sheep, probably based on his obser-vation of 'old' Leicestershire and Lincolnshire sheep, whose most notable characteristic is their size and the length of their wool staple (see, for examples, lines 68–70, and II, lines 386–7). In Book III, indeed, he uses their size to make a comic comparison with North Wales ponies:

> The northern Cambrians, an industrious tribe,
> Carry their labours on pigmean steeds,
> Of size exceeding not Leicestrian sheep.   (III, lines 581–3)

But none of these references have the kind of descriptive detail he gives in his advice on the second ram.

Be this as it may, Dyer's description and recommendation of an improved pasture sheep for the lowland clay-marl areas of Leicestershire is important in two ways. Firstly, it has a historical significance. It is the earliest description of the new kind of sheep I have found; and it adds a little more evidence to the revisions in the dating of the breeding revolution suggested by Kerridge (1967) and pursued in more detail by Russell (1981). In the light of the seriousness of Dyer's purpose, the depth of his research and the high level of his engagement in contemporary economic and agricultural matters, we ought not to be too surprised to find in him an important historical witness, and a far-sighted advocate of new inventions and developments. Dyer is aware, for example, of major new textile technologies, giving rare eye-witness accounts of the new carding and spinning machines of Lewis Paul later in the poem (III, lines 79–85, 292–302), and important statistical information on Thomas Lombe's organzine silk mill at Derby.[22] Dyer's engagement with enclosure, the drainage of the fens, canal-building and cartography, all also suggest an observant engagement with the major economic activities of his time.[23]

Secondly, Dyer's recommendation, in its context, interestingly suggests some of the ambiguities and conflicts of the mid eighteenth century. Dyer turns towards the improving breeders; but how far towards them he moves is not clear. Of course we cannot postulate anything satisfyingly specific, such as a historic encounter between Dyer and Bakewell, in which the young grazier explains to the chronicler of the fleece the significance of his new breed. Were they to have met (which indeed they may have done), though, it seems to me unlikely they would have agreed for very long on the subject of the care of sheep. Dyer's gentle, almost fussy concern for the welfare of the animal, as well as its fleece, seems out of step with the toughness of the improving graziers. The poet's attitude to animals is cited by Keith Thomas as an example of a new, humane sensibility. For Dyer, 'Even to the reptile, every cruel deed / Is high impiety' (II, lines 22–3), as Thomas has noted.[24] By contrast Bakewell, relentlessly putting fathers to daughters and sons to mothers in his 'in-and-in' breeding methods, manipulating the incidence of liver-rot and foot-rot, tying up and force-feeding sheep before killing and weighing them, and generally doing anything he had to do the better to turn grass into flesh and flesh into money, seems to epitomise Thomas's characterisation of eighteenth-century breeders as 'ruthlessly eugenic'.[25] In Dyer's description and recommendation of the New Leicester the two outlooks are at their closest, as the poet attempts to include in his advice the work of the mutton-growing breeders. Elsewhere, his sensibility has a more aestheticised and philosophical, less functional aspect, a long way indeed from the procedures of the south Leicestershire graziers and breeders.

'Silurian'

We left Dyer's second sheep, the 'fairer species' of 'milder hills', in a kind of ovine limbo: half-way between the barren mountains of Wales and the fertile lowlands of Leicestershire; half-way between the control of God and the control of man; half-way between the free-ranging scavengers of the unfenced mountainsides, and the lowland sheep, fenced-in and force-fed on lush pastures. A half-way position is appropriate. If for Cowper, God made the country, and man made the town, then for Dyer, God populated the mountainside, and man must stock the fields of the lowlands. The middle sheep's role in this scheme is ambiguous. It cannot be so easily defined as the other two, and this is most apparent if we try and identify it in terms of breed or type. The description is as follows:

> But hills of milder air, that gently rise
> O'er dewy dales, a fairer species boast,
> Of shorter limb, and frontlet more ornate:
> Such the Silurian. If thy farm extends
> Near Cotswold Downs, or the delicious groves
> Of Symmonds, honour'd thro' the sandy soil
> Of elmy Ross, or Devon's myrtle vales,
> That drink clear rivers near the glassy sea,
> Regard this sort, and hence thy sire of lambs
> Select: his tawny Fleece in ringlets curls;
> Long swings his slender tail; his front is fenc'd
> With horns Ammonian, circulating twice
> Around each open ear, like those fair scrolls
> That grace the columns of th'Ionic dome.   (lines 200–13)

This is not quite as plain as it seems. Hills of 'milder air' that 'gently rise', that is to say green or rolling hills, have a 'fairer species' of sheep on them than the mountains; it has shorter legs than the mountain sheep, and a 'more ornate' forehead.[26] The 'Silurian' is an example of this type. If your farm is in the milder areas of Gloucestershire, Herefordshire or Devon, says Dyer, consider this type, and pick your breeding ram from there. He has ('should have' is implied) a tawny, ringletted fleece, a long slender tail, and double-circling horns framing open ears.

In fact the areas named (the Cotswolds, the Symond's Yat/Ross-on-Wye area, and the valleys of Devon), are all examples of the type of environment mentioned ('hills of milder air'), which seems at first sight to make the advice seem banal: if you live in mild rolling hills select a ram from the kind of sheep that live on mild rolling hills. This could perhaps be paraphrased as: pick a good ram from an area similar to the one your farm is in; which is more meaningful. The description of the sheep that inhabit milder hills is ambiguous. Many sheep have shorter legs than mountain sheep; and an ornate frontlet may mean either a forehead ornamented with a tuft or poll, or one decorated with horns. It seems to be an aesthetic, impressionistic description rather than an identifying one.

However, Dyer gives an example, 'Such the Silurian'. Now 'Siluria' is a mytho-topographical concept of some elasticity, embracing notions of the Welsh Marches and their bordering counties in general, and the rich agricultural landscape of Herefordshire in particular. But whatever Dyer means by 'Siluria', what he means by the 'Silurian' sheep can be identified as one of two breeds by other references in the poem to it and to its wool. There are three: two are to high-quality wools, and the third is to the practice of 'cotting' sheep.[27] Both subjects plainly indicate that the 'Silurian' is either the Cotswold or the Ryelands sheep. Their unique high-quality wools have been mentioned earlier; and they were the only breeds still being 'cotted' in the eighteenth century whose mention would be credible in this context.[28] A close interpretation of the concept of 'Siluria' would tend to point to the Ryelands, the indigenous sheep of Herefordshire. The text becomes increasingly ambiguous, however. The advice given to those living in the areas named is to 'Regard this sort', which may mean either the 'fairer species' or the 'Silurian' which is an example of it, a general type or a particular breed. The particular characteristics for selection are then given, and as we have seen, they include 'horns Ammonian, circulating twice / Around each open ear' (lines 211–12). The problem here is that whatever this ram may be, it cannot be a 'Silurian', since neither the Cotswold nor the Ryelands were horned sheep: both were, and as far as is known had always been, polled.

On the other hand, Dyer has given as the third of his three named locations 'Devon's myrtle vales', and this does indeed suggest a horned sheep, namely the South-Western Horn, part of Russell's Group 2, and the prototype of the modern Dorset Horn. Sheep were more commonly horned than polled in the eighteenth century, but horns 'circulating twice / About each open ear' are distinctive. The rams of some sheep types (the Norfolk Horn, the Spanish Merino, and the black-faced sheep of Scotland and northern England) had them; but in the context the horn shape strongly suggests the Dorset and its predecessor. It is not compatible in any way with the Cotswold or the Ryelands, both members of a different group in Russell's model.[29]

If we are looking for a real breed here, the best we can say is that Dyer is confusing different ways of classifying sheep. He is not distinguishing between descriptions of breeds, locational types and favoured features. The impression given, in fact, is not of a real breed, but of a range of features, appropriated and blended together to make a literary ideal; and we need to look at the literary side of this if we are to pursue it further. John Barrell's comments on Dyer's sheep descriptions are particularly useful here. He quotes the two verse-paragraphs describing the 'fairer species' (lines 200–13) and the lowland sheep (lines 214–24), and concludes as follows:

There are quite clearly two tones and two sorts of diction in these two paragraphs. In the first, the Silurian sheep, a 'fairer species' than the mountain breeds of sheep just discussed, is described in a diction as ornate and classicising as, according to Dyer, its own appearance is. Its fleece is tawny (*fulvus*), curled in ringlets, and its horns curled also, in the shape of the horns of Jupiter Ammon, or the scrolls of an Ionic column. This writing is formal enough, but it has nothing mock epic about it ... It is a language which, not especially simple in itself, directs attention to the simplicity of the shepherd's lot: if his sheep are Silurian, he need concern himself, it seems, with their beauty only, while less fortunately situated shepherds must worry about profitability.[30]

This is well described: I can add one annotation. Barrell is right to stress the allusion to the ram horns of the Roman (originally Egyptian) god Jupiter Ammon; Dyer uses this to give his 'Silurian' ram heroic and classical dignity, as he uses the reference to scrolls of an Ionic column. But the double-circling horn shape in itself attracted Dyer's enquiring mind and artist's eye. In the 'Commercial Map' (fo. 19v) are two drawings of fossils. The note above them reads: 'Turbinated shells < & e > – in y[e] Earth – y[e] Nautili – & Conchee Ammonica of y[e] same sort are found in Gloucester & Warwicksh[ire]'. The two illustrations which follow are captioned 'y[e] Nautili' and 'Conchee Ammonica'. Both are simple sketches of spiral ('turbinated') fossils. The 'Conchee Ammonica' is noticeably double-circled. That he seems to have found these fossils in Gloucestershire and Warwickshire, that is, on the borders of 'Siluria', possibly helped spark the descriptive connection with the 'Silurian' sheep (fossils similarly occur in the phrase 'shells deluvian', lines 30–1).

Barrell contrasts the 'ornate and classicising' language of the 'Silurian' description with that of the New Leicester description, which he aptly calls 'language an auctioneer would understand' (p. 94). It does seem to be the case that Dyer is here concerned with a classicised ideal. He is positing a perfect sheep, whose description suggests, as Barrell says, interest in the beauty rather than the practical value of the sheep.

I find Barrell's reading of the frontispiece illustrations to the first two editions of the poem (1757 and 1761) less persuasive, though it is also worth examining. He writes:

The first two editions of *The Fleece* were both issued with frontispieces of sheep grazing. The first edition showed a breed unrecognizable at least from the various descriptions of sheep Dyer gives in his poem; the second shows one which is recognizably the Silurian – its tail thin, its fleece curled, and the ram with

Ammonian horns. In bothering to get the illustration changed, Dyer or his publishers, the Dodsleys, underlined the fact that the poem's centre was Siluria.[31]

'Dyer or his publishers' gives a misleading sense of authorial involvement. The second edition of the poem came out four years after Dyer's death, and as none of the textual changes Dyer had asked for had been made, it is unlikely he would have had a posthumous influence on the choice of illustration. It is more likely that this reflects the sensibilities of his publisher Dodsley, who of course had written his own georgic poem, 'Agriculture' (1753) and was sufficiently interested in *The Fleece* to tinker with the text. Neither do I agree that either illustration shows sheep grazing. Both show a family group: in the first frontispiece (1757) a ewe is standing, apparently guarding her two lambs, while a ram (or, less probably, a second ewe), to the left of the picture, is ruminating. In the second frontispiece (1761) the ewe is suckling a half-grown lamb while the ram, whose head is the only part of him shown, is either sleeping or ruminating. The horns of the second ram do not seem to be 'double-circling' in the distinctive way Dyer describes, though they are certainly of a 'circling' (as opposed to a 'goat horn') type. The fleece quality in the second illustration does indeed have a greater quality of curliness (though I do not see 'ringlets'); but I think this may simply reflect that it is a better and more detailed drawing.

In short, neither illustration is particularly helpful in making conclusions about Dyer's sheep types, though they are interesting for other reasons. Both, for example, sustain the anthropomorphic fantasy that sheep live in family groups (real sheep always live in matriarchal flocks). If there is a major change between them, other than in quality, it concerns roles. The ewe in the first illustration has the role of guard; but in the second she is suckling the lamb, while the ram guards the family group (though not very efficiently if – as it seems – he is fast asleep). Both pictures suggest that the sheep lives a placid life and holds the model of the nuclear family dear. This may indeed be a 'Silurian' ideology, but Barrell's reading of Dyer's language is more convincing evidence of the centrality of 'Siluria'.

What has happened, then, in the description of the middle sheep is that Dyer, finding himself in his favourite mental landscape of Siluria, half way between the sublimity of the North Wales mountains and the agricultural imperatives of Leicestershire, has retreated into the classicised imagery of the golden age of British wool. The double-circled horns suggest classical and prehistoric natural images as well as the specific, aesthetically pleasing horn-shape of the South-Western Horn; while the tawny ringletted fleece suggests the 'Cotswold Lion', and 'Lemster Ore', the 'golden fleece' of the Ryelands sheep.[32] Barrell's glossing of 'tawny' as the Latin word 'fulvus' is apt. It is a word used by the Roman poets, notably Lucretius (V, line 899) in the phrase 'corpora fulva leonem', 'the tawny bodies of lions'. Dyer is always aware of the mythology of the Golden Fleece: he gives a heroic narration of the Jason story in Book II (lines 218–310), and Longstaffe records that the poem itself was headed the 'Golden Fleece' in an early draft manuscript.[33]

Dyer's topographical machinery is again brought into play here, in the imagery of 'Cotswold Downs', 'Symmonds', 'elmy Ross' and 'Devon's myrtle vales' (lines 204–6). The first and the last of these nicely extend the catalogue of first-rate sheep-grazing land given earlier (Banstead, Dorchester, Dover, etc., lines 37–66). We may add 'Devon' to the long ribbon of good grazing lands extending along the south coast; while Cotswold is quasi-Silurian, and evokes a strongly idyllic tradition of English wool and sheep. The other two places bring us back to Dyer's Siluria. Ross we have considered, while Symmonds (nowadays 'Symonds Yat') is a little further down the Wye, between Goodrich Castle and Monmouth.

The poet's advice on types of sheep, then, shows a range of concerns and approaches. There are three basic stances. The mountain sheep, its hardy characteristics sketched by the poet, may be left alone. The intermediate sheep of rolling hills seems to demand intervention, but the emphasis is on its natural beauty, and one feels no real practical imperative here. For the heavy clays and heavy fleeces of Leicestershire, by contrast, a careful phenotypal identification ensures the shepherd can aim for the kind of animal which was indeed to dominate the future of British sheep production, a prototype of the New Leicester.

The economic historian might remain sceptical about a writer who puts a 'fantasy sheep' alongside what, I am claiming, is an important, first-hand, early description of a New Leicester. It does not quite answer the case to say that there have always been powerful aesthetic motivations involved in animal breeding, even for hard-headed characters like Bakewell.[34] Nevertheless it is so; and there is an even stronger case to argue that the wool industry is inherently 'aesthetic' in its requirements. The age-old prejudice against mixed-colour fleeces, for example, is market determined, hence both 'aesthetic' and 'practical'.[35] Ultimately, though, the answer to why Dyer mixes fantasy and reality lies with the 'poetic', the visionary side of his work. A powerful imaginative impulse is involved in the creation of the 'Silurian' sheep, as we can see if we look at another of William Youatt's quotations from the poem. As I noted above, Youatt uses Dyer's lowland sheep description to head his chapter on 'The New Leicester Sheep'. But he also uses Dyer's 'Silurian' description, this time as an opening epigraph for his chapter on the Cotswold sheep. However, he quotes it rather selectively, as follows:

If thy farm extends

Near Cotswold Downs————————————
Regard this sort, and hence thy sire of lambs select.[36]

Clearly Youatt has recognised that there is a problem with Dyer's description, and he deals with this by simply removing all the descriptive phrases. One can better understand why Youatt nevertheless persists in quoting Dyer here when one notices that in the first few paragraphs of his chapter on the Cotswold sheep he cites Camden, Drayton and Stow, mentions Henry VIII, Henry VI and Edward IV, and recycles the romantic story about the English crown giving Cotswold wool and Cotswold sheep to the Castilians in the fifteenth century. The purpose of this story had always been to prove that the Spanish originally derived their Merino (the fly in the ointment of supremacist feelings about English wool) from our Cotswold sheep.[37]

Youatt, in other words, though he is writing a highly practical treatise on sheep, recognises, partly through Dyer and his 'Silurian' fantasy, that the Cotswold is also the powerful symbol of an imagined national past, a symbol that he simply cannot ignore. For all the enthusiasm that writers like Dyer and Youatt showed for improvement and change, there is a parallel and equally powerful emotional and imaginative engagement with an older way of farming, which the mythology of the 'Cotswold Lion' seemed to encapsulate. This is one of the ways in which aesthetic and imaginative responses could be as much a part of the discourse of agriculture, breeding programmes and the human uses of animals, as practicality, rationalism and science. Youatt needs to bring the imaginative and mythical structures of Dyer's poetry into his practical treatise on sheep and shepherding, just as Dyer brought the practical and the agricultural into his poetry. There is here an important reciprocal interaction between aesthetics and agriculture.

9

The care of sheep

The art of preserving health

In starting with terrain, weather and breed, the three major variables of shepherding, Dyer has prepared the shepherd to begin his task. The rest of his advice concentrates more literally on 'the care of sheep'. The next priority is to rehearse the major diseases of sheep and their possible preventions and remedies, which the poet does next (lines 251–320). William Youatt describes the shepherding and veterinary advice of an earlier agricultural writer, William Ellis (1744), as 'a singular compound of good sense and quackery', and he might have extended the remark to characterise mid eighteenth-century veterinary practice in general.[1] On the one hand certain essentials had been understood, such as the ability of various antiseptic, astringent and mordant chemicals to work positively on external parasites and infections. On the other hand, shepherds and veterinarians were unable to understand or treat effectively a number of important parasite and micro-organism borne diseases. Dyer uses the image of 'whole flocks' being 'swept away' twice, to describe the effect of the 'coughing pest' (lines 264–5), and flash-floods in the South Wales valleys (lines 593–600). The readiness with which this imagery of instant and overwhelming disaster comes to him reflects Dyer's awareness of the lack of control which still marked the shepherd's relationship with the environment, and the vulnerability of even the hardy English sheep to disease and inclemency in the climate.

Thus disease, and the preservation of health, are fundamental to Dyer and to the shepherding advice in *The Fleece*; and the key message is a familiar one: forewarned is forearmed:

> Sagacious care foreacts. When strong disease
> Breaks in, and stains the purple streams of health,
> Hard is the strife of art. (lines 262–4)

The skill in shepherding, then as now, was to take preventive measures, and where disease did break out, to notice the cough or the limp as quickly as possible and act before further damage could be done.

The manner of this important precept is significant. Here we have again the epic style, distinctly heroic and war-like in its imagery of invasion and 'strife'. The phrase 'stains the purple streams' uses exactly the kind of language we would expect to find in an eighteenth-century military epic, Pope's *Iliad*, perhaps, or Chatterton's 'Battle of Hastings'.[2] Once again the shepherd is revealed as having the potential qualities of the epic hero, capable of brilliant feats of foresight and saving the day. In forestalling disease, the language suggests, he will enact the archetypal heroic deed of pre-empting a military catastrophe. Dyer also takes care, again, to tie his epic language to the task in hand. As with the 'people's Shepherd', he does this here by literalising: the blood ('purple streams') of epic battle becomes the blood of sheep invaded by disease.

Dyer's specific advice on health begins as advice on types of grass. But he has little to add on that subject; and he quickly turns towards the subject of disease prevention:

> Of grasses are unnumber'd kinds, and all
> (Save where foul waters linger on the turf)
> Salubrious. Early mark when tepid gleams
> Oft mingle with the pearls of summer showers,
> And swell too hastily the tender plains;
> Then snatch away thy sheep: beware the rot;
> And with detersive bay-salt rub their mouths,
> Or urge them on a barren bank to feed,
> In hunger's kind distress, on tedded hay;
> Or to the marish guide their easy steps,
> If near thy tufted crofts the broad sea spreads.   (lines 251–61)[3]

There are some good details here, in both descriptive and prescriptive terms. Dyer observantly notes the range of grasses: there are hundreds, and although we might now distinguish more strongly between qualities than he does, they are all essentially beneficial (he has described the best kind of pasture earlier). The contrasting of 'tepid gleams' with the 'pearls' of summer showers effectively serves the more than poetic function of stressing the difference between stagnant and fresh water. The word 'tepid' has the usual meaning of 'lukewarm': one of the *OED* citations is suggestive in the present context: '1626 Bacon, *Sylva* 346 For as a great heat keepeth bodies from putrefaction, but a tepid heat inclineth them to putrefaction'. Dyer warns repeatedly in the poem against putrid or stagnant water, and wet ground in general. In the absence of modern knowledge of infection control and eradication this was one major variable which could be controlled in a way that would reduce disease.

In fact the more general mixture of strengths and weaknesses in the eighteenth-century shepherd's ability to deal with disease is nicely conveyed in this passage. The recognition that stagnant water caused liver-rot (and other infections) had been made, as had the fact that the disease was caused by a parasitic worm (though Dyer does not specifically mention this). What was not known at the time was the chain of its infection, associated with a phase in the cycle of the water-snail; or indeed a cure.[4] Dyer's remedy of removing the sheep from wet areas is a good one as far as it goes, but none of the other things he advises would help much with liver-rot. Removal from the field, a change of diet, especially to hay, and salt are all remedies which were still being recommended for liver-rot eighty years later; but they are all in fact better remedies for other diseases. Putting the sheep on a 'barren bank' and feeding them on hay, a kind of starvation diet, would have been a reasonably good pre-antibiotic way of treating diseases associated with over-rich or over-wet diet, such as entero-toxaemia and redwater. Making the sheep close-crop on a 'barren bank' would also have been good for mineral deficiency ailments such as grass staggers (caused by a magnesium deficiency associated with the kind of over-lush conditions Dyer describes). The close-cropping this necessitated would mean a certain amount of soil, and hence minerals, would be ingested. Rubbing the mouth with bay-salt (i.e. large crystal sea-salt), and grazing the sheep on salt-marsh, would also help with deficiency diseases, by adding trace elements to the diet. Dyer's instincts as regards modulating and supplementing diet seem generally sound. He does not recommend anything that would be likely to harm the animals. Modern veterinary opinion is against sudden changes in diet for sheep; but liver-rot and other infectious diseases demanded drastic measures in the early modern period.[5] In these circumstances, moving to scantier and more arid pastures, and finding ways to supplement minerals, would be fairly good general preventive work.

One notices the skilful way in which Dyer orchestrates his advice here, and the implied role the shepherd has in the drama. The shepherd is an active observer, who must 'mark' the water, 'beware' the rot. Responding to changes in climate and terrain, he dramatically 'snatches' sheep away from one sort of danger, and pastorally 'urges' them away from another. The course he must steer between dynamic action and gentle compassion, toughness and tenderness, is nicely signalled in the oxymoron 'kind distress'. It is traditional for poets to praise the felicities of the shepherd's life, through pastoral imagery. Dyer does this, even in the middle of a passage of advice on disease like this one, through phrases like 'summer showers' and 'tedded hay'. But he also uses the less obviously delightful elements of shepherding to positive effect, so that the threat of disease is allowed to give the shepherd significance: he must be observant, astute, capable on the one hand of heroic feats and on the other of extending the conventional shepherdly virtue of 'gentleness' into a 'kindness' or compassion more usually associated with the Christian idea of 'pastoral care'. Dyer's shepherd is far from being a literary cypher; his calling has here a depth of meaning, and a practical significance usually absent from literary depictions. And although the poet is instructing the shepherd, the impression one gets, through Dyer's skilful mixing of description and prescription, is that the shepherd is a capable, self-motivating figure.

Some problems, however, require the poet to adopt a more directive teaching role. The next verse-paragraph gives more detail on liver-rot:

> That dire distemper, sometimes may the swain,
> Tho' late, discern; when on the lifted lid,
> Or visual orb, the turgid veins are pale,
> The swelling liver then her putrid store
> Begins to drink: ev'n yet thy skill exert,
> Nor suffer weak despair to fold thy arms:
> Again detersive salt apply, or shed
> The hoary med'cine o'er their arid food.   (lines 266–73)

Here the technique of disguising prescription as description has a slightly different emphasis. The swain is ostensibly examining the sheep, but it seems more strongly to be the poet who takes the role of veterinary surgeon, standing astride the animal to lift the eyelid; pointing to the pallor of the blood vessels, explaining how the disease swells the liver and advising the shepherd, with the kind of confidence only doctors and vets can muster, not to panic. Despair is the danger here, and the poet's higher profile aims to counteract its debilitating onset.

Well indeed may Dyer call this the 'dire distemper' and advise the swain not to 'suffer weak despair to fold thy arms'. The fact was that, as Youatt was to concede, once liver rot had set in, 'neither medicine nor management will have much power in arresting the evil'. Dyer again can only offer 'detersive' (i.e. purgative) salt; but eighty years later Youatt had to admit that his own 'account of the treatment of rot must, to a considerable extent, be very unsatisfactory', and could only come up with the same remedy, together with two other purgatives, Epsom salts and calomel with opium.[6] Dyer's advice is bravely optimistic in the face of a disease which would continue to terrorise shepherds and farmers through the eighteenth and nineteenth centuries.

Eighteenth-century practice was very much more competent to deal with external diseases, and Dyer's next two verse-paragraphs reflect this. Firstly, 'halt' or foot-rot:

> In cold stiff soils the bleaters oft complain
> Of gouty ails, by shepherds term'd the Halt:
> Those let the neighb'ring fold or ready crook
> Detain, and pour into their cloven feet
> Corrosive drugs, deep-searching arsenic,
> Dry allum, verdigrise, or vitriole keen:

> But if the doubtful mischief scarce appears,
> 'Twill serve to shift them to a dryer turf,
> And salt again. Th'utility of salt
> Teach thy slow swains; redundant humours cold
> Are the diseases of the bleating kind.   (lines 274–84)

And secondly 'scab', a mange/itch type of skin disease:

> Th'infectious scab, arising from extremes
> Of want or surfeit, is by water cured
> Of lime, or sodden staves-acre, or oil
> Dispersive of Norwegian tar, renown'd
> By virtuous Berkeley whose benevolence
> Explored its pow'rs, and easy med'cine thence
> Sought for the poor.   (lines 285–91)

The curious thing about both these pieces of advice is the disparity between ignorance of cause and knowledge of cure. Both diseases are contagious, caused respectively by a bacterium (not 'cold stiff soils') and a parasitic mite (not starvation or plenty). Sheep diseases are not specifically caused by 'redundant humours cold' (another example of Dyer using Galen's theory), though cold and wet may be contributory factors – as of course starvation or over-rich diet may be. His cures are generally good ones for their time. Nowadays formalin rather than vitriol is used in foot-baths, 'allum' is still used in medicine as a styptic and astringent; and though the copper compound 'verdigrise' has been superseded as a surface antiseptic by compounds such as iodine and potassium permanganate, and copper sulphate (a similar substance) in the treatment of foot-rot, it would have had useful disinfecting and cleaning properties. All these chemicals would have been potentially helpful in the treatment of foot-rot, which demanded substances (such as vitriol) which had mordant as well as antiseptic qualities, to get at the infected areas. Foot rot continues to affect sheep, and apart from the move to less dangerous chemicals than vitriol and verdigris the only new weapons available to modern shepherds are the antibiotics. Dipping the sheep in compounds containing pesticides is the modern solution to skin diseases like scab, which is now more or less eradicated. Dyer's remedies of lime-water, staves-acre (a natural pesticide extracted from the seeds of Larkspur, *Delphinium staphisagria*) and tar-water are inevitably less effective on such a highly infectious condition than specialised modern chemicals (though perhaps also less dangerous to the farmer), but might be expected to kill the mite and not the sheep, which would be as much as one could reasonably hope for at that time.[7]

As his advice on diseases moves to completion Dyer's emphasis on teacherly instruction increases. In the section under discussion (lines 274–91), he addresses the farmer rather than the shepherd ('Th'utility of

salt / Teach thy slow swains', lines 282–3), and having credited Berkeley
with the popularisation of tar-water, urges the poor ('Ye Poor!') to bless
the philosopher 'with grateful voice' (line 291). Bishop Berkeley's influential *Siris: A Chain of Philosophical Reflexions and Inquiries concerning the Virtues
of Tar Water*, had appeared in 1744, though the medicinal use of tar and
tar-water goes back much further than this, and indeed continues today.[8]
Nicholson and Rousseau (1970) have shown that *Siris* was often treated in
its time as a work of medicine, rather than the work of philosophy,
specifically neo-platonic idealism, that Berkeley had intended. Their
otherwise thorough account of the literary response to *Siris* overlooks
Dyer's hymn-like moment, in which the poet characteristically reads
Berkeley's book as a two-fold benefit: a scientific advance, and an act of
benevolence to the poor.[9]

Dyer's move towards paternalism, as he exhorts the poor to praise
Berkeley, coincides with a retreat from human intervention and towards
'natural health'. Sheep suffer 'pleurisies and dropsies', he writes, because
they have been 'driven from Nature's path by artful man' (lines 293–4).
But the 'more humble' swain may leave these things to Nature and to God,
and should:

> thy rural gates
> Frequent unbar, and let thy flocks abroad
> From lea to croft, from mead to arid field,
> Noting the fickle seasons of the sky.
> Rain-sated pastures let them shun, and seek
> Changes of herbage and salubrious flowers.
> By their All-perfect Master inly taught,
> They best their food and physic can discern.   (lines 297–304)

Dyer again has it both ways here. Man must not interfere with the natural
propensity of sheep to seek healthy terrain; but at the same time he must
keep an eye on the weather, keep them out of the wet grass, see that they
seek fresh pasture (with the right sort of flowers) and so on. The poetry
forces a harmony between the opposing tendencies of quietism and intervention. Dyer wants to stress that there is a natural, divinely ordered way
in which sheep may stay healthy. Human intervention, 'science' and
improvement, are not his only scale of recommendations.

In the light of his double-edged attitude to 'nature' it is perhaps
appropriate that the passage ends with an intriguing question:

> O'er the vivid green observe
> With what a regular consent they crop,
> At every fourth collection to the mouth,
> Unsav'ry crow-flow'r; whether to awake
> Languor of appetite with lively change,
> Or timely to repel approaching ills,

Hard to determine. Thou, whom Nature loves,
And with her salutory rules intrusts,
Benevolent Mackenzie! say the cause.
This truth howe'er shines bright to human sense;
Each strong affection of th'unconscious brute,
Each bent, each passion of the smallest mite,
Is wisely giv'n: harmonious they perform
The work of perfect reason (blush, vain Man!),
And turn the wheels of Nature's vast machine.   (lines 306–20)

The progression is an interesting one. Having somehow made the sheep both self-directing and under the control of the shepherd, the poet observes a tiny piece of animal behaviour. It puzzles him, and he offers two possible causes, before admitting that the reason for it is 'hard to determine'. At this point he asks his friend Dr James Mackenzie to explain the phenomenon.

Mackenzie (1680?–1761) is an interesting figure. Educated at Edinburgh and Leyden, he practised for many years at Worcester, and was closely involved in the establishment of Worcester Royal Infirmary, the last of the group of new provincial hospitals founded in the first half of the eighteenth century. His most important work, *The History of Health and the Art of Preserving it* (1758), declares its allegiance to the georgic tradition by echoing the title of John Armstrong's georgic poem *The Art of Preserving Health* (1744). His friends included Lady Mary Wortley Montagu, whose visionary enthusiasm for inoculation he perhaps shared. He met Dyer when the latter lived briefly in Worcester in 1736, and became his lifelong friend and mentor as well as his doctor.[10]

In more then one sense Mackenzie held for Dyer the role Pope ascribes to Dr John Arbuthnot in the 'Epistle to Arbuthnot'. Mackenzie had saved Dyer from life-threatening illness as Arbuthnot had 'prolonged' Pope's life ('Epistle', lines 26–8), supporting and encouraging him in his literary work, particularly *The Fleece*, which Mackenzie seems indeed to have instigated. He is treated as a wise counsellor, a learned doctor who understands the secrets of nature. Pope had asked Arbuthnot ('Epistle', line 29) 'What Drop or Nostrum' could remove his plague of pestering scribblers; while Dyer invites Mackenzie to 'say the cause' of the strange case of sheep eating 'unsav'ry crowflow'r'. Both questions are in fact rhetorical, and both poets, having asked them, push on with their monologues. But unlike Pope, who aims to expand on his dilemma, Dyer needs to move to closure. A truth (but not *the truth*, in the absolute sense) is offered. There must be a good reason for the animal behaviour, as it reflects a work of 'perfect reason'. The movement is from observation and intellectual curiosity to abstraction and pious acceptance, in the face of a purposeful, wise and harmonious 'machine'. Dyer's benevolent deism is

clearly enough expressed, but he leaves the question itself hanging: we are
not finally told why sheep eat crowflowers.

The question is itself an odd one. On the one hand it reflects Dyer's role
as agricultural researcher, measuring and observing; but on the other it
seems to be a poet's question, of the sort Robert Graves attempts to answer
by and through poetry:

> Who cleft the Devil's foot?
> When did the Fifty Danaids come with their sieves to Britain?
> What secret was woven into the Gordian Knot?
> Why did Jehovah create trees and grass before he created the
>   Sun, Moon and stars?
> Where shall Wisdom be found?[11]

It is also, like Pope's question, playful: the poet asks the wise and sober
doctor a fanciful or absurd question, with a slight overtone of bantering
in-jokery as to the doctor's privileged ability to know all there is to know
about medicines (Arbuthnot) or the mysteries of nature (Mackenzie).
Pope allows facetiousness, and Dyer allows bathos, to haunt the question.

With this mixed tonal and structural context in mind we may consider
what it means. The 'crowflower' is almost certainly in this context the
buttercup, which is mildly poisonous and 'unsavoury' to ruminants. The
various types of buttercup, and many other ranunculi, contain a chemical
which tastes unpleasant and is poisonous to cattle, and the question of
animals eating the buttercup was a source of curiosity and the focus of
various myths.[12] 'Every fourth collection to the mouth' seems both poetical (like Keats's declaredly arbitrary 'with kisses four') and observational.
We are used to the monoculture of modern pasture, but eighteenth-
century fields were awash with different flowers and grasses. Thus we may
turn the thing round, and consider that in an eighteenth-century field it
would perhaps be impossible for a sheep to take four bites *without* eating a
buttercup. On such terms poetry and observation of nature may meet.

However Dyer also insists on intentionality; and his two postulated
intentions are both interesting: 'whether to awake / Languor of appetite
with lively change, / Or timely to repel approaching ills' (lines 309–11). I
take Dyer's phrase 'awake / Langour of appetite' to mean 'awake from',
that is, act as a stimulant. The slight bitterness of buttercups might indeed
act in this way, as a kind of appetiser. A traditional shepherd's remedy for
a sheep which will not eat, still used today, is to feed ivy to it. Much more
than the buttercup, ivy is poisonous and bitter, but it can have the effect of
rekindling the sheep's rumen system, and restoring its appetite; if it will
not eat ivy, it will not eat anything. If he is indeed thinking along these
lines, Dyer's phrase 'lively change' is a good one.[13]

His second idea, that sheep eat buttercups 'timely to repel approaching ills' may perhaps suggest a homeopathic protection in which a small amount of slightly poisonous buttercup wards off the effects of the major natural poisons, which were much commoner in the eighteenth century; or it may suggest a purgative or emetic function, in the way, for example, that carnivores sometimes eat grass. Dyer of course passes the question to Mackenzie at this point, before installing it as a source of natural wonder; a question that cannot be answered in any certain way. It becomes, in one aspect, an emblem of Dyer's equivalent to Keats's 'negative capability', showing a poet's concern with mystery and intuition as well as with the curiosity, observation and overview which characterise Dyer's handling of his agricultural theme. The poem encompasses prescriptiveness, rationalism and faith on the one hand, and poetry, vision and intuition on the other. The combination is particularly characteristic of its author.

The shepherd's calendar

With Dyer's curious question about sheep eating crowflowers, the most important areas of basic advice are completed. The shepherd is established on the right kind of soil, with the right kind of sheep, in the land of heroes and fine wool. He knows what can be done to improve his land and his sheep, and how to ward off the major diseases. Once Dyer has dealt with these urgent matters he can allow the poem to move into the cyclical rhythm of the shepherd's year, and fill out his shepherding advice via the traditional literary and didactic form of a 'shepherd's calendar'.[14] This he now does, beginning with some advice on equipment:

> See that thy scrip have store of healing tar,
> And marking pitch and raddle; nor forget
> Thy shears true pointed, nor th'officious dog,
> Faithful to teach thy stragglers to return;
> So may'st thou aid who lag along, or steal
> Aside into the furrows or the shades,
> Silent to droop; or who at ev'ry gate
> Or hillock rub their sores and loosen'd wool.
> But rather these, the feeble of thy flock,
> Banish before th'autumnal months. Ev'n age
> Forbear too much to favour: oft renew
> And thro' thy fold let joyous youth appear.   (lines 321–32)

At the beginning of this passage Dyer is still in the foreground as the 'teacher', kitting out the shepherd (in the manner of a rather fussy parent), before sending him out into the fields to begin his annual round of tasks. But by the end of the passage the shepherd seems restored to his role as the responsible professional, assessing which sheep are to be sold and which to be kept, mixing compassion and utility in a characteristically

Dyeresque manner. This is traditionally the first task of the shepherd's year; and from here to the end of the first book Dyer follows the calendar from this autumn cull (nowadays called 'making up the flock'), through to the summer shearing.[15]

The most important model for this calendar section is Thomson's *Seasons*; and Dyer makes a Thomsonian pattern of seemingly spontaneous digressions, returning each time to the next important moment in the temporal pattern. Dyer is not as skilled in this kind of work as Thomson (there are some awkward transitions, and less sense of structure); and his advice is less full, its subjects more selective than one might expect. In the passage quoted above, for example, he misses out the shepherd's crook, an essential piece of equipment, needed to catch and examine sheep. The equipment he does specify is adequate, and would hold no surprises for the shepherd. The tar-pot was the universal panacea for external infections and injuries, and had been at least since Elizabethan times. Thomas Tusser includes a 'tarpot' and a 'tar kettle' in his 'digression to husbandlie furniture' – though his approach to fly-strike does not suggest he knew much about using them in infection control:

> If sheepe or thy lambe fall a wrigling with taile,
> > go by and by search it, whiles helpe may prevaile:
> That barberlie handled I dare thee assure,
> > cast dust in his arse, thou hast finisht thy cure.[16]

It is hard to imagine Dyer being so casual. As tar was for healing, so pitch was for marking sheep: both are now superseded by the ubiquitous 'blue spray'. Raddle is still used to monitor tupping.

As usual Dyer's observation of sheep is keen. The indications of which sheep to cull (those that lag behind, or have loose wool or sore skin), would not be out of place in a modern manual on condition-scoring, though one would expect some reference to other factors, particularly the condition of teeth, the most important indicator of the animal's age and ability to survive the season. At this moment in the poem, indeed, one gets the impression that the poet's interest in detailed shepherdly advice has waned a little. The major topics of the first half of the book, terrain, weather, animal types and disease prevention, all allowed him to express the major themes of what Goldstein aptly calls his 'elevated pastoralism'. They enable him to show the natural harmony and wisdom of nature, and the value and scope of human intervention; he can vent his patriotic fervour, and testify to his religious convictions. The minutiae of the shepherd's tasks do not always offer the poet such fertile possibilities for maintaining the 'epic' and 'high' side of his poem alongside the 'georgic' and the 'low'.

The result is that Dyer will sometimes sacrifice didactic credibility for the chance of a literary or ideological coup, as for example in the passage that follows the advice on equipment and 'making up the flock' (lines 333–45). Here, Dyer goes for a heroic rendering of 'the season of imperial love'. The comparison he makes between battling rams and battering-rams is no more successful at hitting the true Virgilian note than the passage of Thomson's 'Spring' (lines 789–820) it imitates; nor does it enhance the status of the shepherd's calling, as heroic material tends to do elsewhere in the poem. It does, however, sacrifice the chance to give advice on the agricultural concerns of the season, especially the preparation of rams and ewes for the mating season, which would be as vitally important to shepherdly success as his earlier advice on 'selecting a breed' was.

Even more seriously, from an agricultural point of view, the poet then entirely misses out lambing, the major event of the shepherd's year. We move from battling rams to advice on the castration of ram lambs. It is an odd omission, and a range of possible reasons suggest themselves. One is sorely tempted to pursue a Freudian interpretation of the movement from rutting to castration (perhaps Dyer's anxious equivalent to Thomson's escape into the waters of the 'foaming deep', when the heat of 'fierce desire' became too intense for the other poet, in 'Spring'). More prosaic explanations also offer themselves. Perhaps Dyer felt there was little literary mileage in the subject of lambing. Perhaps he did not feel confident about advising shepherds, with their reputation for fierce independence, on the most difficult and highly skilled of their tasks, the central mystery of their craft. Perhaps he had qualms about addressing a subject whose serious didactic treatment would necessarily be gynaecological.

Whatever the reason for Dyer's reticence on the subject of lambing, he is certainly not squeamish about the subject of castrating ram lambs, and indeed seems to recover his sense of practical engagement, and descriptive strength, in the passage on this subject:

> Wise custom at the fifth or sixth return,
> Or ere they've past the twelfth, of orient morn,
> Castrates the lambkins; necessary rite,
> Ere they be numbered of the peaceful herd.
> But kindly watch whom thy sharp hand has grieved,
> In those rough months that lift the turning year:
> Not tedious is the office; to thy aid
> Favonius hastens; soon their wounds he heals
> And leads them skipping to the flow'rs of May.   (lines 346–54)

The reference to Favonius is a much more credible piece of classicising than Dyer's battering-ram references to the 'tow'rs of Salem' (line 345). It is genuinely appropriate to find in the west wind (also called Zephyrus, and traditionally associated with springtime) a manifestation of the shepherd's renewed pastoral spirit of 'kindness', and a healing agent. An early correspondent in *Notes and Queries* can 'scarcely wonder' no-one reads *The Fleece* when the first book offers the subject of castration in its argument.[17] Had he troubled to read the text he might have been pleasantly surprised by the poet's tactful ability to address the pastoral context of the subject (in the fuller sense of 'pastoral').

Two major set-pieces end this second half of the book; consecutively, a passage (with some global digressions) on moderation as a principle of shepherding (lines 451–554), and the grand finale of the shearing festival (lines 555–720). The interim passages of the 'shepherd's calendar' (lines 355–450), meanwhile, form a loosely constructed miscellany of thoughts on shepherding, with a roughly cyclical progression. Despite the loose-knit structure, there is skilful work in this section, as the poet advises and ponders on the various aspects of the shepherd's life and work. The next section, which begins with an echo of the final word of the previous line ('May'), offers some well-written Maytime advice:

> May! who allows to fold, if poor the tilth,
> Like that of dreary houseless common fields,
> Worn by the plough; but fold on fallows dry.
> Enfeeble not thy flock to feed thy land,
> Nor in too narrow bounds the pris'ners crowd;
> Nor ope the wattled fence while balmy Morn
> Lies on the reeking pasture: wait till all
> The crystal dews, impearl'd upon the grass,
> Are touch'd by Phoebus' beams, and mount aloft,
> With various clouds to paint the azure sky.   (lines 355–64)

So distinctive to the modern ear and eye is the language of eighteenth-century poetry that it is easy to see only the surface polish and the artifice of 'poetic diction'. But we have seen that Dyer can incorporate the rhythm and tone of proverbial folk-wisdom; and here the verse gains strength from another ancient and distinctive mode, that of alliterative verse. The line 'Enfeeble not thy flock to feed thy land' is especially alliterative, as are such phrases as 'fold on fallows' and 'Nor in too narrow'. The manner is rather like that of the earlier agricultural poet, Thomas Tusser, who uses short, anapaestic tetrameters with a range of alliterative echoes and rhymes, to give pith and energy to his advice.

Dyer incorporates this kind of technique into the 'higher' poetic style of Miltonic blank verse. Taken singly, many of Dyer's epithets ('balmy morn', 'crystal dews', 'azure sky') seem merely conventional; yet the cumulative effect of his various verbal and rhythmic techniques, in a passage such as this one, is convincing. One gets a clear feeling of the May morning, and a real sense of the shepherd's decisions and choices, of the contrast between penned and free-roaming sheep, between impoverished and rich land, and between the chilly dampness of the morning and the heat of the day. One notices Dyer's constant sense of physical reality. For every formal poetic phrase like 'azure sky' or 'crystal dews', there is something more down-to-earth, a 'wattled fence' or a 'common field'. The advice, too, is similarly down-to-earth and common-sensical. Giving the sheep space within the fold, and ensuring they have an adequate quality of tilth, are both good advice. The modern farmer would find the idea of keeping the sheep away from the dewy grass very fussy, but the eighteenth-century shepherd can be forgiven for being nervous of wet pastures, for reasons we have seen.

The advice on skin and fleece care in the short verse-paragraph that follows (lines 365–71) is also simple and sensible:

> In teasing fly-time, dank or frosty days,
> With unctuous liquids, or the lees of oil,
> Rub their soft skins between the parted locks:
> Thus the Brigantes: 'tis not idle pains:
> Nor is that skill despis'd which trims their tails,
> Ere summer-heats, of filth and tagged wool.
> Coolness and cleanliness to health conduce.   (lines 365–71)

Dyer recommends the rubbing of oils on the sheep's skin here as a protection against fly-strike and cold, damp or frosty weather. He ascribes the practice to the 'Brigantes', the shepherds of Yorkshire and the north of England, but the practice is an ancient one: Ryder finds in Varro, Columella and Cato evidence that Roman shepherds used olive oil, and other substances including wine, wine lees, wax, lard, and lupin water, to protect the sheep's skin, especially after shearing, and one can find many later examples of such practices.[18] In the days before tails were routinely docked (as they are nowadays), trimming around the tail was a vital task. Even in representations of sheep, apparently, as the painter Constable learned from an intrusive colleague, Sir Francis Chantrey, apropos *The Cornfield* (1826): 'When the picture of the Corn field was at Somerset house previous to the opening of the exhibition Chantry came up and noticing the dark shadows under the tails of the sheep suddenly said why Constable all your sheep have the rot give me the pallet I must cure them ...'[19]

Dyer is preparing here for two related and slightly longer flights. The first is an energetic miscellany of shepherdly tasks, and a sequence on telling the weather:

> To mend thy mounds, to trench, to clear, to soil,
> Thy grateful fields, to medicate thy sheep,
> Hurdles to weave, and cheerly shelters raise,
> Thy vacant hours require; and ever learn
> Quick ether's motions: oft the scene is turn'd;
> Now the blue vault, and now the murky cloud,
> Hail, rain, or radiance; these the moon will tell,

> Each bird and beast, and these thy fleecy tribe.
> When high the sapphire cope, supine they couch,
> And chew the cud delighted; but ere rain
> Eager, and at unwonted hour, they feed.
> Slight not the warning . . .   (lines 372–83)

The opening list typifies Dyer's blending of rural labour and pastoral idyll. The shepherd's constant productive activity is seen as self-determined and pleasurable. He spontaneously fills his 'vacant hours' with work: no Duckian 'Master', Thomsonian sense of communal effort, or Collieresque pressure of practical need is present here, and none seems needed. When the shepherd is not actually digging, tending sheep, or making useful things with his hands, he is educating himself, 'ever learning'. That his subject of study is the weather neatly unites Dyer's faith in folklore and the natural wisdom of shepherds, and his interest in education. Thomson had contrasted the 'amaz'd' response of his swain to the rainbow with Newton's disclosure of its meaning ('Spring', lines 203–17). Dyer's shepherd, a more sophisticated and independent figure, teaches himself to understand meteorology; yet he does so within the observational methodology of shepherdly lore ('telling the weather' being a traditional shepherdly skill). The subject gives Dyer a chance to take further the idea of the natural wisdom of animals, first suggested in the 'crowflower' passage we examined earlier, and it extends the idea of the variety of the shepherd's experience, signalled here as a pleasurable kind of variety.

However, we have noted earlier that Dyer does not gain his sense of pastoral idyll by simply making bad things disappear. The shepherd's is a hard life, as Dyer acknowledges in the context of the swiftly sketched Virgilian/Thomsonian storm that follows the passage on forecasting weather:

> Slight not the warning; soon the tempest rolls,
> Scatt'ring them wide, close rushing at the heels
> Of th'hurrying o'ertaken swains: forbear
> Such nights to fold; such nights be theirs to shift
> On ridge or hillock; or in homesteads soft,
> Or softer cots, detain them. Is thy lot
> A chill penurious turf, to all thy toils
> Untractable? Before harsh winter drowns
> The noisy dykes, and starves the rushy glebe,
> Shift the frail breed to sandy hamlets warm;
> There let them sojourn, till gay Procne skims
> The thick'ning verdure and the rising flow'rs.   (lines 383–94)

The passage has some interesting epithets, in terms of assonance and the mixing of classical and northern words: 'noisy dykes', 'rushy glebe', 'sandy hamlets', etc. Even more interesting is the fact that as Dyer is admitting there are 'bad' lands as well as good, he makes a double-echo of Gray's description of the villager's impoverished life in the *Elegy*, through the phrases 'thy lot' and 'chill penurious turf'. Davies has noted the similarity of the phrase 'chill penurious' to Gray's 'Chill Penury' (*Elegy*, line 51).[20] But Dyer also uses the word 'lot': 'Is thy lot / A chill penurious turf', and 'lot' is a key word in the *Elegy*, where 'Their lot forbade' (line 65), meaning that the villagers were excluded from fame and fortune by their given circumstances. The contexts are similar, for Dyer is also referring to the limits deprivation has put on the villagers' lives. No other echo of the *Elegy* has been noted in *The Fleece* by Dyer's editors. However, I think Dyer's description of his friend Joseph Nutt slightly later in the poem (discussed below), as a man whom 'rude Obscurity severely clasps' (line 447), conflates a series of phrases and ideas from the *Elegy*: 'rude fore-fathers' (line 16), 'destiny obscure' (line 30), 'repressed' and 'froze' (lines 51 and 52: compare 'severely clasps'). Roger Lonsdale gives earlier analogues for all these ideas in Gray's poem, but no specific verbal analogue for the two words both poets use ('rude', and 'obscure' or 'obscurity'). The purpose of this echo would be to ascribe to Nutt an unassuming nobility, which is part of Gray's characterisation of the villager's demeanour.[21] Certainly a consciousness of hardship and difficulty is more freely expressed in this section of the poem, and this may both reflect and draw on ideas from Gray's portrayal of the pathos of village life.

We saw earlier that Thomson, in particular, seems to offer 'compensations' for the hardship of rural life. Dyer's 'compensation', in so far as he offers the shepherd one, is what we would now call 'job satisfaction'. The shepherd is faced with a 'chill penurious turf', but so, even more directly, is the sheep; and it is the shepherd's responsibility to ease conditions for his animals. The pleasure of his life lies in the moral satisfaction of treating his animals with benevolence, and the sense of professional responsibility in the way he can nurture the sheep, saving them from danger by his skill and exertion. Thus Dyer ends the passage quoted, as he does the castration passage, with a joyful emergence into springtime. In both examples this is the reward for the shepherd's pains: the sheep survive to enjoy the safety and pleasure of spring, and the shepherd's pleasure is derived from this success as much as from a direct enjoyment of the new season. Dyer is leading to a formal statement of this view of the shepherd's life. Before he gives this, however, he has two more pieces of description to give, which will add the final touch to this set of illustrations of the shepherd's professional work. They lead on from the passage quoted above:

> And while departing autumn all embrowns
> The frequent-bitten fields, while thy free hand
> Divides the tedded hay, then be their feet
> Accustom'd to the barriers of the rick,

Or some warm umbrage; lest, in erring fright,
When the broad dazzling snows descend, they run
Dispers'd to ditches, where the swelling drift
Wide overwhelms: anxious, the shepherd swains
Issue with axe and spade, and, all abroad,
In doubtful aim explore the glaring waste,
And some, perchance, in the deep delve upraise,
Drooping, ev'n at the twelfth cold dreary day,
With still continu'd feeble pulse of life,
The glebe, their Fleece, their flesh, by hunger gnawed.

(lines 395–408)

We are led into the worst moments of the shepherd's year in this passage. The storm Dyer has just described, the barren fields and the snow drifts are expressed in a less dramatic and sublime way than Thomson's parallel scenes (see 'Autumn', lines 311–50, and 'Winter'), but the dire significance of the withering grass in the 'frequent-bitten fields', and of the arrival of heavy drifting snow, would be immediately apparent to a shepherd. Dyer's shepherd is able to rescue both situations. Into the starving fields he brings hay, dividing it out with a 'free hand', that is, generously; and from the depths of the snowdrift he produces, after twelve days, a living sheep. The models for these two victories are, I think, two of Christ's miracles, the feeding of the five thousand (the shepherd's gesture of dividing up the hay is particularly suggestive), and the raising of Lazarus. The second action also literalises Christ's fable of the lost sheep.[22] We have seen that Dyer elsewhere ascribes the Christian idea of 'pastoral care' to the shepherd; here the parallel is at its most forceful. The shepherd is shown as the saviour of the sheep, a most 'elevated' form of pastoral. In the concluding lines of these two descriptions one notices again a powerful use of an alliterative form ('deep delve', 'dreary day'), and of patterns of assonance in the language. In the last line this is combined with the rhetoric of listing, in a way that focuses the 'miracle' in a manner that is both dramatic and gentle: 'With still continu'd feeble pulse of life, / The glebe, their Fleece, their flesh, by hunger gnaw'd' (lines 407–8). In the resonances between soft fricatives and hard consonants here the contrast between the gentleness and frailty of the sheep and the harshness of the winter; and the contrasting energies of toughness and tenderness in the shepherd's life are precisely expressed.

The passage successfully prepares the way for Dyer's formal statement of the shepherd's role as a pastoral carer; and this in turn provides an appropriate way of addressing the subject of the care of lambs:

Ah, gentle Shepherd! thine the lot to tend,
Of all that feel distress, the most assail'd,
Feeble, defenceless: lenient be thy care;
But spread around thy tend'rest diligence

> In flow'ry spring-time, when the new-dropp'd lamb,
> Tott'ring with weakness by his mother's side,
> Feels the fresh world about him, and each thorn,
> Hillock, or furrow, trips his feeble feet:
> O! guard his meek sweet innocence from all
> Th'innumerous ills that rush around his life.   (lines 409–18)

When Dyer uses the familiar characterisation of the 'gentle shepherd' in his peroration here, one feels he has earned the right to do so, and is not just using the stock phrases of literary pastoral. The moment is right for the statement, between the success of keeping the sheep alive through winter, and the new subject of the care of lambs.

The poet's treatment of this new subject itself goes some way to making up for his omission of lambing. The 'meek sweet innocence' of the lamb may be a literary notion, but it is appropriate to the vulnerability of the lamb the poet goes on to delineate; and no shepherd would argue with the idea that 'innumerous ills ... rush around' the new-born lamb. Quentin Seddon characterises them well:

Shepherds say that the first three weeks are half a sheep's life; in that time it finds as many ways to die as in the rest of its days put together ... Even when safely born, lambs must be closely watched to make sure they get enough milk, resist the wet, avoid the raven and the fox, and through the exhausting weeks of lambing the same patient attention must be paid night and day.[23]

Each of the dangers Seddon mentions receives its share of advice in the passage that follows: shortage of milk (lines 426–7), bad weather (line 425), the predatory crows (line 421) and foxes (lines 421–2); and Dyer also warns of a few dangers no longer faced: the attacks of the 'quick kite' (lines 419–20) and the 'bold bird of prey' (line 428); and the failure of the land to produce an early enough bite of grass (lines 425–6):

> Mark the quick kite, with beak and talons prone,
> Circling the skies to snatch him from the plain;
> Observe the lurking crows; beware the brake,
> There the sly fox the careless minute waits;
> Nor trust thy neighbour's dog, nor earth, nor sky:
> Thy bosom to a thousand cares divide.
> Eurus oft slings his hail; the tardy fields
> Pay not their promis'd food; and oft the dam
> O'er her weak twins with empty udder mourns,
> Or fails to guard when the bold bird of prey
> Alights, and hops in many turns around,
> And tires her, also turning.   (lines 419–30)

This is an impressive passage in didactic and thematic terms; and Dyer draws it to a conclusion well. Hand feeding is recommended as a task for children, so that they learn 'charitable habits in sport'; Dyer finely characterises the shepherd's role again, in the line 'Various as ether is the past'ral care' (line 440). He concludes on a note of exemplary digression, double-punningly pastoralising the name and qualities of his friend Joseph Nutt, whom he presents as a model of modest didacticism:

> The whole long lesson gradual is attain'd,
> By precept after precept, oft receiv'd
> With deep attention; such as Nuceus sings
> To the full vale near Soar's enamour'd brook,
> While all is silence: sweet Hinclean swain!
> Whom rude Obscurity severely clasps:
> The Muse, howe'er, will deck thy simple cell
> With purple violets and primrose flowers,
> Well pleas'd thy faithful lessons to repay.   (lines 442–50)

Nutt (1700–75) is another interesting man, like Mackenzie. Apparently self-taught, he was an apothecary to the poor, and the designer of the 'flooding' system for ironing out bumps in the highway. Dyer's praise of his friend also suggests he was a popular outdoor orator, probably on didactic and religious themes.[24]

Dyer has usually been dismissed as humourless, but the description of his friend here is one of several instances of humorous word-play and punning on names in the poem. Joseph is not only a nut ('Nuceus'), but a 'sweet' nut, as pastoral convention decrees. (The adjective 'Hinclean' brings him into the mytho-topography of Dyer's Tripontium: Nutt lived in Hinckley.) The characterisation of Nutt (lines 444–50) also imitates the invocation of Lucretius' *De Rerum Natura*. This takes the form of what a modern translator calls a 'Prayer to the creative force of Nature to inspire the poet, to bless his patron Memmius and to bring peace to the world'.[25]

Nutt is the last of three individuals, following Berkeley and Mackenzie, whom Dyer has held up to exemplify the ideal of teacherly-pastoral care, and his mention of them consecutively (lines 289, 314, 444) weaves this theme through the middle of his shepherdly advice. At one level his praise of them reflexively defends his own role in writing *The Fleece*. At another level they are models for the shepherd to emulate. We have seen the way Dyer encourages the shepherd to learn about the weather; and his advice throughout this first book offers itself as a way of encouraging the shepherd to learn useful arts. By characterising Nutt as one whom 'rude obscurity severely clasps' Dyer is suggesting, not only a model of modest retirement, but also the possibility that even someone of Nutt's modest background can learn enough to become a teacher, a 'friend to man'. The implication is that the shepherd, through his benevolent and caring role, and his ability to gain and share practical wisdom, has the capability to become a Berkeley, a Mackenzie, a Nutt, or indeed a Dyer. Through the shepherd, the poet implies that each role in society has the potential for expansion beyond its immediate function. In this he differs greatly from his quietist contemporary Gray, even though he borrows Gray's language. Through the figures of the caring shepherd and the exemplary Nutt, Dyer brings the three-fold pastoral role (shepherding, caring and teaching) together neatly to conclude this important part of the poem.

Winter feeding

In his heroic depiction of shepherding, as a calling and a model for a successful society, Dyer has two more cards to play. Both are built around pastoral descriptions of key moments in the agricultural year. The first is centred on winter feeding (the second is the shearing feast of summer, the pleasurable reward for the shepherdly care of winter). Dyer begins the winter passage with a further comment on the subject of climatic moderation. The position of this passage, following the praise of 'Nuceus', amplifies its apparent significance; we get the impression that Dyer is beginning to draw to its conclusion the 'long lesson' whose method of gradual attainment has been the subject of the previous verse-paragraph:

> Sheep no extremes can bear: both heat and cold
> Spread sores cutaneous; but more frequent heat.
> The fly-blown vermin from their woolly nest
> Press to the tortur'd skin, and flesh, and bone,
> In littleness and number dreadful foes!
> Long rains in miry winter cause the halt;
> Rainy luxuriant summers rot your flock;
> And all excess, ev'n of salubrious food,
> As sure destroys as famine or the wolf.
> Inferior theirs to man's world-roving frame,
> Which all extremes in every zone endures.   (lines 451–61)

In fact two of Dyer's earlier subjects are brought together here: climate (see lines 125–84), and disease (see lines 251–320). In uniting them Dyer graphically prepares to particularise the significance of the English climate for shepherding. The extremes of heat and cold are shown as the deadly enemies of health in sheep, thus preparing for an example of the way that the temperate climate of England represents a perfect moderation between the two extremes. The last sentence (lines 460–1) presents an interesting subtext to this: the extreme climates are not condemned *per se*, but only as sites for shepherding. The phrase 'man's world-roving frame' reveals the significance of this stricture; for while in the 'home' climate sheep may thrive under the care of their shepherds, Dyer will later despatch other classes of society (explorers, merchants and traders) to the 'extreme' parts of the earth to buy and to sell. The first preparations for that later movement, and for the idea that it may have a relationship with the idyllic sheep pastures of Albion, are made here.

But the major task in hand is to count the shepherd's blessings in temperate England, and to compare them with less fortunate areas:

> With grateful heart, ye British Swains! enjoy
> Your gentle seasons and indulgent clime.
> Lo! in the sprinkling clouds your bleating hills
> Rejoice with herbage, while the horrid rage
> Of winter irresistible o'erwhelms
> Th'Hyperborean tracks: his arrowy frosts
> That pierce through flinty rocks, the Lappian flies;
> And burrows deep beneath the snowy world;
> A drear abode!
>
> (lines 462–70)

The 'hyperborean tracks' are a purgatory of extended winters ('Twice three slow gloomy months', line 475), which the northern shepherd and his beasts somehow endure by living on fish bones and tree bark:

> His lank and scanty herds around him press,
> As, hunger-stung, to gritty meal he grinds
> The bones of fish, or inward bark of trees,
> Their common sustenance . . .
>
> (lines 477–80)

This is no doubt an exaggerated portrayal: eighteenth-century georgic writers were incurably fascinated by the sublime horrors and depredations of winter; but the contrasted British scene for which this prepares is one of the more successful pastoral moments in the poem:

> while ye, O Swains!
> Ye, happy at your ease, behold your sheep
> Feed on the open turf, or crowd the tilth,
> Where, thick among the greens, with busy mouths
> They scoop white turnips: little care is yours:
> Only at morning hour to interpose
> Dry food of oats, or hay, or brittle straw,
> The wat'ry juices of the bossy root
> Absorbing; or from noxious air to screen
> Your heavy teeming ewes with wattled fence
> Of furze or copse-wood in the lofty field,
> Which bleak ascends among the whistling winds:
> Or, if your sheep are of Silurian breed,
> Nightly to house them dry on fern or straw,
> Silk'ning their Fleeces. Ye nor rolling hut
> Nor watchful dog require, where never roar
> Of savage tears the air, where careless Night
> In balmy sleep lies lull'd, and only wakes
> To plenteous peace.
>
> (lines 480–98)

Every aspiration of the eighteenth-century georgic is present in this passage. The contrast between the rigours of the northern winter, and the ease of folding sheep through root-crops in an English winter, faithfully gives what Addison calls a 'pleasing variety of scenes'. Description and prescription are artfully intertwined; and, again in Addison's terms, Dyer 'makes the driest of [his] precepts look like a description'.[26] Indeed, so far as the major prescription is concerned, Addison's characterisation of 'dry' precepts seems punningly apt, for the issue in lines 484–8 is one of balancing wet and dry foods.

A modern critic has used these particular lines to attack the pretensions of eighteenth-century 'poetic diction'; and we may use his comments as a starting point in examining Dyer's procedures here. He writes:

The more ordinary or utilitarian the subject, the more needful the poet generally felt it to avoid the prosaic word at which his sophisticated readers might laugh. So Dyer in his *Fleece* may let his sheep 'with busy mouths . . . scoop white turnips', but he quickly changes the vulgar turnip to 'the watery juices of the bossy root.' Poetry indeed stood on its dignity when it could not on its inspiration.[27]

It seems to me that one does not best 'avoid' a word by using it, and then drawing further attention to it by reiterating it in periphrasis three lines later. But more importantly, these lines carry a meaning which the critic does not address, and which seems to me to vindicate Dyer's periphrasis. He is concerned to stress the 'ease' of the shepherdly intervention needed in folding; but the 'easy' task he mentions is important, and the descriptive work shows why this is so. The task is: 'Only at morning hour to interpose / Dry food of oats, or hay, or brittle straw, / The wat'ry juices of the bossy root / Absorbing' (lines 485–8). The issue here is dietary balance between roots, which have a high water content (turnips are approximately ninety per cent water), and dry, bulky foods such as oats, hay and straw. The possible danger Dyer has in mind is one of 'extremes' caused by imbalance. What we now call lactic acid poisoning, overeating disease, enterotoxaemia and other such dietary disorders may all be caused by excessive root or concentrate eating, and are best prevented by what the Ministry of Agriculture calls 'careful checks': 'careful feeding management is of the greatest importance. Sudden changes of diet should be avoided and careful checks made on consumption'.[28] One can see how the cause of these diseases might focus particularly, in Dyer's world, on winter crop-folding; and the cure on balancing the diet. The phrase 'watery juices of the bossy root' is designed to make a clear contrast with the previous line's 'Dry food of oats, or hay, or brittle straw', and thus vividly to illustrate by this contrast the nature of the balancing task. The word 'turnip' would hardly achieve this effect.

The contrast in the two lines has also a thematic significance. We have seen that Dyer praises the British climate as 'moderate'; and in the same way he advocates 'moderation' in sheep feeding here, expressed (as with the weather) by means of descriptive contrast. At an immediate level, 'moderation' is of real value in sheep management, whether one considers diet or climate. At another level it is a poetic and philosophical idea which came from Roman culture, particularly through the poetry of Horace, and was much beloved by eighteenth-century Horatians like Pope, and Dyer himself. Thus the poet is again able to tie the literal imperatives of shepherding to his higher ideals. Philosophy and pragmatism, poetry and agriculture, are here in harmonious agreement.

The periphrasis also works if we subject it to close linguistic scrutiny. The turnip is very precisely a 'bossy root'. That it is a root is clear enough; and I am thinking of the first *OED* definition of bossy as 'Swelling in, or like, a boss: projecting in rounded form'. Putting the two words together in a phrase suggests the turnip's physical substantiality (bossy, contrasting and alliterating with the 'brittle straw'), and its discovered quality (root). Appositely, the phrase 'wat'ry juices' describes its content and substance very precisely, though the phrase provides information which is not usually available (except to a sheep). The whole line sensuously delineates the contrast between the solidity and presence of the turnip's appearance, and the juicy richness of its content. This contrasted depiction in turn ties it to its context of sheep feeding with 'busy mouths' – another evocative and precise phrase, as anyone who has observed sheep grazing on turnips will confirm.[29]

James Sutherland wrote of another piece of periphrasis in the poem, 'prickly brambles, white with woolly theft' (line 103), that it showed how Dyer's kind of periphrasis 'could concentrate much meaning in a single phrase'.[30] It could indeed, and the phrase 'watery juices of the bossy root' has the same capability. These lines intelligently engage their subject in a unified and coherent way, working simultaneously in philosophical, didactic and physical, observational ways. Of course they tell us something of 'the care of sheep', which is the first intention; but Dyer also uses the periphrasis and contrast to bring together several layers of thought and observation, in a way that only poetry can do.

I see no evidence in this of 'dignity' taking the place of inspiration; and the idea of the turnip as a 'vulgar' or even an 'ordinary or utilitarian' subject is not really appropriate to a discussion of eighteenth-century agricultural poetry. For those practically or intellectually involved in agricultural developments in the early modern period (including georgic writers and their readers), the turnip was no less than the silicone chip of the New Farming. Its introduction as a field crop in Suffolk during the Interregnum is described by one agricultural historian as having consti-tuted in itself an 'agricultural revolution'; while another goes so far as to declare that the introduction of the turnip and other new fodder-crops on a field scale represented for agriculture 'an innovation equal in signifi-cance to any subsequently applied to industry'.[31] Dyer's powerful attach-ment to the agricultural richness which the turnip and the other new crops were enabling, his 'spacious flocks of sheep, / Like flakes of gold illumining the green' (lines 168–9), offers no concession to our modern narrowness about eighteenth-century poetry. We may believe that the turnip is 'low', but Dyer reasonably supposed it to be in the very vanguard of cultural progress.

The rest of Dyer's description serves to focus and recommend his gentle, benevolent approach to shepherding. The shepherd protects the flock, using hurdles and cots, with a particular emphasis on the care of pregnant ewes. Again one notes the way in which the pastoral does not conceal hardships ('noxious air', 'whistling winds', and so on); the idyllic mood is characteristically based upon acknowledging difficulties, then showing how the shepherd may defeat them by his labour. Although the shepherd is shown as being fortunate in the benevolent character of the English environment and climate, he also creates his own fortune, through labour, and appropriate intervention. The poet is able to merge Horatian and Bakewellian approaches to the rural world, to make a credible, harmoni-ous vision.

Dyer ends the section by making further foreign contrasts with his English idyll. The 'terror' of the earthquake zones is briefly historicised (lines 498–505), reflecting the poet's twin interests in ruins and volcanoes.[32] The 'Furies, famine, plague, and war' of 'neighb'ring realms' (lines 506–7) are implicitly contrasted with the peace of Albion, while its temperate climate is contrasted with the heat and drought of the desert and the Bible lands (with digressions to Arcadia and to the story of Jacob and Rachel, lines 514–50). The message is clear, and by now familiar: Albion, almost uniquely, provides a perfect and moderate climate in which the shepherd is spared all manner of hardships, expenses and dangers ('perils' and 'toils', line 551). A modest (and pleasurable) amount of continuing careful labour, informed by a spirit of didacticism and observational learning, will serve, in the poet's view, to make a favourable land idyllic.

10

The shepherd's harvest

The shearing

So far as the agricultural theme is concerned, three related tasks remain
for the poet. He has given most of his advice, and drawn together the
major aspects of the shepherdly role: practical tasks, learning and teaching, benevolent care and the balancing in moderate harmony of the given
conditions. Now he will complete the theme by particularising and localis-
ing the experience, rewarding the shepherd and connecting shepherding
with the wider worlds of work which are his second and third theme. All
this is done through the advice on shearing (lines 555–600), and the
shearing festival (lines 601–720). This grand finale to the book has caught
the attention of many readers and critics, with its striking blend of
first-person narrative, pastoral eclogue, mythologising and lyric celebration. The poet creates an Edenic pastoral scene, incorporating ideas of
childhood, innocence and communal rural delight, and set emphatically
in the mytho-topographical land of Siluria.

Dyer announces his final theme with energy and impatience, as if he
were by now becoming a little bored by the easy trick of contrasting
foreign lands with Albion, and felt anxious to move on to the excitement of
Silurian memories:

> Such are the perils, such the toils, of life,
> In foreign climes. But speed thy flight, my Muse!
> Swift turns the year, and our unnumber'd flocks
> On Fleeces overgrown uneasy lie.
>   Now, jolly Swains! the harvest of your cares
> Prepare to reap, and seek the sounding caves
> Of high Brigantium, where, by ruddy flames,
> Vulcan's strong sons, with nervous arm, around
> The steady anvil and the glaring mass
> Clatter their heavy hammers down by turns,
> Flatt'ning the steel: from their rough hands receive
> The sharpen'd instrument that from the flock
> Severs the Fleece.   (lines 551–63)

The excitement and expectation of the new theme is, typically, communicated in terms of georgic urgency: the sheep need shearing, and we must get on with it. More surprising, at first sight, is the fact that the new subject opens on an industrial note. The 'Sounding caves / Of high Brigantium' (lines 56–7) indicate the steel manufacturing centre of Sheffield. The description of its steel-workers, with 'nervous arm', appropriately echoes the 'sinewy arm' of the poem's first reference to 'Tripontian' labour (lines 68–9): like 'Tripontium', 'Brigantium' is more suggestive of georgic labour than of pastoral idyll. The activity of the forges and steel mills is another example of Dyer's heroic depiction of labour, seen in the classical reference to 'Vulcan's strong sons' (line 558). It is characteristic of Dyer's imaginative boldness that he should begin a pastoral description of sheep-shearing with an entirely industrial scene; yet it makes perfect sense: his advice is serious, and the serious priority when it comes to sheep-shearing is sharp clippers. The reputation of Sheffield steel in this context remains sufficiently potent for us to need no further explanation of Dyer's 'Brigantium'.[1]

That he is able to bring the steel-forging Brigantes into the charmed circle of his 'jolly Swains' is also remarkable, but again makes sense. The poet's constant refusal to distinguish between pastoral idyll and postlapsarian labour has partly prepared us for the new phenomenon of industrial-pastoral.[2] The specific way in which the steelmakers join the circle is by being made a part of the poet's first piece of advice to shepherds on shearing, where the second, following naturally on, has a different tone:

> If verdant elder spreads
> Her silver flow'rs; if humble daisies yield
> To yellow crow-foot, and luxuriant grass,
> Gay shearing-time approaches.   (lines 563–6)

This is pastoral, folkloric, proverbial and poetic. It is flower-lore, but it also unites with the first piece of advice as serious prescription. The shepherd, by now established as an intelligent observer, as naturally learns the seasons of flowers as he does the best place to buy good shears, and thus non-shepherdly industry is portrayed as being part of the same process as pastoral activity.

Of the plants Dyer mentions, the elder (*Sambucus nigra*) features frequently in poetic tree-lore as well as folklore, folk medicine and folk recipes. It flowers in large white clusters from May to June. The daisy (*Bellis perennis*), Chaucer's favourite flower, according to the prologue to *The Legend of Good Women* (lines 40–63), flowers between March and October. Dyer's 'yellow crow-foot', like his 'crow-flow'r' (line 309), is a buttercup, in this instance the creeping buttercup (*Ranunculus repens*), which flowers from May to September. The poet's flower lore points to

May to June for washing and shearing the sheep. The humble daisies 'yield' to the buttercup in the sense of being superseded as the primary colour of the field. As has been written of the latter's close relative the meadow buttercup, 'There is hardly a meadow that does not become a blaze of buttercup yellow between May and July'.[3]

The passages that follow, on washing and shearing sheep, show that Dyer had read *The Seasons* carefully and intelligently. Like Thomson, he concentrates on the energy and movement of sheep-washing, especially expressed through his verbs, 'Drive', 'plunge', 'sinks', 'glisten', 'seize', 'bears', 'laves'. The shearing advice follows, with the shepherdly gentleness the task requires played lightly in this instance (Thomson, as we saw, melodramatically overplayed it), and the skill of shearing emphasised. A smaller-scale version of Thomson's destroying autumn storm emphasises the need for post-shearing care, and moves us to the Welsh valleys ('Cambrian glades'), in preparation for the shearing festival (whose location is 'along the lively vales', line 601). For the storm itself (in fact a flash-flood) Dyer uses for the second time the image of flocks being swept away by a natural disaster, (the first was used to describe the 'coughing pest', lines 264–5). However, the emphasis here is slightly different. The 'coughing pest' disaster is formulated in terms of scale as well as suddenness. 'From their green pasture' it 'sweeps whole flocks away'. The flash-flood description concentrates on pathos as well as suddenness:

> Then thunder oft with pond'rous wheels rolls loud,
> And breaks the crystal urns of heav'n; adown
> Falls streaming rain. Sometimes among the steeps
> Of Cambrian glades (pity the Cambrian glades!)
> Fast tumbling brooks on brooks enormous swell,
> And sudden overwhelm their vanish'd fields:
> Down with the flood away the naked sheep,
> Bleating in vain, are borne, and straw-built huts,
> And rifted trees, and heavy enormous rocks,
> Down with the rapid torrent to the deep.   (lines 591–600)

Dyer's flash-flood, though in style (particularly in its final lines) it imitates the storm in Thomson's 'Autumn' (lines 311–50), seems also to have been observational; and such floods still occur from time to time in the valleys of South Wales.

The year's work is now completed, and there will be no more georgic prescription in this book of the poem (though work is never quite forgotten). Instead, we are moved by degrees, through a series of increasingly lyrical passages, towards what John Barrell has called the 'extraordinary sentence' that ends the first book. Both Barrell and Feingold have made important analyses of this final scene. Unlike earlier commentators, who have usually been content simply to point to the lyrical beauty of the passage, both read it as central to Dyer's attempt to reconcile the pastoral with the labouring world. My reading owes much to their important comments.[4]

First, moving smoothly on from the floods that overwhelm 'Cambrian glades', Dyer describes another phenomenon of the valleys, in general, customary terms:

> At shearing-time along the lively vales
> Rural festivities are often heard;
> Beneath each blooming arbour all is joy
> And lusty merriment. While on the grass
> The mingled youth in gaudy circles sport,
> We think the Golden Age again return'd,
> And all the fabled Dryades in dance:
> Leering they bound along, with laughing air,
> To the shrill pipe, and deep remurm'ring-cords
> Of th'ancient harp, or tabor's hollow sound.   (lines 601–10)

There is a great deal of the communality of Thomson's harvest scenes in this, though dancing is here more explicit than it is in *The Seasons*. The thought that the 'Golden Age' has 'again return'd' gives the poet a fairly credible excuse to sketch in the classical, Arcadian details of Dryades, and the rather more Welsh instruments of harp, voices, and pipe and tabor. Drayton, in Song VI, tells of how the 'Bards with furie rapt, the British youth among' once sang the glories of Plinlimmon 'Unto the charming Harpe'.

What is most notable in this passage, though, is the rare use of the first-person plural 'We'. The use of the first person is not unknown in eighteenth-century georgic, but the poets tended to save it for special occasions, maintaining the persona of responsible public utterance, expressed in the second and third person, through most of their texts. Dyer, for example, uses the first-person only for special effects: in the invocation (lines 1–2), and the 'I knew a careful swain' exemplum (line 108 ff.); and in his Miltonic autobiographical declaration ('For this I wake the weary hours', etc., II, line 503 ff). Yet this pastoral ending of the first book contains much first-person utterance. 'We', here, brings the poet himself into the circle of the celebrating shepherds, giving a personal, autobiographical flavour to the pastoral.

A second verse paragraph (lines 611–24) shows 'th'old apart, upon a bank reclin'd'. Thomson involved older people in his harvest work, but for Dyer they provide an audience for the music which is a major part of his pastoral celebration. The music itself suggests another line of thought, this time concerning the loss of innocence:

Music of Paradise! which still is heard
When the heart listens, still the views appear
Of the first happy garden, when Content
To Nature's flowery scenes directs the sight.
Yet we abandon those Elysian walks,
Then idly for the lost delight repine;
As greedy mariners, whose desp'rate sails
Skim o'er the billows of the foamy flood,
Fancy they see the lessening shores retire,
And sigh a farewell to the sinking hills.   (lines 615–24)

The simile seems extraordinary because, as Barrell notes, these 'mariners' are shortly to be praised for their part in world trade; yet here their 'greed' is compared to the causes of the loss of pastoral innocence.[5] Apart from Goldstein's important comment, which I quoted earlier, about Dyer being 'loyal to irreconcilable myths', two thoughts on this occur.[6] The contradiction may reflect the degree to which Dyer is able to give himself up to the music of a pleasant memory, and abandon (albeit temporarily) the imperatives of didacticism. We saw in his idealised 'Silurian' sheep that thoughts of Siluria could have this effect of modifying the poet's need to control and instruct. There is also a sense in which the occasion demands a cessation of industrious activity, a moment in which to acknowledge that there are other values than those of labour. The first stage in the fleece's progress is safely completed, and the poet can afford to make his mariners wait, and even acknowledge that their task may be destructive of the 'Golden Age' values which are (temporarily) in the ascendant. They will re-establish their control in the later sections of the poem. Here, as both Feingold and Barrell observe, the mariners, in the very last image of the first book (lines 718–20) trim their sails respectfully, and 'Linger among the reeds and copsy banks', content, like the poet, simply to enjoy the pastoral music of the shepherds' celebration.[7]

Dyer's first-person approach to the shearing festival is now intensified, though it is almost immediately distanced again:

Could I recall those notes which once the Muse
Heard at a shearing, near the woody sides
Of blue-topp'd Wreakin! Yet the carols sweet,
Through the deep maze of the memorial cell
Faintly remurmur. First arose in song
Hoar-headed Damon, venerable Swain!
The soothest shepherd of the flow'ry vale,
'This is no vulgar scene; no palace roof
Was e'er so lofty, nor so nobly rise
Their polish'd pillars as these aged oaks,
Which o'er our Fleecy wealth and harmless sports

> Thus have expanded wide their shelt'ring arms,
> Thrice told an hundred summers. Sweet Content,
> Ye gentle shepherds! pillow us at night.'   (lines 625–38)

Early in this passage the poet's recollection is displaced into a formal eclogue between 'Damon' and 'Colin' (both traditional English pastoral names). To the post-Romantic sensibility, used to poets' first-person accounts of childhood and the experience of nature, it will seem strange and disappointing that Dyer should seem able to manifest his recollection only in the rather stilted terms of the eighteenth-century pastoral eclogue; and the fact that the eclogue itself shows signs of the influence of Ambrose Philips can only make things worse.[8]

But Dyer has serious reasons for moving into the eclogue form. These may be summarised under the headings of dramatisation and ritualisation. The whole first book has been concerned to show that the shepherd's life is happy, rewarding and meaningful not only in itself, but as a model for other, higher roles in society. The most effective way in which the poet can enforce this message is to put it into the mouths of shepherds. The dialogue form avoids the impression that this is simply the poet making a speech; and allows the shepherds to draw the meaning of their roles from their own experience; or rather, from Dyer's experience: for as he directly remembers a shearing feast on the slopes of the Wrekin (lines 625–7), so his shepherd remembers climbing Breidden Hill 'After a kidling' (lines 654–5), describing the experience in entirely Dyeresque terms of scenery and prospect. The shepherd has the articulacy and sensibilities of the author, and can dramatically exemplify Dyer's view of the shepherd's life, arguing against the idea that it is 'mean' (line 670); and articulating what has been implied throughout the first book, that king and priest are 'also shepherds' (line 673), and thus by implication that the shepherd's is a noble and spiritual, a teacherly and nurturing occupation, of the greatest antiquity and significance.

Ritualisation goes alongside the 'elevated pastoralism' expressed here. Colin and Damon complete their recollections and opinions, then Damon interrupts himself to begin the 'rites' of the festival:

> 'But haste, begin the rites: see purple Eve
> Stretches her shadows: all ye Nymphs and Swains
> Hither assemble. Pleas'd with honours due,
> Sabrina, guardian of the crystal flood,
> Shall bless our cares, when she by moonlight clear
> Skims o'er the dales, and eyes our sleeping folds;
> Or in hoar caves around Plynlymmon's brow,
> Where precious minerals dart their purple gleams,
> Among her sisters she reclines; the lov'd
> Vaga, profuse of graces, Ryddol rough,

Blithe Ystwith, and Clevedoc, swift of foot;
And mingles various seeds of flow'rs and herbs,
In the divided torrents, ere they burst
Thro' the dark clouds, and down the mountain roll.
Nor taint-worm shall infect the yeaning herds,
Nor penny-grass, nor spearwort's pois'nous leaf.' (lines 676–91)

The poetic mood shifts slightly here: the careful arguments of 'Colin' and 'Damon' seem to be informed by the eloquence of the Elizabethan pastoral poets. This passage is more attuned to the sensibilities of the seventeenth century, echoing Milton's *Comus* (1637) and *Lycidas* (1638) as well as Drayton, and reminding one of the Christianised paganism of that other clergyman-poet, Robert Herrick (another flower enthusiast).[9]

The ritual is solemn (the food for the feast must remain 'untouch'd', until it is completed, line 703), and elaborate: there are, for example, three distinct stages in the plant lore. Firstly, Sabrina, the presiding spirit of the river Severn, 'mingles various seeds of flow'rs and herbs' into the headwaters of the rivers that rise on Plinlimmon (lines 687–9). None of Dyer's editors have annotated these lines (other than to locate the Miltonic echoes), and I have not been able to trace the origin of this 'seeding', which may form a subtext to the Sabrina myth (discussed below), and/or relate to the folk-custom of sprinkling flowers on the river Severn at shearing festivals (itself the subject of the third stage of the flower-lore). Secondly, and perhaps relatedly, 'Damon' adds: 'Nor taint-worm shall infect the yeaning herds, / Nor penny-grass nor spearwort's pois'nous leaf' (lines 690–1). This seems to be expressed, not as a hope, plea or prayer, but as something determined, a sort of spell, or a formulaic phrase as part of a pre-ordained ritual.[10] Sabrina, seeding various flowers and herbs which are good for grazing, is being asked to be careful not to sow anything bad which might cause illness in the sheep. *OED* defines 'taint-worm' as an archaic word meaning 'a worm or crawling larva supposed to taint or infect cattle, etc.' (the word 'cattle' here, like Dyer's 'herd', means sheep as well as cows). Penny-grass could mean one of three species, but almost certainly means marsh pennywort (*Hydrocotyle vulgaris*), traditionally (and wrongly) thought to cause liver rot in sheep. Similarly 'spearwort' may indicate one of a number of species, but Dyer's indication that it is poisonous, and a suggestive quotation in the *OED* from Gervase Markham about a plant 'unwholesome for Sheepe', points to *OED* 'spearwort' definition 3, 'One or other of several species of ranunculas, esp. R. Flammula'; that is to say, lesser spearwort. Kerridge defines spearwort as 'sheep-rot'.[11] Dyer's interest in the relationship between sheep and the ranunculi seems unabating; but the main theme behind this incantation is the fear of sudden illness, especially in the 'yeaning' (pregnant or lambing) ewes. The sources are clearly folkloric, though the diction is classical and poetic.

Dyer has saved the most vivid folk custom until the end of the ritual. This is, in the words of the poet's 'Argument', the 'Custom in Wales of sprinkling the rivers with flowers', and it directly follows Damon's ritualising speech:

> He said: with light fantastic toe the nymphs
> Thither assembled, thither every swain;
> And o'er the dimpled stream a thousand flow'rs,
> Pale lilies, roses, violets and pinks,
> Mix'd with the greens of burnet, mint, and thyme,
> And trefoil, sprinkled with their sportive arms.   (lines 692–7)

Apart from the singularity of the custom itself, several things distinguish this passage within the Miltonic pastoral tradition it represents. A faint Dyeresque pun on 'flow'rs' (flow-ers as rivers as well as blooms) enriches the language. One notices the 'sportive arms' of the flower-strewing nymphs and swains: we have seen 'sinewy', 'labour-strengthen'd' and 'nervous' arms in the labouring section (lines 68, 111, 558); the energy of labour is clearly also present in this scene of relaxation. The 'greens' of 'burnet, mint, and thyme' serve the double purpose of setting off the flower colours (suggesting again a painterly sensibility), and of whetting the appetite for the feast which is to come. Lesser or salad burnet (*Sanguisorba minor*), was infused in wine as an antidote to melancholy; the varieties of mint were universally used as a stimulant and *digestif*; while thyme, which aids the digestion of fatty food, was (and is) widely used as a potherb. The trefoils, members of the pea family, would be both lucky and decorative in this context. One notices that all the flowers are richly perfumed species; and that the herbs are all creeping plants which are good for sheep to eat (see lines 19 and 26–8, discussed above). There are rituals of luck-making, fertility and sympathetic magic here, as well as sensuous and celebratory stimulation. The parallel passage in Milton's *Comus*, with its more conventional 'pansies, pinks and gaudy daffodils' (line 851) lacks these nuances, which I think represent Dyer's own contribution to the pastoral tradition.[12]

Topographical mythology

Thus visually and gustatively stimulated, and with the fertility and propitiation rituals complete, Dyer's shepherds can now enjoy their pastoral feast, which they proceed to do, ending the scene in life-affirming triumph, with food, drink and music (lines 702–20). The most powerful element within this final section of the first book is not, however, its flower lore, or even its idyllic festivity, but its sense of topography; and I shall conclude this reading of Dyer's agricultural theme by looking briefly at the poet's topographical referencing in this important pastoral passage.

Topographical naming, the sense of place, is an important and ever-intensifying presence in *The Fleece*, beginning in the opening passage of shepherdly prescription, and culminating in the fourth book, which offers a kind of gazetteer of world trade. We have seen a number of the topographic concepts Dyer sets up in the first book: the cluster of good pasture areas and more personal idyllic locations (lines 38–66); 'Dimetia', the agriculturally neglected lands of south-west Wales (lines 104–5); 'Darwent' in the Peak District and 'Snowden', 'Plynlymmon', 'Cader-ydris' in mid and north Wales, the mountainous regions where sheep roam free. Most importantly, we have noted Dyer's 'Siluria' and 'Tripontium', sites of particular agricultural significance, embodying several pairs of related or contrasting aesthetic and agricultural ideas, and the prescribed territory for two very differently conceptualised types of sheep. Dyer habitually forms topographical matrices of this sort, and they provide both a sophisticated epic machinery, and (as Barrell has noted) a measure of the poet's ideological frames of reference, and his modulation of georgic and pastoral elements in the poem.

There is also an important personal mythology embedded in Dyer's topographical referencing. Humfrey calls the poem a 'tapestry or living landscape' of the poet's own life, as indeed it is: 'Dimetia' is the land of his youth; 'Siluria', north Wales, and the English and Welsh border counties are the territory of his early adulthood, the years of itinerant painting and of the poet's first experience of farming. Thereafter Dyer moved inexorably eastwards from Bromyard, across the Midlands, living in Worcester ('Vigornia', III, line 433), Nuneaton and then Catthorpe; so that 'Tripontium', with its sterner and more practical imperatives, represents the landscape of his middle years, and of his new role as parish priest and philanthropic tutor to the poor. The final stage of Dyer's personal topographic journey, just to complete the picture, was 'the levels green of Lincoln' (II, line 385) where, as he wrote rather forlornly on 20 December 1751:

> At length 'mong reeds and mud my bark sticks fast;
> So Fate thinks proper, who can now sustain
> My tribe with delicacies, frogs and eels,
> 'Mong reeds and mud; begirt with dead brown lakes,
> Whose, perhaps pleasant, shores lie far unseen:
> Nor will their habitants the decent face
> Of civil man or woman deign approach:
> Ev'n Rumour comes not here!

Poor Dyer: but at least, as Humfrey remarks, the 'new diet of frogs and eels' had the advantage that it 'certainly speeded the composition of *The Fleece*'.[13]

We have also seen that Dyer uses topographical reference to contrast an idyllic national agricultural experience with the various hardships faced by foreign shepherds; thus the classical Falernum/Vesuvius/Herculanean/ Pompeian area (lines 64–6), shows by contrast Britain's freedom from volcanoes and ruins; and the 'Hyperborean tracks' passage (lines 464–80) and its various exotic/extreme opposites (such as Sabaea/Chaldaea/ Egyptus/Cyrene/Zembla, lines 230–4) show by contrast the moderation of the British climate. As well as the implied contrast with temperate Albion, the message in much of this topography is that each location and each climate has its appropriate role in an ordered scheme of natural and human production.

So far as British topography is concerned, Dyer's models are Camden's *Britannia* (translated by William Gibson, 1695), and Drayton's *Poly-Olbion* (1613–22), both of which provide analogues for most of his references; and of course Defoe's *A Tour Thro' the Whole Island of Great Britain* (1724–6), a project which Dyer's own unpublished 'Commercial Map of England' was to have extended into new areas of economic and cartographic information. Camden had aimed to 'restore antiquity to Britaine, and Britaine to his antiquity', and Drayton gave the subject epic treatment, offering his readers 'the Rarities and Historie of their owne Country delivered by a true native Muse'.[14] The practical purposefulness which was Defoe's particular contribution to the topographic tradition appealed to Dyer, as his 'Commercial Map' notes show; and so too did the poetic and epic traditions of topographic naming. Pat Rogers has suggested that the Renaissance tradition of river-poetry is still unexpectedly alive in the 'rich and complex utterance' that is Pope's *Windsor Forest*; this specialised area of the topographic tradition is alive, too, in the ending of the first book of *The Fleece*.[15]

But most strikingly, in this final section of the first book, Dyer gives us mountains. We have seen the way in which the poet selects the vantage point within a landscape. In this last section he encircles the pastoral, and the land of Siluria, with vantage points. The eclogue began with Dyer's memory of a shearing 'near the woody sides / Of blue-topp'd Wreakin' (lines 626–7). Rising to the west of Telford, in Shropshire, near the north-east bank of the Severn, the Wrekin is a craggy hill, 1,300 feet high. It marks the north-eastern border of Dyer's Siluria. A modern gazetteer notes two other archetypally Dyeresque features: 'The summit commands an extensive prospect, and is occupied by ancient fortifications, called Heaven's Gate and Hell's Gate Camps.' Like Dyer, the shepherd Colin next recalls a moment of epiphany, climbing a mountain, 'Huge Breaden' (lines 654–5). And again, Breidden Hill (Welsh 'Craig-ap-Wridden') is a prominent hill, this time on the north-west bank of the Severn, to the north-east of Welshpool, in Powys. It marks the north-western border of Siluria, and again is, according to the gazetteer, 'Crowned with [an] ancient camp'.[16]

The topographic neatness, and the way in which these two hills focus a number of roles, (historical and geographical prominence, places of prospect and Silurian 'border markers') is striking. They also possess considerable connotative power in the resonances of their names. 'Wreakin' (to use Dyer's spelling) is also the name Drayton uses on the map accompanying Song XXVI to indicate the river Wreake, which flows in an appropriately Tripontian way through Leicestershire and into the Soar. That Dyer's shearing took place 'near the woody sides' of the Wrekin suggests that its massive bulk offered safety and reassurance to the shepherdly pastoral and youthful innocence which the poet offers in this section. The occasion Dyer describes is celebratory, and the Wrekin would be particularly appropriate for such an occasion. In the eighteenth century, and probably earlier, there was a local toast in the Shropshire area, invoked by George Farquhar in the 'Epistle Dedicatory' to his play *The Recruiting Officer* (1706), to 'All friends round the Wrekin'.[17]

Dyer's spelling of 'Breaden' perhaps also connotes a second mountain, Bredon Hill, situated north of Cheltenham, in Worcestershire. Though not especially high (950 feet), Bredon Hill stands strikingly clear of its mainly flat surroundings, and has, again, an iron age fort on it. It commands a view of England to the east, and Siluria and Wales to the west, and is, as the builders of its fort obviously realised, a perfect border post for the eastern flank of Siluria.[18]

Thus the poet's topography here marks the borders of the land of Siluria, using mountains which both protect and oversee. Their prospect is a double one, looking inwards with pleasure to the cherished landscape of Siluria, and outwards with excitement to the world beyond, to England, to trading lines, centres of manufacture, industry and consumption. The aesthetic is one of prominence ('huge Breaden', 'blue-topp'd Wreakin'), as the poet finds vantage points, even greater than Grongar Hill, from which he can bestride the world and give a prospect of society in terms of a vision of harmony.

One more prominence completes this pattern of prospect and enclosure. Dyer writes of the flower rituals:

> Such custom holds along th'irriguous vales,
> From Wreakin's brow to rocky Dolvoryn.   (lines 698–9)

The epithet 'irriguous vales' echoes Thomson's 'Autumn' (line 751), 'th'irriguous Vale'. The fact that this is drawn from Thomson's speculative account of the water cycle is interesting in the light of the mountain and river-lore in this passage of *The Fleece*. 'Wreakin' has been discussed: its presence is reiterated here. Dolforwyn Castle (Dyer's 'Dolvoryn') is a ruin on the west bank of the Severn, as it flows north from Newtown to Welshpool, in Powys. If we follow the Severn's arc from Dolforwyn, past

Breidden Hill, past the Wrekin (and possibly, as in the connotation I mentioned, past Bredon Hill), we can see that 'Dolvoryn' completes the pattern of Siluria's encirclement by the Severn, or rather, by the Severn's attendant landmarks.

Thus of course 'Sabrina', the spirit of the Severn, is the living heart of this topographical pattern. The ritual speech (lines 678–89, quoted above, pp. 172–3) reflects her mythology.[19] In the myth Sabrina, daughter of Locrine and granddaughter of Brute, the mythical first King of England, escapes from her vengeful stepmother Guendolen by jumping into the Severn. She thus becomes the river's presiding spirit; and the flow of the Severn represents her eternal flight.[20] The associated topography in the ritual speech places her. Plinlimmon (Welsh *Pumlumon Fawr*), the high point (2,500 feet) of the great central moorland of mid Wales, contains the head waters of numerous rivers, flowing in all directions from this central eminence, including the two rivers that enclose Siluria, the Severn and the Wye. Drayton, in Song VI, draws attention to the Bardic and Cambrian significance of Plinlimmon; it is also mentioned by John Philips in *Cyder* (1708) and is part of Gray's sublime machinery in his dramatic Cambrian ode *The Bard* (1757). Sabrina's four sisters are major rivers flowing from Plinlimmon. Vaga is the river Wye, so styled by John Philips (*Cyder*) and Pope ('Epistle to Bathurst', in relation to the 'Man of Ross'), as well as Dyer. The river Rheidol (Dyer's Ryddol) flows west, as does the more southerly Ystwith, both reaching the sea at the coastal town of Aberystwyth. The Clywedog (Dyer's Clevedoc) flows east from the Clywedog lake to the head of the Severn.[21]

Sabrina, the guardian of the Severn and of the land the Severn encloses, seeds the waters, an action imitated by the shepherds who cast flowers on the water. Both gestures make, in one sense, a kind of mime or dumb-show to represent the next stage in the fleece's progress, where the wealth of Siluria is itself floated away on the water, to distant lands. The river is appropriately allowed to complete the topographical referencing in the book, with the phrase 'Majestic wave of Severn slowly rolls' (line 716). Sabrina is at her most powerful here, as she marks out the borders of Siluria, wraps it comfortingly up and is celebrated as its life-giving maternal deity. The mood in the last section of the book is one of reverence for her power, and reassurance in the comfort of the pastoral environment she provides. How she provides it in the real, commercial, georgic world, is by carrying the 'trading bark with low contracted sail' (line 718), which stops to listen and to 'view' the paradisal scene of the shepherd's feast in the very last line of the book. The bark's real purpose, of course, is to collect the fleeces, the cider, the produce of a fertile land: and the most important function of Sabrina, the ever-fleeing, encircling river, is to bring and to take the goods that are the life-blood of Dyer's Siluria.

In the remaining books of the poem the ripples of Dyer's topography will spread wider and wider, through the different areas of Britain with their various kinds of productive activity, and ultimately out to the trade routes and the world. A kind of climax is reached in Book III, where a great cluster of Latin town and river names shows the way in which (in Dyer's own phrase) 'o'er the hospitable realm they spread' (III, line 430). What is spreading here, as it happens, is the ideal of 'golden-footed Sciences' (III, line 405), but the phrase could equally well describe the fleece's spread, the 'naval wave' (III, line 421) of seaborne trade, or indeed the network of topographical reference that Dyer uses to convey what he sees as the splendour and complexity of human productive labour.

Conclusions

Dyer embarked on the longest and last literary journey of his life determined to teach, as he put it, 'th'inactive hand to reap / Kind Nature's bounties, o'er the globe diffused' (II, lines 501–2). His major ideological tools were the rationalistic 'benevolent' Christianity he had learned with the help of John Hough, Bishop of Worcester, whose portrait he painted in 1740–1; the practical didacticism which James Mackenzie, having nursed him through his sickness and depression of 1741, encouraged him to apply to the new project; and an enduring belief, tested extensively in practice, that agricultural activity and especially shepherding were of central economic significance, and possessed important social and spiritual dimensions. He chose the best literary medium available, the Addisonian English georgic, which merged Virgilian and Miltonic traditions into a popular 'middle style', able to address most areas of human experience, and especially capable of dealing with major socioeconomic themes such as 'the care of sheep, the labours of the loom, and arts of trade', which earlier genres could only speak of in humorous or sanitised terms.

If the result has often been felt to be rather less successful than my reading of the agricultural theme would suggest, this is at least partly a trick of the light caused by subsequent events. The two great rural poems of the later eighteenth century, Oliver Goldsmith's *The Deserted Village* (1770) and George Crabbe's *The Village* (1783), dealt terrible blows to Dyer's particular form of rural idealism. What is more, they did so from within his own medium of serious, socially conscious rural poetry. Enclosure, for Dyer a great improving development (II, lines 107–33), undoubtedly became a major cause of rural depopulation, the tragedy at the heart of *The Deserted Village*. The workhouse, praised as the saviour of the poor by Dyer (III, lines 259–303), is the terrifying central image of

Crabbe's exposure of rural deprivation in *The Village*. And time has continued to chip relentlessly away at the idealism of Dyer's visionary poem.

We can fairly apply hindsight in the case of the workhouse. Dyer's language ('constraint ... compell'd ... Rigour ... detain', III, lines 234 ff.) indicates that he is aware of the compulsion of the workhouse system, and may be criticised for failing to acknowledge the implications of this compulsion. It would not, however, be at all clear in the 1750s that enclosure was to prove disastrous for the rural poor; quite the contrary. And other examples of Dyer's idealism show the dangers of applying hindsight indiscriminately. In Book II, for example, the poet celebrates a marvellous discovery: 'In Euboa's isle / A wondrous rock is found, of which are woven / Vests incombustible' (II, lines 396–8). The carcinogenic properties of asbestos have now of course been revealed to us, and the material removed from buildings and identified as a source of fear rather than wonder. But for more than two hundred years after Dyer wrote these lines few would have argued that it was anything other than a 'wondrous' substance. Similarly Dyer celebrates the draining of the fens by Lord Russell as a great progressive move (II, lines 159–83). It is just beginning to become apparent, as the peat of the fens gradually shrinks away, and green consciousness increases, that the drainage programme may have set in motion a long-term ecological disaster. If we are only just learning this, we cannot expect Dyer to treat the subject in any terms other than delight at the conquest of the unhealthiest environment in the country, and the opening up to agriculture of millions of productive acres. At the time Dyer wrote *The Fleece* arable land represented mere oases on an island dominated by scrub, heath, marshland, forest and rough grazing, a long way indeed from the neat patchwork of tilled fields and pastures we see today. The production of food had a significance and urgency we can no longer envisage in Britain. Dyer was essentially, as Wordsworth recognised, 'a tender-hearted friend of humanity', and would naturally support any development he thought would help feed the poor.[22]

The literary side of his work also raises issues of hindsight. Georgic poetry, indeed didactic poetry, is no longer written.[23] This is in some ways a pity. Dyer's handling of his agricultural theme, if we put aside modern prejudice against the genre, is often excellent. As we have seen, his agricultural observation is typically perceptive and intelligent; and he manages in most cases to make the poetry a suitable vehicle for prescriptive work, without sacrificing agricultural meaning, poetic skill, or his larger engagement with rural life and the metaphysics of shepherding. The eighteenth century in English verse was, according to T.S. Eliot, 'cursed with a Pastoral convention ... and a ruminative mind'.[24] Rereading *The Fleece* does not suggest to me that these were necessarily curses: in the right hands, indeed, they could even be blessings.

Appendix A 'Siluria'

'Siluria' is glossed by Dyer (*The Fleece*, I, line 57, n) as 'the part of England which lies west of the Severn, viz. Herefordshire, Monmouthshire, etc'; whereas Camden had included in his Siluria 'Herefordshire, Radnorshire, Brecknockshire, Monmouthshire and Glamorganshire'. Clearly the concept is a flexible one, but Dyer's Siluria seems to be trans-Severn England, and in particular, Herefordshire. In a useful short essay on the subject (in *The Dark Side of the Landscape*, p. 173 n. 99) John Barrell traces the significance of Siluria as a 'pastoral-georgic haven in a newly indus-trialised Britain', through the poetry of John Philips, William Diaper, Pope and Dyer, and even in the prose of John Duncumb, in the Board of Agriculture report on Herefordshire (1805). We can find the roots of the 'Silurian' ideal in Drayton (Song VII), Camden (p. 574) and in the writings of early travel writers like Celia Fiennes (1696), and Daniel Defoe (1724–6, vol. II, p. 448).

As this might suggest, we can trace the idea of Siluria through what we may tentatively characterise as a distinctly 'Silurian' literature. Some of its key texts have been identifed above. Such a tradition might perhaps look back to William Langland's *Piers the Plowman*, whose central matter begins 'on a morning in May, among the Malvern Hills'. It would certainly include the work of the seventeenth-century poets Thomas Traherne (born in Hereford), and Henry Vaughan (born in Brecknock) who styled himself 'The Silurist', and John Milton's *Comus* (1637), composed for a Silurian setting (Ludlow), and appropriately stocked with Silurian imagery. Apart from *The Fleece*, perhaps the most interesting eighteenth-century text is John Philips's *Cyder* (1708), a seminal celebration of Silurian pomaceous-ness. Wordsworth's 'Lines Composed above Tintern Abbey' (1798) seems to be the major Romantic Silurian text: by then, of course, the Wye Valley had become a focus for picturesque tourism, for which William Gilpin's *Observations on the River Wye* (1782) was the essential guidebook. In the Victorian period Francis Kilvert's *Diary* (written 1870–9, published 1944) is Silurian in much of its setting and content. In the modern period 'Silurian' texts would include A. E. Housman's *A Shropshire Lad* (1896), especially I, XXI, XXVIII and XXXI; and its (even darker) shadow,

Dennis Potter's *Blue Remembered Hills* (1979). Mary Webb's novels (*Gone to Earth*, 1917; *Precious Bane*, 1924) are also to the point. In different ways all these modern texts remind us that there is a dark side to Silurian pastoral: for a glimpse of that darkness in an earlier period, see Chris Fitter, 'Henry Vaughan's Landscapes of Military Occupation'. Perhaps one might conclude this brief survey with Bruce Chatwin's border novel, *On the Black Hill* (1982), whose pastoral nostalgia is finely modulated by a sense of mortality and 'Et in Arcadia Ego'.

Appendix B
Eighteenth-century sheep breeds

1 Problems of identification

Russell, p. 241, states the problem of identifying pre-improvement breeds cogently, citing four faults in modern systems, which may be summarised as follows:

i   Treating early post-improvement sources such as the Board of Agriculture reports and Youatt's *Sheep* (1837) as primary sources.
ii Lack of system or incomprehensibility.
iii Over-reliance on modern versions of early breeds.
iv Artificial classifications, not based on biology.

It is difficult to avoid all these pitfalls, though Russell's own classification steers a fairly skilful course between the Scylla of generic chaos and the Charybdis of over-simplification. For the major discussions of the problem see Robert Trow-Smith, *A History of British Livestock Husbandry to 1700*, pp. 230–2, and *A History of British Livestock Husbandry, 1700–1900*, pp. 36–41 and 121–53; Eric Kerridge, *The Agricultural Revolution*, pp. 311–16; M. L. Ryder, 'The History of Sheep Breeds in Britain', and *Sheep and Man*, pp. 484–95; N. C. Russell, 'Animal Breeding in England', pp. 242–52.

2 Evidence that Dyer's 'second sheep' is a prototype New Leicester

In addition to the evidence I cited in the text, my evidence for identifying Dyer's 'second sheep' as a prototype New Leicester is largely negative. The best model available is Russell's, pp. 242–51, who (in what for the literary critic is a pleasingly Empsonian fashion) distinguishes seven types of pre-improvement sheep, with some sub-types. Dyer's phrase 'That larger sort' rules out his Group 7 (described as 'Small'), and gravitates against (though does not exclude) his Groups 3 and 4, both described as 'Small and Middle Sized'. The phrase 'of head defenceless' (i.e. polled rather than horned) rules out his Groups 2, 3, 5 and 6 (all horned). This leaves Group 1, and, less probably, Group 4. Russell characterises Group

4 as: 'Small and Middle-sized Grey. Brown or Speckled Faced, Polled
Down of [for 'or'] Fallow sheep. These were either fine or middle woolled.'
Group 4 seems unlikely. Apart from their lack of size, it seems probable
Dyer would make some reference to pigmentation were it present, or to the
fleece shade (as he does to the 'tawny' fleece in his second example). And
while down or fallow sheep would fatten well on the south Leicestershire
pasture land Dyer is concerned with, they would not be a very appropriate
choice (see Kerridge, p. 313 for fallow sheep on pasture, and pp. 311–14
for the various agricultural roles of the pre-improvement types). Russell
locates his two sub-groups (4a and 4b) to, respectively, the chalk downs
and heaths of south and south-east England; and the 'heaths, forests and
poor arable' areas of the west Midlands. It is improbable Dyer would
recommend either for south Leicestershire pasture land.

   This leaves Group 1, described as, 'Largely unpigmented, hornless
sheep types, often with a top-knot of wool on the forehead. Fleece types
various, fine, medium or long woolled. All fleeces with a high reputation
for whiteness.' There are four sub-types in the group (a-d) corresponding
approximately to the types more commonly known, respectively, as the
Ryelands, Cotswold, Leicester/Lincolnshire and Cheviot. Russell purposely avoids these terms as tending to a fallacious confusing of pre- and
post-improvement types, and to give himself a closer generic accuracy
than these titles imply (his type 1b, for example, includes the sheep of the
Lincolnshire uplands as well as the Cotswolds). This is scrupulous, but
limits our ability to pursue in his model some of the phenotypical and
observational details Dyer gives. We need to revert to the older categories
to find descriptions of this sort, though we must keep in mind Russell's
categories and his reasons for using them. Youatt's *Sheep* (1837) is an
excellent source of information by breed and location titles ('Cotswold',
'Ryelands', etc.), although Russell warns us (p. 241) that he should be
used as a 'secondary source', being on the other side of the improvement
'divide'. In fact although Youatt uses many species titles, his major
ordering is by location, with an overall division between middle wool
(which includes what we would call short-wool) and long-wool types.
Both means of categorising are rational, though not (in Russell's phrase,
p. 242) 'biological or historical'. Youatt is scholarly, careful and historically minded (drawing on many valuable earlier sources), however; and in
what follows I shall use his descriptions, though rather cautiously.

   We may eliminate at once the Cotswold sheep (linked with the Lincolnshire upland sheep as Russell's type 1b). Youatt provides no illustration
for the breed, for as he says (p. 340) 'Very few flocks of pure Cotswolds
now exist, and these are rapidly diminishing.' By 1837 the Cotswold had
become so heavily infused with New Leicester genes as to be unrecognisa-
ble in terms of the old breed. He describes the 'unimproved' Cotswolds as

'taller and longer than the improved breed, comparatively flat-sided, deficient in the fore-quarter, but full in the hind-quarter; not fattening so early, but yielding a longer and heavier fleece' (p. 340). Kerridge (p. 312) adds: 'Old Cotswolds were small-faced, white-skinned and polled, with long, spare, big-boned frames, long necks, square bulks and broad buttocks.' The 'deficient fore-quarter' of Youatt's description is not compatible with Dyer's 'breast and shoulders broad'; nor is Kerridge's description of the head and frame.

Youatt's description of the Ryelands (pp. 258–61; Russell's type 1a) is slightly unsatisfactory, as he does not make it clear whether it is a of a pre- or post-improvement sheep; though it is clear that, like the Cotswold, the breed had been thoroughly infused with New Leicester genes. However, Dyer cannot be describing it here: it is 'small' and 'round', and judging by the illustration Youatt provides (p. 261) could not be said to have a 'stretch'd head'.

In the case of the Cheviot (Russell's type 1d), Youatt clearly distinguishes pre- and post-improvement types, drawing on an earlier account by Sir John Sinclair (1792) for the pre-improvement description. It has much in common with Dyer's description. What eliminates this sheep is its long-leggedness (noted by Sinclair), and its lack of 'depth in chest', noted as a pre-improvement feature by George Culley (both sources as cited by Youatt, pp. 285–6). This defect, as Youatt records, was remedied by crossing with the New Leicester.

Finally, we have Russell's type 1c, the 'Lowland Pasture Longwools'. Conversion into breed names is more complex here, as Russell includes in this type the 'Pasture sheep of the Midland counties' and the 'Marsh sheep of Lincolnshire' (p. 244), and locates them to Lincolnshire, Yorkshire, Durham, Northumberland, Leicestershire, Rutland, Northamptonshire, Cambridge, Warwickshire, Oxfordshire, Somerset, Devon and the East of Kent (the North and West Midlands, Teeswater and Durham are also mentioned). Their 'epicentre', so to speak, is Leicestershire and Lincolnshire. It would be tedious to rehearse here each of the sheep Youatt finds in these areas (though I have checked and eliminated them all to my own satisfaction). Russell is clearly referring to what Youatt (p. 341) calls 'The Midland Long-woolled Sheep', specifically the 'Old Leicesters' and 'The Lincoln Sheep'; the descendants of the 'pasture sheep' that Lord Ernle (*English Farming*, 1961, pp. 138–9) quotes a sixteenth-century source as locating to 'all Leicestershire, Buckinghamshire, and part of Nottinghamshire'; and a comparison with these types will be adequate. The Old Leicester was, writes Youatt:

large, heavy, coarse-woolled [with] a white face, no horns – it was long and thin in the carcass, flat-sided, with large bones – thick, rough, and white legs ... It was covered with wool from 10 to 14 or 15 inches in length, coarse in quality, and weighing from 8 to 13 lbs. The pelt and offal were thick and coarse; the animal, a slow feeder, and the flesh was coarse-grained, and with little flavour.   (p. 313)

This is nothing like Dyer's straight-backed, compact-shaped ram. Of the Lincolnshire long-woolled sheep it is sufficient to note that Ellis, writing in 1749 (cited by Youatt, p. 331), finds it the 'longest legged and largest carcassed sheep of all others'. Dyer's ram is indeed a 'larger sort' but it is 'short-limb'd', and while 'long' and 'short' are relative terms, 'longest' is clearly not compatible with 'short'.

The positive evidence for Dyer's 'second sheep' being a prototype new Leicester is largely visual. Descriptions of the New Leicester are many and detailed. Marshall describes the Ewe as follows:

The head long, small, and hornless, with ears somewhat long, and standing backward, and with the nose shooting forward. The neck thin, and clean toward the head; but taking a conical form; standing low, and enlarging every way at the base; the forend, altogether, short. The bosom broad, with the shoulders, ribs, and chine extraordinarily full. The loin broad, and the back level. The haunches comparatively full toward the hips, but light downward; being altogether small, in proportion to the fore parts. The legs, at present, of a moderate length; with the bone extremely fine. The bone, throughout, remarkably light. The carcase, when fully fat, takes a remarkable form: much wider than it is deep; and almost as broad as it is long. Full on the shoulder, widest on the ribs, narrowing with a regular curve towards the tail; approaching the form of the Turtle, nearer than any other animal I can call to mind. The pelt thin, and the tail small. The wool, shorter than long wools in general; but much longer than the middle wools; the ordinary length of staple, five to seven inches: varying much in fineness and weight.

(*The Rural Economy of the Midland Counties*, 1790, vol. I, pp. 388–9)

Every major feature the poet describes is confirmed here, apart from the legs, which Marshall describes as 'of moderate length' rather than 'short'. However a later note by Marshall (p. 409, n) says 'the legs of the improved breed have been considerably lengthened, since their first stage of improvement'. It seems likely, therefore, that Dyer saw the creature at the 'first stage of improvement'. All other accounts of the sheep I have seen confirm Dyer's accuracy. See, for example, Youatt (p. 110) and J. Mac-Donald, quoted by James Burnley (*The History of Wool*, p. 16).

3 The date of the breeding revolution

Major earlier agrarian historians, such as Lord Ernle (*English Farming, Past and Present*), J. A. S. Watson and M. E. Hobbs (*Great Farmers*) and H. C. Pawson (*Robert Bakewell*), make no reference to any predecessor to Bakewell in the invention of the New Leicester; but Kerridge (pp. 322–3), and Russell (pp. 290–4) argue that the new breed had a much earlier and more widespread ancestry. *DNB*, 'Bakewell'; Youatt (p. 315, n); and

Pawson (p. 18) all give 1760 as the year the New Leicester was made public. Youatt (p. 316, n) dates the beginning of Bakewell's most successful ram-hiring to 1780, though other sources put this earlier. William Marshall quotes Pitt's Leicestershire (1807) as saying that 'the enterprize among breeders remains undiminished' (*The Review and Abstract*, vol. IV, p, 234). By 1837 Youatt records that the New Leicesters:

have within little more than half a century spread themselves from their native county over every part of the United Kingdom, and are now exported in great numbers to the continents of Europe and America. Such, indeed, have proved to be their merits, that at the present day there are very few flocks of long-woolled sheep existing in England, Scotland, or Ireland, which are not to some degree descended from the flock of Mr Bakewell. (p. 318)

Notes

Note: the full titles of all works cited are given in the Select bibliography below.

Introduction

1 James Thomson, 'Winter' (1746 version, lines 389–413). See also Keith Thomas, *Man and the Natural World*, p. 273.
2 Unsigned 'Introductory Note' in John Gay, *The Shepherd's Week. In Six Pastorals* [facsimile edition, 1969, unnumbered page].
3 Defoe, vol. II, p. 659; John Latimer, *Annals of Bristol in the Eighteenth Century*, as cited in E. H. W. Meyerstein, *A Life of Thomas Chatterton*, p. 15.
4 Raymond Williams, *The Country and the City*; John Barrell, *The Idea of Landscape*, *The Dark Side of the Landscape*, *English Literature in History*, 'The Golden Age of Labour', *Poetry, Language and Politics*, and 'Sportive Labour'.
5 James Turner, *The Politics of Landscape*, p. 185.
6 William Wordsworth, Preface to *Lyrical Ballads*, p. 245.
7 David Nokes, *Raillery and Rage*, p. 122.
8 For English didactic verse to 1650 see Dwight L. Durling, *Georgic Tradition*, pp. 3–19; Anthony Low, *The Georgic Revolution*.
9 Dwight L. Durling, *Georgic Tradition*, p. 19.
10 Margaret Anne Doody, *The Daring Muse*, p. 67.
11 For some indication of the range in subject matter of the English georgic see Dwight Durling, *Georgic Tradition*, pp. 59–121.
12 For eighteenth-century developments in the pastoral eclogue see Harold Mantz, 'Non-Dramatic Pastoral in Europe in the Eighteenth Century'; Richard F. Jones, 'Eclogue Types in English Poetry of the Eighteenth Century'; A. J. Sambrook, 'An Essay on Eighteenth Century Pastoral'; Nigel Wood, 'Collins and the End of Shepherd Pastoral'. On eighteenth-century topographical poetry see Robert A. Aubin, 'Materials for a Study of the Influence of Cooper's Hill', and *Topographical Poetry in XVIII-Century England*; John Wilson Foster, 'A Redefinition of Topographical Poetry', and 'The Measure of Paradise'. The essential study of eighteenth-century Horatian poetry remains Maren-Sofie Röstvig, *The Happy Man*.
13 Reuben A. Brower, *The Poetry of Allusion*, p. 48.
14 On the eighteenth-century georgic see also John Chalker, *The English Georgic*; Paul H. Johnson, 'Turnips and Romanticism'; Clark Emery, 'The Poet and the Plough'; Bonamy Dobree, 'The Theme of Patriotism'; Earl R. Wasserman, *The Subtler Language*; Ivanka Kovacevic, 'The Mechanical Muse'; O. H. K. Spate, 'The Muse of Mercantilism'; Richard Feingold, *Nature and Society*; A. D.

Harvey, 'First Public Reactions to the Industrial Revolution'; John Barrell, *The Dark Side of the Landscape*.

1 Thomson, Duck, Collier and rural realism

1 *Swift-Wogan*, July–2 August 1732; *Swift-Pope*, 30 August 1716.
2 Introduction to James Thomson, *The Seasons*, ed. James Sambrook, pp. xvii–xxxiv, xxiv.
3 Samuel Johnson, *The Lives of the English Poets*, vol. III, p. 299.
4 Stephen Duck, *Poems on Several Occasions*, Introduction by John Lucas, p. xv.
5 John Barrell and John Bull (eds.), *The Penguin Book of English Pastoral Verse*, pp. 377ff.
6 William Diaper, 'Brent', line 71, in *The Complete Works of William Diaper*; 'No chearful Sound diverts our list'ning Ear' (1736). Duck might have seen an early broadside version of 'Brent', published in Bury St Edmunds in 1720 as *Lincolnshire*. Other possible influences include Thomas Richards's *Hogland* (1728). This was a translation of the same author's *Hoglandiae Descriptio* (London, 1709), and was reprinted in 1738 as *A Satyr on Lincolnshire*. Rather less obscurely, the antipastorals of Swift and Gay could perhaps have been influential.
7 ''Tis all a gloomy, melancholy Scene' (1736).
8 Mary Collier, *Poems on Several Occasions*, p. iv.
9 Rayner Unwin, *The Rural Muse*, pp. 62–3; Alan Warner, 'Stephen Duck', 41–2; H. Gustav Klaus, *The Literature of Labour*, p. 13; Donna Landry, 'The Resignation of Mary Collier', pp. 114–15, and *The Muses of Resistance*, pp. 68–9; Morag Shiach, *Discourse on Popular Culture*, pp. 41–3; Ralph Cohen, 'Notes on the Teaching of Eighteenth-Century Poetry of Natural Description'; John Barrell, 'Sportive Labour', pp. 116–19; Richard Greene, *Mary Leapor*, chapter 3.
10 For inter-influence between Thomson and Duck, see below, chapters 4–5; for Thomson's influence on other self-taught poets see Rayner Unwin, *The Rural Muse*, pp. 37–46.
11 Mary Collier, 'Remarks of the Authors Life', and 'Elegy upon Stephen Duck' in *Poems* (1762). Roger Lonsdale (ed.), *Eighteenth Century Women Poets*, p. 171, dates Mary Collier's birth to *c.* 1690.
12 See John Barrell, *The Dark Side of the Landscape*, pp. 6–7, 9–11. For some broadly similar conclusions about seventeenth-century poetry see James Turner, *The Politics of Landscape*, p. 165, and Keith Thomas, *Man and the Natural World*, pp. 250–2.
13 Rayner Unwin, *The Rural Muse*, pp. 62–3, Alan Warner, 'Stephen Duck', 41–4; H. Gustav Klaus, *The Literature of Labour*, p. 15; Donna Landry, *The Muses of Resistance*, pp. 61–9; John Barrell, 'Sportive Labour', pp. 118–20; Moira Ferguson (ed.) *The Thresher's Labour*, pp. iii–x; E. P. Thompson and Marian Sugden (eds.), *The Thresher's Labour and The Woman's Labour*, pp. viii–xii. See also P. M. Ashraf, *Introduction to Working Class Literature in Great Britain*, vol. I, pp. 30–2; H. Gustav Klaus, 'Stephen Duck und Mary Collier'; Morag Shiach, *Discourse on Popular Culture*, pp. 51–3; John Goodridge, 'Some Predecessors of Clare'.

14 James M. Osborne, 'Spence, Natural Genius and Pope', pp. 128; Stephen Duck, 'An Account of the Author' and 'On Poverty', in *Poems* (1736), pp. xv and 5–9.
15 Mary Collier, *Poems* (1762), pp. [iii]–v.
16 'And to the Hedge they soon for shelter run' (1736).
17 'There silent sit, and All at once is hush' (1736).
18 Joseph Addison, *The Spectator*, no. 160 (3 September 1711), no. 62 (11 May 1711), no. 303 (16 February 1712), in *Critical Essays from the Spectator*, ed. Donald S. Bond, pp. 251, 16, 95.
19 I have restored the first edition italicisation of '*Cocks in equal Rows*', which is designed to focus the phrase as an accusing echo of Duck's lines (the editors have put this in Roman).
20 See Keith Thomas, *Man and the Natural World*, pp. 286 and 397 n. 88. For more on Shenstone's aesthetics see 'A Description of the Leasowes' in *The Works of Shenstone*, vol. II, pp. 287–320.
21 Pat Rogers, *Hacks and Dunces*, p. 6.
22 E. P. Thompson and Marian Sugden (eds.), *The Thresher's Labour and The Woman's Labour*, p. ix.

2 Initiations and peak times

1 *TE*, vol. I, pp. 74, 63, 25.
2 Robert Bloomfield, *The Farmer's Boy*, 'Summer', p. 34; James Thomson, 'A Hymn on the Seasons', line 2 in *The Seasons*.
3 The changes to this passage in 1736 are substantial: Duck omits the couplet about rent, changes the threshers to reapers and classicises extensively:

> SOON as the golden Harvest quits the Plain
> And CERES' Gifts reward the Farmer's Pain;
> What Corn each Sheaf will yield, intent to hear,
> And guess from thence the Profits of the Year,
> He calls his Reapers forth.   (1736, p. 11)

4 'As he directs, to distant Barns we go' (1736).
5 Raymond Williams, *The Country and the City*, p. 133.
6 1762 has 'chairing', probably a variant spelling, though it is not listed as such in *OED*.
7 Alan Warner, 'Stephen Duck', p. 42; James Thomson, *The Seasons*, ed. James Sambrook, p. 345 n. 361.
8 John Barrell, 'Sportive Labour', p. 114.
9 See for example, the range of responses to haymaking extracted in Neil Philip (ed.), *Between Earth and Sky*, pp. 142–7; and (for the pains and pleasures of communal work in another kind of harvest), Gilda O'Neill, *Pull No More Bines*. M. K. Ashby evokes the mixed feelings of Victorian fields workers towards haymaking and harvest, when she writes: 'How few now know what it was ninety years ago to get in a harvest! Though the disinherited had no great part in the fruits, still they shared in the achievement, the deep involvement and the

joy of it.' See *Joseph Ashby of Tysoe*, chapter 3. See also E. P. Thompson, *Customs in Common*, p. 361.

10 In *Agrarian History*, vol. V, part i, p. 42; J. C. Morton (ed.), *A Cyclopaedia of Agriculture*, vol. II, p. 15.

11 Andrew Marvell, *Selected Poems*, p. 101 and note.

12 'The Bottle and the Beer are both too small' (1736).

13 Neil Philip, *Between Earth and Sky*, no. 179, quotes a nineteenth-century female farm worker, who says 'When a lot of women get together it's the pleasantest, for then there's company; but often we work alone – yesterday I was in this field alone, hoeing, from eight till five, all day.'

14 Donna Landry, *The Muses of Resistance*, p. 63.

15 'each Mower takes his proper Place' (1736).

16 'the Work they mind' (1762).

17 J. C. Morton, (ed.) *A Cyclopaedia of Agriculture*, vol. II, p. 16.

18 R. Bradley, *Farmer's Monthly Directory*, pp. 51–4.

19 John Barrell, 'Sportive Labour', p. 117.

20 See *The Letters of Robert Burns*, vol. I, p. 137, letter 125, undated; *The Poems and Songs of Robert Burns*, vol. I, p. 3, no. 1 and vol. III, p. 1003 n. 1.

21 David Daiches, *Robert Burns*, p. 288; *OED*, 'haymaker', def. 3.

22 Henry Stephen, *The Book of the Farm*.

23 Richard Jefferies records that 'Large numbers of women still work in the hayfield, but they are not used in gangs so much as formerly.' See *The Toilers of the Field*, p. 87.

24 I necessarily summarise and generalise about haymaking and harvesting here, and it is an article of faith in modern agrarian history that local variations are as important as general practices. I have drawn on many sources, of which the following are the most important: Thomas Tusser, *Five Hundred Points of Good Husbandry*; R. Bradley, *Farmer's Monthly Directory*, pp. 51–4, 80–1; J. C. Morton (ed.), *A Cyclopaedia of Agriculture*; Lord Ernle (R. E. Prothero), *English Farming*, pp. 360–1; George Ewart Evans, *Ask the Fellows Who Cut the Hay*, pp. 85–97; Thomas Hennell, *The Old Farm*, pp. 101–21, 136–42; G. E. Fussell, *The Farmer's Tools*, pp. 115–51; *Agrarian History*, vols. IV, V, part i, V, part ii, and VI; Michael Roberts, 'Sickles and Scythes', 3–28.

25 'And view the various Scenes its Beauties yield' (1736). Mary Collier echoes the phrase Duck uses here, 'where-e'er our Course we bend', in her description of gleaning, p. 19.

26 Flora Thompson, *Lark Rise to Candleford*, p. 234.

27 For 'John Barleycorn' see, for example, Alfred Williams, *Folk Songs of the Upper Thames*, p. 246. For the killing of the corn king see J. G. Frazer, *The Golden Bough*, pp. 560–7.

28 Thomas Tusser, *Five Hundred Points of Good Husbandry*, p. 122; George Ewart Evans, *Ask the Fellows Who Cut the Hay*, p. 91.

29 Flora Thompson, *Lark Rise to Candleford*, p. 235.

30 George Ewart Evans, *Ask the Fellows Who Cut the Hay*, pp. 86–7.

31 Thomas Hennell, *The Old Farm*, pp. 114–5. *OED* ('Harvest', sb. 7. special combinations) gives 'Harvest rig', Scotland, as: (a) a ridge, rig, or 'land' of a harvest field, between two furrows; the harvest field so divided; and (b) the

couple, man and woman, who reap together during the harvest, cutting a 'rig' conjointly. See also 'Hairst', *The Scottish National Dictionary*, ed. William Grant and David D. Murison, vol. V, pp. 2–3.

32 Artist unknown, *c.* 1730, Cheltenham Art Gallery, described as 'British Provincial School, Eighteenth Century'. An apparent companion piece, *Dixton Manor*, also *c.* 1730, is in the same gallery. Together the two paintings give a panoramic view of trans-Severn Gloucestershire in the haymaking and sheep-shearing season. The painting is discussed by John Barrell in 'Sportive Labour', pp. 110–12, and (without being identified) by Quentin Seddon in *The Silent Revolution*, p. 25.

33 John Barrell, 'Sportive Labour', pp. 114–15; see also p. 105 and the argument developed in the early part of his essay.

34 James Thomson, *The Seasons*, ed. James Sambrook, p. 335 n. 830–2.

35 Thomas Hennell, *The Old Farm*, p. 114.

36 'uncloath the Mead' (1736); Donna Landry, *The Muses of Resistance*, p. 295 n. 14.

37 See *OED*, Supplement, 'spend', sb. 2; 'spend' v. II. 15. c; Rochester, 'The Imperfect Enjoyment' (1680): 'In liquid raptures I dissolve all o'er, / Melt into sperm, and spend at every pore', in *The Complete Poems Of John Wilmot, Earl of Rochester*, p. 38.

38 In an interview on 'Woman's Hour', BBC Radio 4, 11 April 1990. See also Whitney Chadwick, *Women, Art and Society*; Rozsika Parker and Griselda Pollock, *Old Mistresses*, pp. 163–4.

39 'Weary indeed! but 'tis not worth our while' (1762).

40 Donna Landry, *The Muses of Resistance*, p. 57; Mary Collier, *Poems on Several Occasions*, p. v.

3 Three types of labour

1 George Ewart Evans, *Ask the Fellows Who Cut the Hay*, p. 96.

2 'Soon as the golden Harvest quits the Plain' (1736).

3 'Yet little Time' (1736).

4 Donna Landry, The *Muses of Resistance*, p. 68. See also her entry for Mary Collier in Janet Todd (ed.), *Dictionary of British Women Writers*.

5 1736 has a number of variant lines: 'The Voice is lost, drown'd by the louder Flail', 'Our Eye beholds no pleasing Object here', 'No chearful Sound diverts our list'ning Ear', 'Inspir'd with all the Beauties of the Spring', ''Tis all a gloomy melancholy Scene'.

6 George Ewart Evans, *Ask the Fellows Who Cut the Hay*, chapters 1–3. Compare W.H. Hudson, *A Shepherd's Life*; Sheila Stewart, *Lifting the Latch*. There are also some good seventeenth-century sources, of which perhaps the most interesting is: Henry Best, *Rural Economy in Yorkshire*, ed. Charles Best Robinson (Durham, 1857). See Robert Trow-Smith, *A History of British Livestock Husbandry to 1700*, pp. 241–50, for more on these sources.

7 Samuel Law, *A Domestic Winter-Piece*. Law is mentioned by E. P. Thompson in *The Making of the English Working Class*, p. 324, and is the subject of an interesting historical poem by David Crabtree, 'A Secret: Four Images'.

8 'At proper Distance, Front to Front we stand'; 'That once secure, we swiftly whirl them round' (1736).

9 Alistair Elliot (ed.), *Virgil's Georgics*, pp. 150–1, Virgil, Book IV, lines 170 ff., Dryden lines 245 ff.

10 George Ewart Evans, *Ask the Fellows Who Cut the Hay*, pp. 96–7.

11 Stephen Duck, 'Description of a Journey', *Poems on Several Occasions*, pp. 207, 212. Between his meeting with the queen in 1730 and his suicide in 1756 Duck was successively made a Yeoman of the Guard (1733), Librarian of 'Merlin's Cave' in Richmond Park and 'Governor of Duck Island in St James's Park' (1735: the latter presumably a Duck-joke at the poet's expense rather than a real job), a Regimental Chaplain (1746), Preacher at Kew Chapel (1751) and rector of Byfleet (1752). See Rose Mary Davis, *Stephen Duck*, pp. 33–8, 67, 69–74, 99–101, 104.

12 See John Barrell, 'The Golden Age of Labour'.

13 William Cowper, *The Task*, Book I, pp. 19–20. See also John Constable's painting *Flailing Turnip-heads*, c. 1812–15, reproduced in Leslie Parris and Ian Fleming-Williams, *Constable*, Plate 38 and pp. 106–7.

14 John Clare, *Autobiographical Writings*, p. 3.

15 George Ewart Evans, *Ask the Fellows Who Cut the Hay*, p. 96.

16 In E. P. Thompson and Marian Sugden (eds.), *The Thresher's Labour and The Woman's Labour*, pp. xi–xii.

17 Eric Kerridge, *Textile Manufactures*, p. 204.

18 See Neil McKendrick, John Brewer and J. H. Plumb, *The Birth of a Consumer Society*, pp. 34–99.

19 See John Smith, *Chronicum Rusticum*; Eric Kerridge, *Textile Manufactures*, p. 122.

20 Apart from the obvious words 'Bees' and 'Hive' the verbal echoes between Collier's four-line simile of bees, and Mandeville's *Fable* and its accompanying material are as follows, where (C) = Collier, and (M) = Mandeville: (C) Gains, (M) gain (p. 66); (C) hourly, (M) Two hours (p. 74); (C) industrious, (M) Industry (p. 63); (C) Pains, (M) Pains (p. 75); (C) poorly, (M) Poor / The Poor (pp. 67, 69, 72); (C) do hourly strive, (M) daily forc'd (p. 73); (C) reap the Gains, (M) reap the Fruits (p. 86); (C) sordid Owners, (M) sordid Selfishness (p. 83). Other verbal similarities between the two texts include: (C) Drudgery (p. 15), (M) these Holy Drudges (p. 66); (C) for Slavery design'd (p. 15) / Their Slaves (p. 17), (M) Slaves (p. 63) / slaved (p. 66); (C) show'rs of gold (p. 16), (M) bribed with Gold (p. 67) / Cloth of gold (p. 74) / Golden Dream (p. 152). See Bernard Mandeville, *The Fable of the Bees*; E. P. Thompson and Marian Sugden (eds.), *The Thresher's Labour and The Woman's Labour*, pp. xiii, 24.

21 Collier's sources for the Danaus and Danae stories are not known; however, both appear in the third book of Horace's *Odes* (numbers xi and xiv). Apart from Richard Bentley's edition of Horace (1711), translations and imitations were fairly common in the period.

22 See Alistair Elliot (ed.), *Virgil's Georgics*, p. 148 ff., Virgil IV, lines 149 ff., Dryden lines 220 ff; George Ewart Evans, *The Pattern Under the Plough*, pp. 97–103; Flora Thompson, *Lark Rise to Candleford*, pp. 82–3, 87; Iona Opie and Moira Tatem (eds.), *A Dictionary of Superstitions*, pp. 17–20. See also

T. Sharper Knowlson, *The Origins of Popular Superstitions*, pp. 207–10; Arthur Robinson Wright, *British Calendar Customs*, vol. I, p. 81; Stith Thompson, *Motif-Index of Folk-Literature*, vol. II, D1441.2; vol. III, G225.1; Index 'Bees'.

23 Moira Ferguson (ed.), *The Thresher's Labour*, p. viii; M. Dorothy George, *London Life in the Eighteenth Century*, p. 207.

24 Printed in *Eighteenth-Century Women Poets*, no. 202.

25 Moira Ferguson (ed.), *The Thresher's Labour*, p. iii; Donna Landry, *The Muses of Resistance*, p. 63; E. P. Thompson and Marian Sugden (eds.), *The Thresher's Labour and The Woman's Labour*, p. x.

26 It should be noted that the sheep-shearing (lines 371–422) and the patriotic exclamation (lines 423–31) were both added to the poem in 1744.

27 For Kings and Queens of Harvest see J. G. Frazer, *The Golden Bough*, pp. 542–607; *OED* 'Corn' sb. IV. attrib. and Comb. 11 Special combinations: 'corn-mother', 'corn-queen', 'corn spirit'; 'Harvest' sb. 3. b. Proverbs and phrases. Lady of the Harvest (a); 'Harvest Queen' (b). For election of 'Captains' see Thomas Tusser, *Five Hundred Points of Good Husbandry*, pp. 122, 303; Flora Thompson, *Lark Rise to Candleford*, p. 235; George Ewart Evans, *Ask the Fellows Who Cut the Hay*, pp. 45, 90–1; Thomas Hennell, *The Old Farm*, p. 107 ff; *OED* 'Harvest' sb. 3.b. Proverbs and phrases. Lord of the harvest (b), Lady of the Harvest (b); 'Harvest'. 7. special combinations. harvest-lady and harvest-lord; 'Harvest Queen' (c).

28 Apart from this and other examples discussed in the text we find cloying mawkishness in the interaction of Shepherd and Milkmaid ('Summer', lines 1664–70), in the 'snatchd' kissing of the 'sidelong Maid' ('Winter', line 625), and in Thomson's two appeals to the 'British Fair' ('May their tender Limbs / Float in the loose Simplicity of Dress!') in 'Autumn', lines 570–609 and 'Summer', lines 1580–94.

29 Eric Rothstein, 'Discordia Non Concors', notes ambivalences in attitudes to bloodsports among georgic writers, from Sir John Denham's *Cooper's Hill* through to the Romantics. Other important poetry sources include Pope's *Windsor Forest*, lines 123–34, *TE*, vol. I, p. 162; *An Essay on Man*, Epistle III, lines 27–70, *TE*, vol. III, part i, pp. 95–9; William Somerville, *The Chace*; John Armstrong, *The Art of Preserving Health*, Book I, lines 206–10; William Cowper, *The Task* (1785), Book VI, lines 231 ff; and John Clare's poetry, especially 'To the Snipe' and 'The Badger'. For the wider context see Keith Thomas, *Man and the Natural World*.

30 For some points of comparison, see the literary shearing feasts portrayed in John Dyer's *The Fleece*, Book I, lines 625–720 (discussed in Part II, below); Shakespeare, *The Winter's Tale*, IV, iii, 31 ff and IV, iv; and Thomas Hardy, *Far From the Madding Crowd*, chapters 22–3.

4 Compensations

1 As well as being a way of supplementing income, and (in pastoral) a signifier of autumnal richness, nutting had important folkloric connotations, particular related to divination and sexuality. Compare John Philips, *Cyder*, Book II, lines 46 ff; John Gay, 'Thursday or the Spell', in *The Shepherd's Week*; William Wordsworth, 'Nutting' in *Wordsworth and Coleridge, Lyrical Ballads*; John Keats,

'To Autumn'; John Clare, 'Nutting' in *Selected Poetry*, p. 7. See also John Brand, *Observations on Popular Antiquities*, pp. 192, 207; George Deacon, *John Clare and the Folk Tradition*, pp. 285, 289n; *Agrarian History*, vol. V, part i, p. 108; Iona Opie and Moira Tatem (eds.) *A Dictionary of Superstitions*, p. 289.

2 *The Idylls of Theocritus*, p. 36.

3 Joseph Addison, 'An Essay on Virgil's *Georgics*'.

4 Compare Miriam Allott's annotation to the second stanza of 'To Autumn'. Allott suggests parallels with paintings by Poussin and Guilio Romano, and with W. Hamilton's engraving of the *Reaper's Repose*, printed in the 1807 edition of Thomson's *Seasons*. See John Keats, *Poems*, p. 652.

5 E. P. Thompson and Marian Sugden (eds.), *The Thresher's Labour and The Woman's Labour*, p. 29.

6 James Thomson, *The Seasons*, p. 380, n1232–4. For a suggested chronology and means by which Thomson could have borrowed from *The Thresher's Labour* for 'Autumn', see chapter 5.

7 E. P. Thompson and Marian Sugden (eds.), *The Thresher's Labour and The Woman's Labour*, p. 29. All the sources I have checked confirm a strict separation of harvesting and gleaning in the cornfield. See for example Thomas Tusser, *Five Hundred Points of Good Husbandry*, p. 124; Thomas Hennell, *The Old Farm*, p. 133; Flora Thompson, *Lark Rise to Candleford*, p. 28; George Ewart Evans, *Ask the Fellows Who Cut the Hay*, p. 98 ff.; see also my discussion of male/female pairs, chapter 2, above.

8 John Barrell also notes this influence, and his comparative discussion of the two texts is useful and astute: see 'Sportive Labour', pp. 117–19.

9 R. W. Malcolmson, *Life and Labour in England*, p. 166 n. 30.

10 *OED* does not help much with this, which is part of a larger problem of identifying classes and social roles in *The Seasons*. It defines 'Husbandman' (1) as 'A man who tills or cultivates the soil; a farmer'. This could include anyone who actually works the land, be they employer or employee. John Barrell, 'Sportive Labour', p. 118, considers that by husbandman Thomson means 'farmworker', here and elsewhere.

11 William Cobbett, *Rural Rides*, vol. I, p. 94.

12 John Barrell, *The Dark Side of the Landscape*, p. 2.

13 The first two lines, containing the charitable appeal, are not present in the 1730 version (pp. 10–11), some of the other lines have been reordered, and there are a number of minor alterations. The 1730 text is:

Each Morn we early rise, go late to bed,	1
And lab'ring hard, a painful life we lead.	2
For Toils, scarce ever ceasing, press us now,	3
Rest never does, but on the Sabbath show,	4
And barely that, our Master will allow.	5
Nor when asleep are we secure from Pain;	6
We then perform our Labours o'er again;	7
Our mimic Fancy always restless seems,	8
And what we act awake, she acts in Dreams.	9
Hard Fate! Our Labours ev'n in Sleep don't cease;	10
Scarce *Hercules* e'er felt such Toils as these.	11

The 1736 text, quoted in the text, has the two new lines, followed by 3, 4, 5, 2, 1, 6, 7, 8, 9, 10, 11.

14 E. P. Thompson and Marian Sugden (eds.), *The Thresher's Labour and The Woman's Labour*, p. xiii. For Morland see John Barrell, *The Dark Side of the Landscape*, pp. 89–129.

5 Homecomings

1 Sappho, *Poems and Fragments*, no. 110.

2 John Barrell, *The Dark Side of the Landscape*, pp. 66–77.

3 'Homewards we move, but spent so much with Toil' ; 'We slowly walk, and rest at ev'ry Stile'; 'Got to the Door, soon eye us in the Way'; 'And out we set again, our Work to try' (1736).

4 The words 'dumpling' and 'bacon' are italicised in 1739, as echoes of Duck. 'Weary, indeed! but 'tis not worth our while'; 'We find again our Work but just begun' (1762). 'Froward' means refractory, perverse, unreasonable: see *OED*, 'froward', a., adv., prep., 1 and 2.

5 Thomas Hennell, *The Old Farm*, p. 134.

6 See, for example, Michael Roberts, 'Sickles and Scythes', 9.

7 Sheila Rowbotham, *Woman's Consciousness, Man's World*, p. 67.

8 'The sweat, the Dust, and suffocating Smoak' (1736).

9 David Dabydeen, *Hogarth's Blacks*, pp. 17–40.

10 'When angry Masters view the blotted Book' (1736).

11 James Thomson, *The Seasons*, ed. James Sambrook, p. 380 n. 1232–4.

12 In E. P. Thompson and Marian Sugden (eds.), *The Thresher's Labour and The Woman's Labour*, p. ii.

13 For evidence of this and other interactions between Thomson and Duck see Rose Mary Davis, *Stephen Duck*, pp. 32–5, 40 and 131; 81; 97; 153; Stephen Duck, 'A Description of a Journey To Marlborough, Bath, Portsmouth, &c', in his *Poems on Several Occasions*, pp. 213–14; Douglas Grant, *James Thomson*, pp. 175–6; James Thomson, *The Seasons*, ed. James Sambrook, p. xlvi ff. See also my discussion of gleaning in chapter 4, above.

14 See Robert Graves, *The Greek Myths*, vol. I, pp. 216–20. Both Duck and Collier use the spelling 'Sysiphus', though Duck corrects this to 'Sisyphus' in 1736.

15 See Robert Graves, *The Greek Myths*, vol. I, pp. 238, 200–5, 352–5, and *The White Goddess*, pp. 64, 67, 129.

16 Donna Landry, 'The Resignation of Mary Collier', p. 114, revised in her *The Muses of Resistance*, p. 69. Landry changes her phrase 'self-regarding sympathetic pastoralism' (1987) to 'olympian pastoralism' (1990), which seems to me rather less incisive.

17 See Keith Thomas, *Man and the Natural World*, pp. 111 and 117; John Brand, *Observations on Popular Antiquities*, pp. 686–7; Flora Thompson, *Lark Rise to Candleford*, p. 153; Iona Opie and Moira Tatem (eds.), *A Dictionary of Superstitions*, pp. 328–30.

18 See Raymond Williams, *The Country and the City*, p. 18. Roger Lonsdale's thorough gloss to the parallel scene in Gray's *Elegy* tells us all we need to know about its precedents. See Roger Lonsdale (ed.), *The Poems of Gray, Collins and Goldsmith*, p. 121 n. 21–4.

19 As my reading ascribes fundamental significance to the 'death of the swain' passage, I should note that it first appeared in the 1730 version of the poem. My reading of *Winter* (1726) would be in this respect a very different one from my reading of *The Seasons* (1730).
20 R. S. White, *Innocent Victims*, p. 1.
21 George Crabbe, *The Village*, Book I, line 5; James Thomson, 'Hymn to the Seasons', line 2, in *The Seasons*.
22 Stephen Duck, *Poems on Several Occasions*, p. vii.
23 For the history of workplace and proletarian poetry see especially Robert Southey, *The Lives and Works of Our Uneducated Poets*; Rayner Unwin, *The Rural Muse*; P. M. Ashraf, *Introduction to Working Class Literature in Great Britain*; Brian Maidment (ed.), *The Poorhouse Fugitives*; Donna Landry, *The Muses of Resistance*; John Goodridge (ed.), *The Independent Spirit*.
24 Tillie Olsen, *Silences*.
25 Childbirth, poverty, gin-drinking, overwork, poor working conditions, small-pox and other diseases combined to make working-class women exceptionally vulnerable to premature death. See R. W. Malcolmson, *Life and Labour in England*, pp. 60–1, 70–1, 76–7, 154–7; M. Dorothy George, *London Life in the Eighteenth Century*, pp. 35–115, 173–4.
26 Susan Griffin, *Made From this Earth*, p. 197.

6 Sheep and poetry

1 Michael Stapleton, *The Cambridge Guide to English Literature* (Cambridge, 1983), p. 265; J. A. Cuddon, *A Dictionary of Literary Terms* (Harmondsworth, 1977), p. 751 ('Vulgarity'); Emile Legouis and Louis Cazamian, *A History of English Literature* (London, 1930), p. 850; Revd E. Cobham Brewer, *The Reader's Handbook* (London, 1898) ('Fleece'); Leslie Stephen, 'John Dyer', *DNB*.
2 For the problem of editions see Textual Note, p. xiv, above.
3 See Penny Boumelha, 'John Dyer, 1699–1758', p. 341.
4 This was first included in Johnson's edition (1779–81), and reprinted in all subsequent editions to carry a portrait until the Wilmott edition of 1855, which finally got the right Dyer in the form of a print loosely based on the poet's self-portrait. The self-portrait itself is printed in Ralph M. Williams, *Poet, Painter and Parson*, and Belinda Humfrey, *John Dyer*.
5 Ralph M. Williams, *Poet, Painter and Parson*, p. 139; Belinda Humfrey, *John Dyer*, p. 97.
6 Laurence Goldstein, *Ruins and Empire*, pp. 25–58; Richard Feingold, *Nature and Society*, pp. 1–17 and 83–119; John Barrell, *English Literature in History*, pp. 90–109. See also Dwight L. Durling, *Georgic Tradition*, pp. 73–5; Bonamy Dobree, 'The Theme of Patriotism'; O. H. K. Spate, 'The Muse of Mercantilism'; John Chalker, *The English Georgic*, pp. 51–5; John Barrell, *The Idea of Landscape*, pp. 12–13, 34–6; Raymond Williams, *The Country and the City*, pp. 69, 125; John Barrell, *The Dark Side of the Landscape*, p. 173 n. 99; Belinda Humfrey, *John Dyer*, pp. 77–104; John Lucas, *England and Englishness*, pp. 38–9, 42, 66–7; Ferdinand Mount, 'Commentary: On Grongar Hill Now'.

7 A few factual corrections to Goldstein's fine essay should be made. He says that 'No anecdotes of Dyer's childhood exist' (p. 25). The manuscript of Dyer's autobiographical 'Journal of Escapes' is lost, but the following interesting childhood entries are quoted in W. H. D. Longstaffe, 'Notes respecting the life and family of John Dyer the Poet', 264:

1704. Fell, when a child, into a tub of scalding wort.
1704. Fell on a case-knife, which wanting a handle, was stuck upright in the ground, and which went deep into my throat, but missed the windpipe.
1709. Fell into a well. – Job's Well, Carm'thens.
1714. Ran from school and my father, on a box of the ear being given me. Strolled for three or four days – found at Windsor, &c.

Goldstein uses Fausset's faulty text (1930), and so repeats Fausset's mistake of 'Dream not', for 'Deem not' (line 670, quoted on p. 55). On the same page he says that 'the shepherd leads his flock from tedded hay or marsh grass'. Dyer in fact advises the shepherd to do the opposite (see lines 259–60).

8 See Boris Ford (ed.), *The Pelican Guide to English Literature 4*, p. 87.
9 J. G. E. Davies, 'An Edition of the Poetical Works of John Dyer', p. 210, following the collations made by Dyer's descendant W.H.D. Longstaffe from (now lost) manuscripts, has:

> Whom public Voice to the great Charge assigns,
> Or Lot of Birth! ye Good of all Degrees,
> Parties and Sects! be present to my Song.   (lines 5–7)

The Wilmott edition of 1855, p. 43, footnotes this variant, with 'choice' for 'Voice', citing *Dyer-Dodsley*, 12 May 1757: but as published in *GM* (1835), 47, the word given in *Dyer-Dodsley* is 'voice'.

10 John Sitter, *Literary Loneliness*.
11 Percy Bysshe Shelley, from *A Defence of Poetry* (1821), extracted in *Percy Bysshe Shelley: Selected Poetry and Prose*, pp. 485–6.
12 Keith Thomas, *Man and the Natural World*, p. 286.
13 For the agricultural revolution see also William Marshall, *The Rural Economy of the Midland Counties*, and *The Review and Abstract*; J. A. S. Watson and M. E. Hobbs, *Great Farmers*; Robert Trow-Smith, *A History of British Livestock Husbandry to 1700*, and *A History of British Livestock Husbandry, 1700–1900*; Eric Kerridge, *The Agricultural Revolution*; A. H. John, 'The Course of Agricultural Change'; E. L. Jones, 'Agricultural Origins of Industry'; N. C. Russell, 'Animal Breeding in England'; *Agrarian History*, vol. V, part ii, pp. 533–89, and vol. VI, pp. 314–35; J. V. Beckett, *The Agricultural Revolution*. See also the next two notes.
14 For these changes see John Smith, *Chronicum Rusticum*; William Youatt, *Sheep*, especially pp. 71, 192–227; Edward Baines, *The Woollen Manufacture of England*; James Burnley, *The History of Wool*; Herbert Heaton, *The Yorkshire Woollen and Worsted Industries*, especially pp. 251–8; Ephraim Lipson, *The History of the Woollen and Worsted Industries*, especially. pp. 215–17; R. M. Hartwell, 'A Revolution in the Character and Destiny of British Wool'; G. D. Ramsay, *The English Woollen Industry*; Eric Kerridge, *Textile Manufactures*.

15 William Youatt, *Sheep*, p. 314; J. D. Chambers and G. E. Mingay, *The Agricultural Revolution*, p. 33; R. M. Hartwell, 'A Revolution in the Character and Destiny of British Wool', p. 328; G. E. Mingay, *The Agricultural Revolution*, p. 29; M. L. Ryder, *Sheep and Man*, p. 486; Keith Thomas, *Man and the Natural World*, p. 26; *Agrarian History*, vol. VI, p. 314.

16 For the pastoral farming of south and east Leicestershire see Defoe, vol. II, p. 488; William Marshall, *The Rural Economy of the Midland Counties*, vol. I, and *The Review and Abstract*, vol. IV, pp. 188–93, 232–9; G. E. Fussell, 'Four Centuries of Leicester Farming'; H. C. Pawson, *Robert Bakewell*, pp. 18–24; Eric Kerridge, *The Agricultural Revolution*, pp. 109–12; *Agrarian History*, vol. V., part i, pp. 89–128.

17 William Marshall, *The Rural Economy of the Midland Counties*, vol. I, p. 295. On pre-Bakewell Leicestershire breeders see also Eric Kerridge, *The Agricultural Revolution*, pp. 318–23; N. C. Russell, 'Animal Breeding in England', pp. 290–4.

18 For Dyer as a farmer see Edward A. Parker and Ralph M. Williams, 'John Dyer, the Poet, as Farmer'; Ralph M. Williams, *Poet, Painter and Parson*, pp. 85–90, 99–100, 102, 117; Belinda Humfrey, *John Dyer*, pp. 61–2, 74–5. For his Leicestershire years see Ralph M. Williams, *Poet, Painter and Parson*, pp. 114–24. Dyer glosses 'Tripontian fields' as 'The country between Rugby in Warwickshire and Lutterworth in Leicestershire'. I have not found any other poets using the term 'Tripontium': Camden, p. 430, mentions it, but locates it at Torcester (now Towcester, in Northamptonshire, some twenty-five miles south of Dyer's 'Tripontian fields'). Drayton, as he travels south-west past Leicester, notes the area's agricultural richness and the meeting of routes: see Song XXVI, lines 37–43.

19 See Eric Kerridge, *Textile Manufactures*; G. D. Ramsay, *The English Woollen Industry*.

20 For the Cotswold and Ryelands sheep and their traditions see Camden, p. 238; Drayton, Song XIV, lines 250–278; Defoe, vol. II, pp. 430–1; William Youatt, *Sheep*, pp. 258–61, 338–41; David Low, *The Breeds of Domestic Animals*, pp. 47–8, 65–6, and Plates XIII and XVIII; J. C. Morton (ed.), *A Cyclopaedia of Agriculture*, vol. II, pp. 282–3, 836; Lord Ernle (R. E. Prothero), *English Farming*, p. 98; John Wrightson, *Livestock Handbooks No. 1*, pp. 29–33, 43–7; Robert Trow-Smith, *A History of British Livestock Husbandry to 1700*, pp. 162–6, 207–8; Ralph Whitlock, *A Short History of Farming in Britain*, pp. 133, 135; Edith Brill, *Life and Tradition on the Cotswolds*, pp. 108–18; H. P. R. Finberg, *The Gloucestershire Landscape*, pp. 57–8, 123; N. C. Russell, 'Animal Breeding in England', pp. 243–4; M. L. Ryder, *Sheep and Man*, pp. 460, 464–5, 469, 487; J. B. Skinner, D. E. Lord, and J. M. Williams (eds.), *British Sheep and Wool*, p. 83.

21 For Dyer's years as an itinerant painter see Ralph M. Williams, *Poet, Painter and Parson*, pp. 81–3; Belinda Humfrey, *John Dyer*, pp. 159–60, 62. Dyer's only direct statement on the matter (cited by Humfrey, p. 47) is: 'After having been an itinerant painter in my native country (S. Wales) and in Herefordshire, Worcestershire, &c. &c. I married, and settled in Leicestershire.'

22 For 'Siluria' see Appendix A.

7 'Soil and clime'

1 *OED* cites the line 'Long rains in miry winter cause the halt' from *The Fleece* under its definitions of 'halt' (sb. 2, 2): the citation should be to I, 456 rather than '56'.

2 On sheep diseases see William Youatt, *Sheep*, pp. 361–556; J. C. Morton, *A Cyclopaedia of Agriculture*, vol. II, pp. 842–53; *Ministry of Agriculture, Sheep Breeding*, pp. 50–4, 57–8; Robert Trow-Smith, *A History of British Livestock Husbandry, 1700–1900*, pp. 40–1, 212–13; 322–3; W. B. Martin, *Diseases of Sheep*; *Agrarian History*, vol. VI, pp. 358–60.

3 A. R. Clapham, T. G. Tutin, and E. F. Warburg, *Excursion Flora of the British Isles*, pp. 25, 147, 152; W. J. Stokoe, *The Observer's Book of Trees*, p. 146.

4 J. G. E. Davies, 'An Edition of the Poetical Works of John Dyer', p. 212, following the collations made by Dyer's descendant W. H. D. Longstaffe from (now lost) manuscripts, has:

> Where moss-grey Stonehenge, lonely-solemn, nods,
> Ruin of Ages; such the matted Leas
> And ruddy tilth.   (lines 48–50)

As Davies notes, p. 356n, *Dyer-Dodsley*, 12 May 1757, gives two alternatives to the lines that were printed: this one, and: 'Where solitary Stonehenge, solemn, nods'. Dyer added in the letter, 'Grey with moss is not so poetical'. The Wilmott edition (1855), p. 44 n. 4, notes the proposals but maintains the original lines.

5 Lord Ernle (R. E. Prothero), *English Farming*, p. 178; *TE*, vol. IV, p. 67; Defoe, vol. I, p. 159.

6 Defoe, vol. I, p. 188; Camden, p. 43; Drayton, Song II, line 19.

7 There are several other verbal similarities between Dyer's lines and *King Lear*: compare e.g. *King Lear*, IV.i.72, IV.vi.1–24 and 57.

8 See for example, Drayton, Song III, lines 41–65; John Dryden, 'To My Honour'd Friend, Dr Charlton', in *The Poems and Fables of John Dryden*, p. 32; Thomas Chatterton, 'Battle of Hastings [No. 1]', lines 301–2, 'Battle of Hastings [No. 2]', lines 541–50, in his *Poems*, pp. 224, 264–5; William Wordsworth, *The Salisbury Plain Poems*. See also Francis Celoria, 'Chatterton, Wordsworth and Stonehenge', 103–4; Stephen Gill, *William Wordsworth*, pp. 75 and 439 n. 27.

9 *DNB*, 'Sir Gilbert Heathcote'; Vicary Gibbs *et al.* (eds.), *The Complete Peerage* (new edition, thirteen volumes, London, 1910–59), 'Ancaster', 'Aveland'; Peter Townend (ed.), *Burke's Complete Peerage and Baronetage* (105th edition, London, 1970), pp. 72–5 ('Ancaster'), pp. 1302–5 ('Heathcote'), pp. 1709–11 ('Mackworth'); *Bartholemew's Gazetteer of the British Isles* (ninth edition, Edinburgh, 1970), p. 512 ('Normanton'); Nikolaus Pevsner, *Leicestershire and Rutland*, p. 311; G. E. Mingay, *English Landed Society*, pp. 11, 238; *TE*, vol. III, part ii, p. 99, 98n; *TE*, vol. IV, pp. 181–2, 365.

10 The sources do not date Sir John's death, but his wife died in 1772. (They married in 1720.)

11 G. E. Mingay, *English Landed Society*, p. 11; *Agrarian History*, vol. V, part ii, p. 238; Nikolaus Pevsner, *Leicestershire and Rutland*, p. 311.

12 William Gilpin, *Observations on the River Wye*, p. 6. For Urchinfield see Camden, p. 573 ff. ('Herefordshire'), and map between pp. 572 and 573; H. J. Massingham, *The Southern Marches*, pp. 170–87 ('Archenfield').

13 *TE*, vol. III, part ii, p. 113–15; John Barrell, *The Dark Side of the Landscape*, p. 173 n. 99; William Gilpin, *Observations on the River Wye*, p. 6. See also H. J. Massingham, *The Southern Marches*, pp. 267–70; *DNB*, 'John Kyrle (1637–1724)'. For the commercial aspect of Ross see Defoe, vol. II, p. 450; *Agrarian History*, vol. V, part ii, p. 345.

14 In *The Old Straight Track*. Alfred Watkins finds many ley lines, alignments and sighted tracks in Siluria and the Welsh Marches. For Leominster see Camden, p. 577; Drayton, Song VII, lines 151–60; Defoe, vol. II, pp. 447–8; H. J. Massingham, *The Southern Marches*, pp. 231–5.

15 Dyer's note on 'Croft' (1757) is 'a seat of Sir Archer Croft'. Dyer's brother-in-law Sir Archer Croft, the Second Baronet (1683–1753), was MP for Leominster (1722–7), later for Winchelsea and then Deeralston. His eldest son the Third Baronet (also Sir Archer Croft) assumed the title in 1753. See Edward A. Parker, 'A Study of John Dyer', pp. 27, 64; Ralph M. Williams, *Poet, Painter and Parson*, pp. 82 n. 3; H. J. Massingham, *The Southern Marches*, pp. 239–44; Peter Townend (ed.), *Burke's Complete Peerage and Baronetage*, pp. 686 ff. ('Croft of Croft Castle'); *Who's Who* (129th edition, London, 1977).

16 *Agrarian History*, vol. V, part ii, p. 133; E.S. Roscoe, *Robert Harley*, p. 6.

17 *DNB*, 'Edward Harley (1689–1741)'; Brian W. Hill, *Robert Harley*, p. 226.

18 Linda Colley, *In Defiance of Oligarchy*, p. 72. See also Linda Colley, 'The Loyal Brotherhood and the Cocoa Tree'. For more on the Yorke family see Philip C. Yorke, *The Life and Correspondence of Philip Yorke*.

19 Dyer's note on 'Eywood' (1757) is 'of the Earl of Oxford'. For the Harley/Oxford family and their Herefordshire seats see also *DNB*, 'Sir Edward Harley, 1624–1700', 'Sir Edward Harley, 1664–1735', 'Edward Harley, Second Earl of Oxford', 'Robert Harley, First Earl of Oxford'; Vicary Gibbs, *Complete Peerage* ('Oxford and Mortimer'); Ralph M. Williams, *Poet, Painter and Parson*, p. 82, n3; Peter Townend (ed.), *Burke's Landed Gentry* (eighteenth edition, three volumes, London, 1965–72), vol. II, p. 287 ff. ('Harley of Brampton Bryan').

20 Dyer's note on 'Shobden' (1757) is 'of Lord Bateman'. For Bateman and Shobden see Linda Colley, *In Defiance of Oligarchy*, pp. 127–8; Vicary Gibbs, *Complete Peerage* ('Bateman', 'Bateman of Shobden'); H. J. Massingham, *The Southern Marches*, pp. 235–6; Ralph M. Williams, *Poet, Painter and Parson*, pp. 40 n. 20, 82 n. 3; Belinda Humfrey, *John Dyer*, p. 15.

21 Here the Edward Thomas edition incorporates one of Dyer's amendments, to line 72. J. G. E. Davies, 'An Edition of the Poetical Works of John Dyer', p. 213, following Longstaffe's collations, has: 'Or Depth of heavy Marl, be then thy choice', where the original 1757 line had been: 'Or Marl with Clay deep mix'd'.

22 See especially Dyer's passage on weather (lines 125–84), and Thomson's two passages on the 'water cycle' ('Autumn', lines 736–835; 'Winter', lines 993–1023).

23 Line 89 incorporates another of Dyer's amendments from *Dyer-Dodsley*, 12 May 1757. J. G. E. Davies, 'An Edition of the Poetical Works of John Dyer',

p. 213, also has the new line; but the Wilmott edition (1855), p. 45, keeps the original, which is: 'At a meet distance from the upland ridge'.

24 My claim for Dyer's accuracy here is based on my own observation of sheep, confirmed by discussion with shepherds.

25 Eric Kerridge, *The Agricultural Revolution*, p. 37.

26 *Ibid*. See also J. C. Morton, *A Cyclopaedia of Agriculture*, vol. I, pp. 668–710 ('Drainage'), pp. 836–62 ('Fences').

27 Dyer glosses 'Dimetians' as 'Dimetia, Caermarthanshire in South Wales'. The contents page of Camden lists the 'Dimetae' counties as 'Caermarthanshire, Penbrokshire, and Cardiganshire'.

28 Eric Kerridge, *The Agricultural Revolution*, p. 155.

29 Belinda Humfrey, *John Dyer*, p. 85. In Book III (lines 436–45) Dyer writes more gently and autobiographically of:

> that soft track
> Of Cambria deep embay'd, Dimetian land,
> By green hills fenc'd, by ocean's murmur lull'd,
> Nurse of the rustic bard who now resounds
> The fortunes of the Fleece.

30 Alistair Elliot (ed.), *Virgil's Georgics*, pp. 148–9, Virgil, lines 121–48, Dryden lines 186–219.

31 Thomas G. Rosenmeyer, *The Green Cabinet*, p. 20.

32 Keith Thomas, *Man and the Natural World*, p. 196; *OED*, 'thorn', sb., IV. 8. attrib. and Comb. A. Attributive, 'thorn-set'; *OED*, 'mound' sb. 3. 1; Virgil, *Eclogues*, translated by John Dryden (1697), no. x, line 83, in *The Poems of John Dryden*, vol. II, pp. 909–12.

33 For eighteenth-century developments in fertilisers see Eric Kerridge, *The Agricultural Revolution*, pp. 240–50.

34 Compare *OED*, 'Cake', sb. 1. b and c; E. P. Thompson and Marian Sugden (eds.), *The Thresher's Labour and The Woman's Labour*, pp. 7, 17.

35 For later interest in transhumance and the Merino see Arthur Young (ed.), *The Annals of Agriculture*, vol. XXXIII, pp. 154–68; Robert Trow-Smith, *A History of British Livestock Husbandry 1700–1900*, pp. 151–3.

36 See John Smith, *Chronicum Rusticum*, vol. I, pp. 250–1, 330; vol. II, pp. 322, 422, 427, 436, 437n; Dyer's Notebooks, as cited in Edward A. Parker, 'A Study of John Dyer', p. 138. See also Herbert Heaton, *The Yorkshire Woollen and Worsted Industries*, pp. 192–4, 249–51; Ephraim Lipson, *The History of the Woollen and Worsted Industries*, pp. 24–5, 87–95; *Agrarian History*, vol. V, part ii, pp. 363–6.

37 John Chalker, *The English Georgic*, pp. 51–5.

38 For a range of comparable English anti-French cultural statements (on food, clothing, education, sexuality, manliness and social behaviour) see Shakespeare, *Henry V*, I, i, 111–14; *The Poems of John Dryden*, vol. III, pp. 1019, 1048; Jonathan Swift, *Irish Tracts 1728–1733*, ed. Herbert Davis (Oxford, 1964), p. 50; John Arbuthnot and Alexander Pope, *Memoirs of the Extraordinary Life*, p. 106; *The Tatler*, ed. Donald F. Bond (three volumes, Oxford, 1988), vol. II, p. 360; *The Prose Works of Alexander Pope: II. The Major Works 1725–1744*, ed. Rosemary Cowler (Oxford, 1986), p. 454; Alexander Pope, *Brutus*, Lib. 2, as

printed in Friedrich Brie, 'Pope's Brutus', *Anglia*, 63 (1939), 150; *Montagu-Pope*, October 1718, in *The Correspondence of Alexander Pope*, ed. George Sherburn (five volumes, Oxford, 1956), vol. I, pp. 519–21; Henry Fielding, *The History of Tom Jones* (1749), Book 12, chapter 14 (where 'a certain nation' is France); John Gay, *Poetry and Prose*, ed. Vinton A. Dearing and Charles E. Beckwith (Oxford, 1974), vol. I, pp. 208–14; Samuel Johnson, *London*. The contemporary equivalent is the anti-French, anti-EC campaigns whipped up by the *Sun* newspaper in the 1980s, epitomised in the slogans: 'Hop off, you Frogs', and 'Up yours, Delors'. I am grateful to Carolyn Williams for many of the earlier citations given here.

39 J. B. Skinner, D. E. Lord and J. M. Williams (eds.), *British Sheep and Wool*, p. 9.
40 *Agrarian History*, vol. VI, p. 314; J. D. Chambers and G. E. Mingay, *The Agricultural Revolution*, p. 199.

8 Environment and heredity

1 Cowper-Unwin, 11 September 1784, as cited by Robert Inglesfield in his Introduction to *The Task*, (facsimile edition, unnumbered page).
2 For Dyer as an advocate of enclosure see Book II, lines 107–33. For mountain sheep management in eighteenth-century Wales see M. L. Ryder, *Sheep and Man*, p. 501. H. C. Pawson, *Robert Bakewell*, p. 79, notes that 'Bakewell, was, of course, concerned with lowland and not hill sheep.'
3 N. C. Russell, 'Animal Breeding in England', p. 279.
4 R. M. Hartwell, 'A Revolution in the Character and Destiny of British Wool', p. 325.
5 Eric Kerridge, *The Agricultural Revolution*, p. 315; N. C. Russell, 'Animal Breeding in England', pp. 247, 250 (types 2 and 4b); M. L. Ryder, *Sheep and Man*, p. 460.
6 Drayton, Song XXVI, lines 397–538; Defoe, vol. II, p. 564 ff. See also P. N. Hartle, 'Defoe and *The Wonders of the Peake*'.
7 *Kilvert's Diary*, p. 10.
8 Robert Trow-Smith, *A History of British Livestock Husbandry to 1700*, pp. 231–2; N. C. Russell, 'Animal Breeding in England', pp. 242–52. See also Appendix B, above.
9 See Defoe, vol. II, pp. 487–9, 502, 547–51; William Cobbett, *Rural Rides*, vol. II, pp. 662–3.
10 As cited in William Marshall, *The Review and Abstract*, vol. IV, pp. 188–9; J. T. Coppock, *An Agricultural Atlas*, p. 178. See also G. E. Fussell, 'Four Centuries of Leicestershire Farming'.
11 See *Agrarian History*, vol. V, part i, pp. 93–4; William Marshall, *The Rural Economy of the Midland Counties*, vol. I, pp. 188–96; 268–92; John Monk, *General View of the Agriculture of the County of Leicester*, pp. 8–9; William Marshall, *The Review and Abstract*, vol. IV, pp. 198–9; H. C. Pawson, *Robert Bakewell*, pp. 18–19; Eric Kerridge, *The Agricultural Revolution*, pp. 91–113; *Geological Survey Ten Mile Map (South Sheet)*.
12 *Dyer-Dodsley*, 12 May 1757, *GM* (1835), 47. One is reminded of Gray's complaint that 'Nurse Dodsley' had given his *Elegy* 'a pinch or two in the

cradle' (*Gray-Walpole* dated Ash Wednesday, 1751). See also Richard Wendorf, 'Robert Dodsley as Editor'.

13 Eric Kerridge, *The Agricultural Revolution*, p. 319; N. C. Russell, 'Animal Breeding in England', pp. 280, 391 n. 100.

14 N. C. Russell, 'Animal Breeding in England', p. 279. For cotting see William Youatt, *Sheep*, pp. 338, 259–60; Eric Kerridge, *The Agricultural Revolution*, pp. 67, 147, 149, 312; M. C. Ryder, *Sheep and Man*, p. 498; OED, 'cot' v. 1. 2.

15 N. C. Russell, 'Animal Breeding in England', p. 298.

16 For the status of the 'arguments' see W. H. D. Longstaffe, 'Notes respecting John Dyer the Poet', 221; *The Poetical Works of Mark Akenside and John Dyer*, p. 42.

17 William Youatt, *Sheep*, p. 313; John Barrell, *English Literature in History*, p. 94.

18 William Youatt, *Sheep*, p. 110; David Low, *The Breeds of Domestic Animals of the British Isles*; H. C. Pawson, *Robert Bakewell*, opp. p. 33. Detailed evidence of identification is set out in Appendix B, above. Of the other breeds illustrated by Youatt, only the Southdown (p. 233) and the Cheviot (p. 284) lack a pronounced curve to their backs; but these are not as level as the New Leicester's back.

19 See *Agrarian History*, vol. VI, p. 317, and Appendix B, above.

20 Ralph M. Williams, *Poet, Painter and Parson*, p. 122. The passage under discussion could conceivably have been added later.

21 William Marshall, *The Rural Economy of the Midland Counties*, vol. I, p. 295; Eric Kerridge, *The Agricultural Revolution*, pp. 318–23; N. C. Russell, 'Animal Breeding in England', pp. 277–81, 290–2, 391 n. 101. For Bakewell's father see H. C. Pawson, *Robert Bakewell*, pp. 14–18. The stock-moving and breeding activity of 1747 is recorded by William Pitt in his report of 1809: see William Marshall, *The Review and Abstract*, IV, p. 232. See also Appendix B, above.

22 'Commercial Map', fo. 28. Dyer's descriptions of Paul's two inventions have been used by the following textile historians: Herbert Heaton, *The Yorkshire Woollen and Worsted Industries*, pp. 324, 331–2, 339–40, 342, 355–6; Ephraim Lipson, *The History of the Woollen and Worsted Industries*, pp. 92, 129, 133, 137, 140, 147–8, 180, 182; Walter English, *The Textile Industry*, pp. 1, 40, 99; and 'A Technical Assessment', 80–2; Edward Baines, *The Woollen Manufacture of England*, p. 58 n. 28; Eric Kerridge, *Textile Manufactures*, pp. 150–1, 159, 170, and various notes. See also Ivanka Kovacevic, 'The Mechanical Muse', 270–1, and *Fact into Fiction*, p. 21.

23 For enclosure see Book II, lines 107–33. For fen drainage see Book II, lines 159–83. For canals see Book III, lines 602–32; 'Commercial Map', fos. 20b, 37–42; Edward A. Parker, 'A Study of John Dyer', pp. 126–7. For maps and cartography see 'Commercial Map', fo. 30 (reproduced by Parker, p. 121b), Belinda Humfrey, *John Dyer*, pp. 89–90; Ralph M. Williams, *Poet, Painter and Parson*, pp. 98–101.

24 Keith Thomas, *Man and the Natural World*, p. 173.

25 *Ibid.*, p. 60. For Bakewell's 'in-and-in' breeding methods see N. C. Russell, 'Animal Breeding in England', pp. 285–7, and the Bakewell-Culley letters printed by H. C. Pawson in his *Robert Bakewell*, for example *Bakewell-Culley*, 8 Feb 1787, 2 May 1787, 30 June 1787.

26 *OED* defines 'frontlet' (2) as 'forehead', citing, *inter alia*, the usage under discussion.

27 The other references to the 'Silurian' sheep and wool are at lines 492–4; Book II, lines 370–2, and Book IV, lines 181–2.

28 See Eric Kerridge, *The Agricultural Revolution*, pp. 67, 147, 52.

29 N. C. Russell, 'Animal Breeding in England', pp. 255–60.

30 John Barrell, *English Literature in History*, p. 94.

31 *Ibid.*, p. 95.

32 For an appropriately lyrical summary of this network of mythology see H. J. Massingham, *The Southern Marches*, pp. 56, 231.

33 W. H. D. Longstaffe, 'Notes respecting John Dyer the Poet', vol. 5, 221.

34 According to Ernle, 'The points which [Bakewell] wished to develop and perpetuate were beauty combined with utility of form', *English Farming*, pp. 179, 185. For Uvedale Price's (equally aesthetic) rejection of Bakewellian 'beauty', see Keith Thomas, *Man and the Natural World*, pp. 285–6. Thomas also marshalls interesting evidence of a much wider tendency towards aesthetic and other non-rational interests in the colour, shape and general 'meaning' of domestic animals (pp. 70–77).

35 Virgil advises the wool-growing shepherd to reject a ram if even his tongue is marked, for fear of spotted fleeces. M. L. Ryder explains: 'Wild sheep, and many primitive domestic breeds, are coloured; but most modern breeds are white, at any rate in the main fleece area. Apart from not being wanted in white garments, pigment interferes with dyeing; and the desire to eliminate naturally coloured wool fibres from fleeces may have begun with the discovery of dyeing.' See Alistair Elliot (ed.), *Virgil's Georgics*, pp. 124 ff., Virgil, III, line 384 ff., Dryden line 590 ff.; M. L. Ryder, *Sheep and Man*, p. 45.

36 William Youatt, *Sheep*, p. 338.

37 For further information on this story and the other traditions discussed by Youatt, see John Smith, *Chronicum Rusticum*, vol. I, pp. 60–78. Smith dismisses the story in a magisterial footnote (pp. 69-70), concluding that far from taking our fine wool, 'Spain and Portugal were anciently famous for Sheep and Wool, and the former for fine Cloth, before the English knew what it was to be cloathed.'

9 The care of sheep

1 William Youatt, *Sheep*, p. 389n.

2 Thomas Chatterton, *Poems*, p. 222, line 260. For uses of 'purple' in eighteenth-century and earlier literature see John Arthos, *The Language of Natural Description*, pp. 280–1.

3 J. G. E. Davies, 'An Edition of the Poetical Works of John Dyer', p. 357n, notes a line in the collations made by Dyer's descendant W. H. D. Longstaffe from (now lost) manuscripts, in place of line 252: 'Where ling'ring waters rankle not the turf'. Edward A. Parker, 'A Study of John Dyer', p. 165, describes the same line as being deleted in the MS, before line 252.

4 For liver-rot or liver fluke, and the history of knowledge about it see William Youatt, *Sheep*, pp. 445–63; Robert Trow-Smith, *A History of British Livestock Husbandry, 1700–1900*, pp. 40, 213; W. B. Martin (ed.), *Diseases of Sheep*, pp. 62–70.

5 See for example *Ministry of Agriculture, Sheep Breeding*, pp. 50, 53.

6 William Youatt, *Sheep*, pp. 456–9.

7 For foot-rot, scab ('psoroptic mange'), foot-bathing and dipping see W. B. Martin (ed.), *Diseases of Sheep*, pp. 98–103, 181–5; *Ministry of Agriculture, Sheep Breeding*, pp. 62–3; *OED* 'Alum' 1., 'Stavesacre', 'Verdigris' 1., 'Vitriol' 1.

8 See, for example, Thomas Tusser, *Five Hundred Points of Good Husbandry*, p. 33; *British National Formulary*, pp. 450–1 (Index, 'Coal Tar').

9 Marjorie Hope Nicholson and G. S. Rousseau, 'Bishop Berkeley and Tar-Water'.

10 See entries for Mackenzie in *DNB*; R. W. Innes Smith, *English-Speaking Students of Medicine*; P. J. and R. V. Wallis, *Eighteenth Century Medics*. See also J. G. E. Davies, 'An Edition of the Poetical Works of John Dyer', pp. 163, 201, 434.

11 Robert Graves, *The White Goddess*, p. 9.

12 *OED* defines 'Crowflower' as a 'popular name for the buttercup', though single usages for the ragged robin and bluebell are also cited, as (without citations) are local usages for marsh-marigold (*Caltha palustris*) and wood cranesbill (*Geranium sylvaticum*). The likeliest candidate seems to be the buttercup, the commonest meadow flower of these, and the most usual meaning for the word. See *OED*, 'buttercup' 2, 'butterflower' 1, 'crowflower', 'crowfoot' 1–2; A. R. Clapham, T. G. Tutin, and E. F. Warburg, *Excursion Flora*, pp. 33–4; J. R. Press, D. A. Sutton and B. R. Tebbs, *Field Guide*, pp. 21–2.

13 Anecdotal information on the 'ivy' remedy was given to me by a shepherd. For information on the digestive system of sheep see M. L. Ryder, *Sheep and Man*, pp. 8–10. The concern in the early modern period about the dangers of poisoning, especially from the more poisonous members of the ranunculus family, is reflected by a long note on corn-crowfoot poisoning in William Youatt, *Sheep*, p. 432.

14 For examples of eighteenth century shepherd's calendars see R. Bradley, *Farmer's Monthly Director*; William Ellis, *The Modern Husbandman*. Shepherding advice still tends to include a 'calendar' of the annual tasks, starting in autumn: see, for example, Derek Goodwin, *Sheep Management*, pp. 75–102.

15 For 'making up the flock' (that is, checking the condition of each animal, and culling as necessary) see *Ibid.*, p. 75.

16 Thomas Tusser, *Five Hundred Points of Good Husbandry*, pp. 33, 104. Tusser's eighteenth-century editor Hillman (1710), quoted on p. 104, recommends the application of tar and tobacco-water for the problem.

17 *Notes and Queries*, fourth series, vol. VII (1871), 443–4.

18 M. L. Ryder, *Sheep and Man*, pp. 165–7. Dyer glosses 'Brigantes' (line 368) as 'The inhabitants of Yorkshire'. He seems to have had a special interest in the area: see the description of Sheffield at lines 556–60; also Book III, lines 259–347, and the 'Commercial Map' (fo. 46). Herbert Heaton, *The Yorkshire Woollen and Worsted Industries*, p. 355, considers that Dyer 'certainly knew Yorkshire very well'. For the origin of the Romano-British term 'Brigantes' see I. A. Richmond, *Roman and Native*; Keith Branigan (ed.), *Rome and the Brigantes*. Camden uses the term to cover Yorkshire, Durham, Lancashire, Westmorland, Cumberland and 'Picts-Wall' (see Camden, contents page).

19 Quoted in Leslie Parris and Ian Fleming-Williams, *Constable*, p. 302.

20 J. G. E. Davies, 'An Edition of the Poetical Works of John Dyer', p. 436.

21 See Roger Lonsdale (ed.), *The Poems of Gray, Collins and Goldsmith*, pp. 110–11, 142. There is a possible problem of chronology, in that Dyer took a manuscript of *The Fleece* to London in the summer of 1750, some months before the *Elegy* was published. For these to be genuine echoes he must either have seen the *Elegy* in manuscript, or revised the relevant passages after 1750. Both are possible, though no evidence for either has come to light.

22 See Matthew 14, 15–21; Mark 8, 1–9; Luke 9, 12–17; John 11, 1–46. For the fable of the lost sheep see Luke 15, 4–6.

23 Quentin Seddon, *The Silent Revolution*, pp. 115–16.

24 See *DNB*, 'Joseph Nutt (1700–1775)'.

25 Lucretius, *On the Nature of the Universe*, pp. 27–8, 21.

26 Joseph Addison, 'An Essay on Virgil's *Georgics*', p. 2.

27 See Boris Ford (ed.), *The Pelican Guide to English Literature 4*, p. 129.

28 *Ministry of Agriculture, Sheep Breeding*, p. 53.

29 A modern writer, Frederick Raphael, also uses 'busy mouths' as an appropriate phrase to describe animals eating, in a short story about a young boy: 'The next day he played as usual in Central Park. Red squirrels abounded in urgent stillness when he threw peanuts. They handed them to themselves with busy mouths.' See 'Transatlantic Blues', *The Listener*, 124, no. 3172 (5 July 1990), 20.

30 James Sutherland, *A Preface to Eighteenth Century Poetry*, p. 139.

31 See Defoe, vol. I, p. 58; W. E. Minchinton (ed.), *Essays in Agrarian History*, vol. I, pp. 141–6 and 223–53.

32 For Dyer's interest in ruins see his earlier poem *The Ruins of Rome* (1740); for volcanoes see the list of volcanoes in the 'Commercial Map', fo. 29v.

10 The shepherd's harvest

1 Dyer glosses 'the sounding caves / Of high Brigantium' as 'The forges of Sheffield in Yorkshire where the shepherds' shears and all edge-tools are made'.

2 For the wider context of this aesthetic, see Francis D. Klingender, *Art and the Industrial Revolution*; Ivanka Kovacevic, *Fact into Fiction*.

3 W. J. Stokoe, *The Observer's Book of Trees*, pp. 83–5; Robert Graves, *The White Goddess*, chapter 2, p. 40; A. R. Clapham, T. G. Tutin and E. F. Warburg, *Excursion Flora*, pp. 369, 398, 34; Geoffrey Chaucer, *Complete Works*, p. 483; Arabella Boxer and Philippa Back, *The Herb Book*, p. 39; J. R. Press, D. A. Sutton, and B. R. Tebbs, *Field Guide*, pp. 330, 21–2.

4 John Barrell, *English Literature in History*, pp. 96–9; Richard Feingold, *Nature and Society*, pp. 101–3.

5 John Barrell, *English Literature in History*, p. 96.

6 Laurence Goldstein, '*Ruins and Empire*, p. 55.

7 Richard Feingold, *Nature and Society*, p. 102; John Barrell, *English Literature in History*, p. 98.

8 Damon's speech ends with an echo of Philips's 'Ah silly I! more silly than my Sheep', a line Pope had ironically challenged 'the most common Reader' to

repeat 'without feeling some Motions of Compassion'. Parker shows that Dyer had read Philips's poems and copied extracts from them into his notebooks. See *The Poems of Ambrose Philips*, p. 13; *The Guardian* [1713], ed. John Calhoun Stephens, p. 164; Edward A. Parker, 'A Study of John Dyer', p. 147.

9 For the numerous Miltonic echoes (particularly of *Comus*) in this section of the poem see J. G. E. Davies, 'An Edition of the Poetical Works of John Dyer', pp. 440–1.

10 Compare the incantation made by Guiderius and Arviragus in Shakespeare, *Cymbeline*, IV.ii.277–81 (another literary view of non-classical, Anglo-Welsh mythology and ritual).

11 Eric Kerridge, *The Agricultural Revolution*, p. 358. The other possibilities for 'penny-grass' are navelwort or wall pennywort (*Cotyledon umbilicus*) and yellow-rattle (*Rhinanthus*). See *OED* 'penny-grass'. For details of the tradition associating Marsh pennywort with liver-rot, see J. R. Press *et al.*, *Field Guide*, p. 170.

12 I take trefoil as either red or wild clover, the commonest meanings of the word. A great deal more could be said about Dyer's choice of flowers and herbs: each has a long and full history. For burnet, mint, thyme and trefoil see *OED* 'burnet' sb. 2. 1; Florence Ranson, *British Herbs*, pp. 184, 171–2, 191–2; A. R. Clapham *et al.*, *Excursion Flora*, pp. 183–4, 342–3, 343–4, 157–60; Claire Loewenfeld, *Herb Gardening*, pp. 187–8, 142–56, 205–9; Dorothy Hall, *The Book of Herbs*, pp. 69–71, 145–9, 191–3.

13 Ralph M. Williams, *Poet, Painter and Parson*, p. 126; Belinda Humfrey, *John Dyer*, pp. 93–4, 98.

14 Camden, Preface, [unnumbered pages]; Drayton, 'To the Generall Reader', p. v.

15 Pat Rogers, 'Windsor Forest, Britannia and River Poetry', 283–4.

16 *Bartholemew's Gazetteer of the British Isles* (ninth edition, Edinburgh, 1970), p. 743.

17 George Farquhar, *The Recruiting Officer*, p. 3 and ff. See also *GM*, 55 (1784), 96–7. The Roman fort of Uriconium was a few miles away from the foot of the Wrekin. For an imaginative treatment of the two locations see A. E. Housman, *A Shropshire Lad*, XXXI, in his *Collected Poems*, p. 36.

18 Housman's poem 'Bredon Hill', *Collected Poems*, p. 27, relates.

19 This seems to be Damon's speech, but there is some ambiguity in the typographic conventions, so it may possibly be Colin's.

20 There are a number of versions of the Sabrina story. See for example Geoffrey of Monmouth, *History of the Kings of Britain*, pp. 76–8; Edmund Spenser, *The Fairie Queene*, Book II, Canto x, lines 13–19, in *Poetical Works*; John Fletcher, *The Faithful Shepherdess* (the killing of Amoret at III.i–IV.i echoes the death of Sabrina); Drayton, Songs V and VI; John Milton, *Comus*, [1637], lines 824–921, in *Poetical Works*; Ambrose Philips, 'The Second Pastoral', line 60, in *Poems*, p. 13; Thomas Chatterton, 'Englysh Metamorphosis', in *Poems*, pp. 196–202.

21 Drayton, Song VI, line 105 ff; John Philips, *Cyder*, I, lines 106–7 and 203, in *The Poems of John Philips*; Thomas Gray, *The Bard*, line 34, in Roger Lonsdale (ed.), *The Poems of Gray, Collins and Goldsmith*; Alexander Pope, 'Epistle to Bathurst', line 251, *TE*, vol. III, part ii, p. 251.

22 *Wordsworth-Lady Beaumont*, November 1811.
23 The only twentieth-century English georgic I know for which serious claims might be made is Vita Sackville-West's attractive Virgilian imitation *The Land* (1926), which won several literary prizes. See also her *The Garden* (1946).
24 See Boris Ford (ed.), *The Pelican Guide to English Literature 4*, p. 275.

Select bibliography

For the main editions used see *Textual Note*; see also *Abbreviations*.

Radio broadcast

Chadwick, Whitney, interviewed on 'Woman's Hour', BBC Radio 4, 11 April 1990

Books, articles and theses

Addison, Joseph, 'An Essay on Virgil's *Georgics*' [1697], in *Eighteenth-Century Critical Essays*, ed. Scott Elledge (Ithaca, 1961), vol. I, pp. 1–7
  Critical Essays from the Spectator, ed. Donald F. Bond (Oxford, 1970)
Arbuthnot, John and Alexander Pope, *Memoirs of the Extraordinary Life, Works and Discoveries of Martinus Scriblerus*, ed. Charles Kerby-Miller (New Haven, 1950)
Armstrong, John, *The Art of Preserving Health: a Poem* (London, 1744)
Arthos, John, *The Language of Natural Description in Eighteenth Century Poetry* (London, 1966)
Ashby, M. K., *Joseph Ashby of Tysoe 1859–1919* (London, 1961)
Ashraf, P. M., *Introduction to Working Class Literature in Great Britain* (two volumes, East Berlin, 1978–9)
Aubin, Robert A., 'Materials for a Study of the Influence of Cooper's Hill', *ELH*, 1 (1934), 197–204
  Topographical Poetry in XVIII-Century England (New York, 1936)
Baines, Edward, *The Woollen Manufacture of England, with Special Reference to the Leeds Clothing District* [1875], ed. K.G. Ponting (Newton Abbot, 1970)
Barrell, John, *The Idea of Landscape and the Sense of Place, 1730–1840, an Approach to the Poetry of John Clare* (London, 1972)
  The Dark Side of the Landscape: the Rural Poor in English Painting 1730–1840 (Cambridge, 1980)
  English Literature in History 1730–80: an Equal Wide Survey (London, 1983)
  'The Golden Age of Labour', in *Second Nature*, ed. Richard Mabey (London, 1984), pp. 177–95
  Poetry, Language and Politics (Manchester, 1988)
  'Sportive Labour', in *The English Rural Community: Image and Analysis*, ed. Brian Short (Cambridge, 1992), pp. 105–32
Barrell, John and John Bull, (eds.), *The Penguin Book of English Pastoral Verse* (Harmondsworth, 1974)

Beckett, J. V., *The Agricultural Revolution* (Oxford, 1990)

Bermingham, Ann, *Landscape and Ideology: the English Rustic Tradition, 1740–1860* (Berkeley, 1986)

Best, Henry, *Rural Economy in Yorkshire in 1641, being the Farming and Account Books of Henry Best, of Elmswell, in the East Riding of the County of York*, ed. Charles Best Robinson (Durham, 1857)

Bloomfield, Robert, *The Farmer's Boy, a Rural Poem* (London, 1800)

Boumelha, Penny, 'John Dyer, 1699–1758', *The Index of English Literary Manuscripts, Volume III (1700–1800), Part I, Addison-Fielding*, ed. Margaret M. Smith (London, 1986), pp. 341–53

Boxer, Arabella, and Philippa Back, *The Herb Book* (London, 1980)

Bradley, R., *The Country Gentleman and Farmer's Monthly Director* (London, 1726)

Brand, John, *Observations on Popular Antiquities* (revised edition, London, 1877)

Branigan, Keith (ed.), *Rome and the Brigantes: the Impact of Rome on Northern England* (Sheffield, 1980)

Brett, R. L. and A. R. Jones (eds.), *Wordsworth and Coleridge, Lyrical Ballads* (revised edition, London, 1965)

Brill, Edith, *Life and Tradition on the Cotswolds* (London, 1973)

British National Formulary, Number 7, ed. K. B. K. Davis *et al.* (London, 1984)

Brower, Reuben A., *The Poetry of Allusion* (Oxford, 1959)

Burnley, James, *The History of Wool and Wool-Combing* [1889] (reprinted in facsimile, New York, 1969)

Burns, Robert, *The Letters of Robert Burns*, ed. J. de Lancey Ferguson, second edition, ed. G. Ross Roy (two volumes, Oxford, 1985)
  The Poems and Songs of Robert Burns, ed. James Kinsley (three volumes, Oxford, 1968)

Bysshe, Edward, *The Art of English Poetry* [1702] (reprinted in facsimile, Menston, Yorkshire, 1968)

Camden, William, *Camden's Britannia [1598], Newly Translated into English with Large Additions and Improvements*, translated and ed. William Gibson (London, 1695)

Celoria, Francis, 'Chatterton, Wordsworth and Stonehenge', *Notes and Queries*, 221 [n.s. 23] (1976), 103–4

Chadwick, Whitney, *Women, Art and Society* (London, 1990)

Chalker, John, *The English Georgic: a Study in the Development of a Form* (London, 1969)

Chamberlain, Mary, *Fenwomen* (London, 1975)

Chambers, J. D., and G. E. Mingay, *The Agricultural Revolution 1750–1880* (London, 1966)

Chatterton, Thomas, *Poems Supposed to Have Been Written at Bristol, by Thomas Rowley and Others, in the Fifteenth Century* (London, 1777)

Chatwin, Bruce, *On the Black Hill* (London, 1982)

Chaucer, Geoffrey, *Complete Works*, ed. F.N. Robinson (London and Oxford, second edition, 1957)

Clapham, A. R., T. G. Tutin and E. F. Warburg, *Excursion Flora of the British Isles* (Cambridge, 1968)

Clare, John, *Autobiographical Writings*, ed. Eric Robinson (Oxford, 1983)

Selected Poetry, ed. Geoffrey Summerfield (Harmondsworth, 1990)

Cobbett, William, *Rural Rides in the Southern, Western and Eastern Counties of England, together with Tours in Scotland and in the Northern and Midland Counties of England, and Letters from Ireland*, ed. G. D. H. and Margaret Cole (three volumes, London, 1930)

Cohen, Ralph, *The Art of Discrimination: Thomson's The Seasons and the Language of Criticism* (London, 1964)

The Unfolding of The Seasons (Baltimore, 1970)

'Notes on the Teaching of Eighteenth-Century Poetry of Natural Description', in *Teaching Eighteenth-Century Poetry*, ed. Christopher Fox (New York and London, 1990)

Colley, Linda, 'The Loyal Brotherhood and the Cocoa Tree: the London Organisation of the Tory Party 1727–60', *Historical Journal*, 20 (1977), 77–95

In Defiance of Oligarchy, the Tory Party 1714–60 (Cambridge, 1982)

Britons: Forging the Nation 1707–1837 (London, 1992)

Collier, Mary, *The Woman's Labour: an Epistle to Mr. Stephen Duck; In Answer to his late Poem, called The Thresher's Labour. To which are added, the Three Wise Sentences, taken from the First Book of Esdras, Ch. III and IV. By Mary Collier, Now a Washer-Woman, at Petersfield in Hampshire* (London, 1739)

Poems on Several Occasions (Winchester, 1762)

Collins, A. H., 'The Life and Writings of John Dyer, LL.B. 1701–1757' (unpublished MA thesis, University of London, 1930)

Congleton, J. E., *Theories of Pastoral Poetry in England 1684–1798* (Gainsville, Florida, 1952)

Cooper, Helen, *Pastoral, Medieval into Renaissance* (Ipswich and Totowa, New Jersey, 1977)

Coppock, J. T., *An Agricultural Atlas of England and Wales* (London, 1964)

Cowper, William, *The Task, a Poem, in Six Books* [1785], Introduction by Robert Inglesfield (reprinted in facsimile, Menston, Yorkshire, 1973)

Crabbe, George, *The Village, a Poem in Two Books* (London, 1783)

Crabtree, David, 'A Secret: Four Images: 1. The Flight of Samuel Law', *Stand*, 31 (1990), no. 4, 66–7

Dabydeen, David, *Hogarth's Blacks: Images of Blacks in Eighteenth Century English Art* (Manchester, 1987)

Daiches, David, *Robert Burns* (revised edition, London, 1966)

Davies, J. G. E., 'An Edition of the Poetical Works of John Dyer' (unpublished MA thesis, University of Wales, Aberystwyth, 1968)

Davis, Rose Mary, *Stephen Duck, the Thresher-Poet* (Orono, Maine, 1926)

Deacon, George, *John Clare and the Folk Tradition* (London, 1983)

Deane, C. V., *Aspects of Eighteenth Century Nature Poetry* (second edition, London, 1967)

Defoe, Daniel, *A Tour Thro' the Whole Island of Great Britain* [1724–6], ed. G. D. H. Cole (two volumes, London, 1968)

Denham, Sir John, *Cooper's Hill* (London, 1642)

Diaper, William, 'Brent', in *The Complete Works of William Diaper*, ed. Dorothy Broughton (London, 1951, first published, in a disguised and unauthorised form, as *Lincolnshire* [Bury St Edmunds, 1720], then in Diaper's *Miscellanea* [London, 1726])

Dobree, Bonamy, 'The Theme of Patriotism in the Poetry of the Early Eighteenth Century', *Proceedings of the British Academy*, 35 (1949), 49–65

Doody, Margaret Anne, *The Daring Muse: Augustan Poetry Reconsidered* (Cambridge, 1985)

Drayton, Michael, *Poly-Olbion. or A Chorographicall description of Tracts, Rivers, Mountains, Forests, and other Parts of this renowned Isle of Greate Britaine* [1613–22], in *The Works of Michael Drayton*, ed. William Hebel, vol. IV (Oxford, 1933)

Dryden, John, *The Poems of John Dryden*, ed. James Kinsley (four volumes, Oxford, 1958)

    The Poems and Fables of John Dryden, ed. James Kinsley (Oxford, 1962)

Duck, Stephen, *Poems on Several Subjects: Written by Stephen Duck, Lately a poor Thresher in a Barn in the County of Wilts, at the Wages of Four Shillings and Sixpence per Week* (London, 1730)

    Poems on Several Occasions [1736], Introduction by John Lucas (reprinted in facsimile, Menston, Yorkshire, 1973)

Durling, Dwight L., *Georgic Tradition in English Poetry* (New York, 1935)

Dyer, John, *The Fleece, a Poem in Four Books* (London, 1757)

    letter to Robert Dodsley, 12 May 1757, *GM* (1835), 47

    poems, in *The Poetical Works of Mark Akenside and John Dyer* ed. Robert Aris Wilmott (London, 1855)

    poems in *Minor Eighteenth-Century Poets: Parnell, Dyer, Green & Anne, Countess of Winchelsea*, ed. Hugh L'Anson Fausset (London, 1930)

Elliot, Alistair (ed.), *Virgil's Georgics with Dryden's Translation* (Ashington, Northumberland, 1981)

Ellis, William, *The Modern Husbandman, or, The Practice of Farming* (four volumes, London, 1744)

Emery, Clark, 'The Poet and the Plough', *Agricultural History*, 16 (1942), 9–15

Empson, William, *Some Versions of Pastoral* (London, 1974)

English, Walter, *The Textile Industry: An Account of the Early Inventions of Spinning, Weaving and Knitting Machines* (London, 1969)

    'A Technical Assessment of Lewis Paul's Spinning Machine', *Textile History*, 4 (1973), 68–83

Ernle, R. E. Prothero, Lord, *English Farming, Past and Present*, ed. G. E. Fussell and O. R. McGregor (sixth edition, London, 1961)

Evans, George Ewart, *Ask the Fellows Who Cut the Hay* (London, 1956)

    The Pattern Under the Plough (London, 1966)

Farquhar, George, *The Recruiting Officer* [1706], ed. John Ross (London, 1977)

Feingold, Richard, *Nature and Society: Later Eighteenth-Century Uses of the Pastoral and the Georgic* (Brighton, 1978)

Ferguson, Moira (ed.), *The Thresher's Labour, Stephen Duck (1736) and The Woman's Labour, Mary Collier (1739)* (Los Angeles, 1985)

Fiennes, Celia, *The Journeys of Celia Fiennes 1685–c. 1712*, ed. Christopher Morris (London, 1947)

Finberg, H. P. R., *The Gloucestershire Landscape* (London, 1975)

Fitter, Chris, 'Henry Vaughan's Landscapes of Military Occupation', *Essays in Criticism*, 42 (1992), no. 2, 123–47

Fletcher, John, *The Faithful Shepherdess* [1610], in *The Dramatic Works in the*

Beaumont and Fletcher Canon, ed. Fredson Bowers *et al.*, vol. III (Cambridge, 1976)

Ford, Boris (ed.), *The Pelican Guide to English Literature 4. from Dryden to Johnson* (Harmondsworth, 1963)

Foster, John Wilson, 'A Redefinition of Topographical Poetry', *JEGP*, 69 (1970), 394–406

'The Measure of Paradise: Topography in Eighteenth-Century Poetry', *ECS*, 9 (1976), 232–56

Frazer, J. G., *The Golden Bough* (abridged edition, London, 1922)

Fussell, G. E., 'Four Centuries of Leicester Farming', in *Studies in Leicestershire Agrarian History*, ed. W. G. Hoskins (Leicester, 1949), pp. 154–76

The Farmer's Tools: The History of British Farm Implements, Tools and Machinery A.D. 1500–1900 (London, 1981)

Gay, John, *The Shepherd's Week. In Six Pastorals* [1714], (reprinted in facsimile, Menston, Yorkshire, 1969)

Gee, Joshua, *The Trade and Navigation of Great-Britain Considered* [1738] (fourth edition, reprinted in facsimile, New York, 1969)

Geoffrey of Monmouth, *History of the Kings of Britain*, translated by Lewis Thorpe (Harmondsworth, 1966)

Geological Survey Ten Mile Map (South Sheet) (London, 1979)

George, M. Dorothy, *London Life in the Eighteenth Century* (Harmondsworth, 1966)

Gill, Stephen, *William Wordsworth: a Life* (Oxford, 1989)

Gilpin, William, *Observations on the River Wye, and Several Parts of South Wales, &c* [1782], Introduction by Sutherland Lyall (reprinted in facsimile, Richmond, Surrey, 1973)

Goldstein, Laurence, '*The Fleece* and the World's Great Age' in his *Ruins and Empire: the Evolution of a Theme in Augustan and Romantic Literature* (Pittsburgh, 1977), pp. 25–58

Goodridge, John, 'Some Predecessors of Clare', *John Clare Society Journal*, 8 (1989), 5–10, and 9 (1990), 17–26

(ed.), *The Independent Spirit: John Clare and the Self-Taught Tradition* (Helpston, Peterborough, 1994)

Goodwin, Derek, *Sheep Management and Production* (second edition, London, 1979)

Grant, Douglas, *James Thomson, Poet of 'The Seasons'* (London, 1951)

Graves, Robert, *The Greek Myths* (revised edition, two volumes, Harmondsworth, 1960)

The White Goddess: a Historical Grammar of Poetic Myth (London, 1961)

Gray, Thomas, *The Correspondence of Thomas Gray*, ed. Paget Toynbee and Leonard Whibley (three volumes, Oxford, 1935)

Greene, Richard, *Mary Leapor, A Study in Eighteenth-Century Women's Poetry* (Oxford, 1993)

Griffin, Susan, *Made From this Earth: Selections from Her Writing 1967–1982* (London, 1982)

Hall, Dorothy, *The Book of Herbs* (London, 1972)

Hammond, J. L. and Barbara, *The Village Labourer, a study in the Government of England Before the Reform Bill* (London, 1911)

Hardy, Thomas, *Far From the Madding Crowd* [1874], ed. John Bayley (London, 1974)

Hartle, P. N., 'Defoe and *The Wonders of the Peake*', *English Studies*, 5 (1986), 420–31

Hartwell, R. M., 'A Revolution in the Character and Destiny of British Wool', in *Textile History and Economic History: Essays in Honour of Miss Julia de Lacy Mann*, ed. N. B. Harte and K. G. Ponting (Manchester, 1973), pp. 320–38

Harvey, A. D., 'First Public Reactions to the Industrial Revolution', *Etudes Anglaises*, 31 (1978), 273–93

Heaton, Herbert, *The Yorkshire Woollen and Worsted Industries* (Oxford, 1920)

Hennell, Thomas, *The Old Farm* (London, 1984, first published as *Change on the Farm*, 1934)

Hill, Brian W., *Robert Harley, Speaker, Secretary of State and Premier Minister* (New Haven, 1988)

Hill, Bridget, *Women, Work, and Sexual Politics in Eighteenth-Century England* (Oxford and New York, 1989)

Hoskins, W. G., *Leicestershire: An Illustrated Essay on the History of the Landscape* (London, 1957)

Housman, A. E., *Collected Poems* (London, 1967)

Hudson, W. H., *A Shepherd's Life* (London, 1910)

Humfrey, Belinda, *John Dyer (Writers of Wales)* (Cardiff, 1980)

Janowitz, Anne, *England's Ruins: Poetic Purpose and the National Landscape* (Oxford, 1990)

Jefferies, Richard, *The Toilers of the Field*, Introduction by Victor E. Neuberg (London, 1981)

John, A. H., 'The Course of Agricultural Change', in *Essays in Agrarian History*, ed. W. E. Michinton (two volumes, Newton Abbot, 1968), vol. I, pp. 221–53

Johnson, Paul H., 'Turnips and Romanticism', *Agricultural History*, 12 (1938), 224–55

Johnson, Samuel, *London: a Poem in Imitation of the Third Satire of Juvenal* [1738] in *The Poems of Samuel Johnson*, ed. David Nichol Smith and Edward L. McAdams (second edition, Oxford, 1974), pp. 66–81

The Lives of the English Poets, ed. George Birkbeck Hill (Oxford, 1905)

Jones, E. L., 'Agricultural Origins of Industry', *Past and Present*, 40 (1968), 58–71

Jones, Richard F., 'Eclogue Types in English Poetry of the Eighteenth Century', *JEGP*, 24 (1925), 33–60

Keats, John, *Poems*, ed. Miriam Allott (Harlow, 1970)

Kent, Robert Warren, 'The Poems of John Dyer, a Critical Edition' (unpublished Ph.D. thesis, University of Minnesota, 1970)

Kerridge, Eric, *The Agricultural Revolution* (London, 1967)

Textile Manufactures in Early Modern England (Manchester, 1985)

Kilvert, Francis, *Kilvert's Diary: Selections from the Diary of the Rev. Francis Kilvert*, ed. William Plomer (London, 1964)

Klaus, H. Gustav, 'Stephen Duck und Mary Collier', *Gulliver*, 10 (1981), 115–23

The Literature of Labour (Brighton, 1985)

Klingender, Francis D., *Art and the Industrial Revolution*, revised and ed. Arthur Elton (Chatham, 1968)

Knowlson, T. Sharper, *The Origins of Popular Superstitions and Customs* (London, 1930)

Kovacevic, Ivanka, 'The Mechanical Muse: the Impact of Technical Inventions on Eighteenth-Century Neoclassical Poetry', *Huntington Library Quarterly*, 28 (1965), 263–81

Fact into Fiction: English Literature and the Industrial Scene 1750–1850 (Leicester and Belgrade, 1975)

Landry, Donna, 'The Resignation of Mary Collier', in *The New Eighteenth Century: Theory, Politics, English Literature*, ed. Felicity Nussbaum and Laura Brown (New York and London, 1987), pp. 99–120

The Muses of Resistance: Laboring-Class Women's Poetry in Britain, 1739–1796 (Cambridge, 1990)

Langland, William, *Piers the Plowman*, translated by J. F. Goodridge (revised edition, Harmondsworth, 1966)

Latimer, John, *Annals of Bristol in the Eighteenth Century* (Bristol, 1893)

Law, Samuel, *A Domestic Winter-Piece: or, a Poem, exhibiting A full View of the Author's Dwelling-Place in the Winter-Season. In two parts. Interspersed with a great variety of Entertaining Reflections* (Leeds, 1772)

Lipson, Ephraim, *The History of the Woollen and Worsted Industries* (London, 1921)

Loewenfeld, Claire, *Herb Gardening: Why and How to Grow Herbs* (London, 1964)

Longstaffe, W. H. D., 'Notes Respecting the Life and Family of John Dyer the Poet', *The Patrician*, 4 (1847), 7–12, 264–8, 420–6, and 5 (1848), 75–81, 218–35

Lonsdale, Roger (ed.), *The Poems of Thomas Gray, William Collins and Oliver Goldsmith* (London, 1969)

The New Oxford Book of Eighteenth-Century Verse (Oxford, 1984)

Eighteenth Century Women Poets: an Oxford Anthology (Oxford, 1989)

Low, Anthony, *The Georgic Revolution* (Princeton, 1985)

Low, David, *The Breeds of Domestic Animals of the British Isles* (two volumes in one, London, 1842)

Lucas, John, *England and Englishness: Ideas of Nationhood in English Poetry 1688–1900* (London, 1990)

Lucretius, *On the Nature of the Universe*, translated by Ronald Latham (Harmondsworth, 1951)

McGonigle, Peter J., 'Stephen Duck and the Text of *The Thresher's Labour*', *The Library*, sixth series, IV (1982), 288–96

McKendrick, Neil, John Brewer and J. H. Plumb, *The Birth of a Consumer Society: the Commercialization of Eighteenth-Century England* (London, 1983)

Mackenzie, James, *The History of Health and the Art of Preserving It* (Edinburgh, 1758)

McKillop, Alan Dugald, *The Background of Thomson's Seasons* (Minneapolis, 1942)

(ed.), *James Thomson (1700–1748), Letters and Documents* (Lawrence, Kansas, 1958)

Maidment, Brian (ed.), *The Poorhouse Fugitives: Self-Taught Poets and Poetry in Victorian Britain* (Manchester, 1987)

Malcolmson, R. W., *Life and Labour in England 1700–1780* (London, 1981)

Mandeville, Bernard, *The Fable of the Bees*, ed. Phillip Harth (Harmondsworth, 1989)

Mantz, Harold, 'Non-Dramatic Pastoral in Europe in the Eighteenth Century', *PMLA*, 31 (1916), 421–47

Marshall, William, *The Rural Economy of the Midland Counties* (two volumes, London, 1790)

The Review and Abstract of the Reports to the Board of Agriculture [1818] (reprinted in facsimile, five volumes, New York, 1968)

Martin W. B. (ed), *Diseases of Sheep* (Oxford, 1983)

Marvell, Andrew, *The Selected Poems of Andrew Marvell*, ed. Frank Kermode (Harmondsworth, 1967)

Marx, Leo, *The Machine in the Garden: Technology and the Pastoral Ideal in America* (Oxford, 1964)

Massingham, H. J., *The Southern Marches* (London, 1952)

Meyerstein, E. H. W., *A Life of Thomas Chatterton* (London, 1930)

Milton, John, *Poetical Works* ed. Douglas Bush (Oxford, 1966)

Minchinton, W. E. (ed.), *Essays in Agrarian History* (two volumes, Newton Abbot, 1968)

Mingay, G. E., *English Landed Society in the Eighteenth Century* (Toronto, 1963)
  The Agricultural Revolution: Changes in Agriculture 1650–1880 (London, 1977)

Ministry of Agriculture Bulletin No. 166: Sheep Breeding and Management (London, 1967)

Monk, John, *General View of the Agriculture of the County of Leicester* (London, 1794)

Morton, J. C. (ed.), *A Cyclopaedia of Agriculture, Practical and Scientific* (two volumes, Glasgow, Edinburgh and London, 1855)

Mount, Ferdinand, 'Commentary: On Grongar Hill Now', *Times Literary Supplement* (27 September 1991), 17

Neeson, J.M., *Commoners: Common Right, Enclosure and Social Change in England, 1700–1820* (Cambridge, 1993)

Nicholson, Marjorie Hope, and G. S. Rousseau, 'Bishop Berkeley and Tar-Water', in *The Augustan Milieu: Essays Presented to Louis A. Landa*, ed. H. C. Miller *et al.* (Oxford, 1970), pp. 102–37

Nokes, David, *Raillery and Rage: a Study of Eighteenth Century Satire* (Brighton, 1987)

Olsen, Tillie, *Silences* (London, 1980)

O'Neill, Gilda, *Pull No More Bines: an Oral History of East London Women Hop-Pickers* (London, 1990)

Opie, Iona, and Moira Tatem (eds.), *A Dictionary of Superstitions* (Oxford, 1989)

Osborne, James M., 'Spence, Natural Genius and Pope', *PQ,* 45 (1966), 123–44

Parker, Edward A., 'A Study of John Dyer in the Light of New Manuscript Materials' (unpublished B.Litt. thesis, Oxford, 1953)

Parker, Edward A., and Ralph M. Williams, 'John Dyer, the Poet, as Farmer', *Agricultural History*, 22 (1948), 134–41

Parker, Rozsika, and Griselda Pollock, *Old Mistresses: Women, Art and Ideology* (London, 1981)

Parris, Leslie and Ian Fleming-Williams, *Constable* (London, 1991)

Patterson, Annabel, *Pastoral and Ideology: Virgil to Valery* (Berkeley, 1988)

Pawson, H. Cecil, *Robert Bakewell, Pioneer Livestock Breeder* (London, 1957)

Payne, Christiana, *Toil and Plenty: Images of the Agricultural Landscape in England 1780–1890* (New Haven and London, 1993)

Pevsner, Nikolaus, *The Buildings of Britain: Leicestershire and Rutland* (Harmondsworth, 1960)

Philip, Neil (ed.), *Between Earth and Sky: Poetry and Prose of English Rural Life and Work Between the Enclosures and the Great War* (Harmondsworth, 1984)

Philips, Ambrose, *The Poems of Ambrose Philips*, ed. M. C. Segar (Oxford, 1937)

Philips, John, *Cyder, a Poem in Two Books* [1708], in *The Poems of John Philips*, ed. M.G. Lloyd Thomas (Oxford, 1927)

Pope, Alexander, *The Twickenham Edition of the Works of Alexander Pope*, ed. John Butt, Maynard Mack *et al.*, Volumes I–X (London and New Haven, 1939–67)

Press, J. R., D. A. Sutton and B. R. Tebbs, *Field Guide to the Wild Flowers of Britain* (London, 1988)

Ramsay, G. D., *The English Woollen Industry 1500–1750* (London, 1982)

Ranson, Florence, *British Herbs* (Harmondsworth, 1949)

Richards, Thomas, *Hoglandiae Descriptio* (London, 1709, reprinted as *Hogland; or a description of Hampshire. A Mock-heroic poem*, 1728, and again as *A Satyr on Lincolnshire*, 1738)

Richmond, I. A., *Roman and Native in North Britain* (London, 1958)

Roberts, Michael, 'Sickles and Scythes: Women's Work and Men's Work at Harvest Time', *History Workshop*, 7 (1979), 3–28

Rochester, John Wilmot, Second Earl of Rochester, *Complete Poems*, ed. David Veith (New Haven and London, 1968)

Rogers, Pat, *Hacks and Dunces: Pope, Swift and Grub Street* (London and New York, 1980, abridged from *Grub Street: Studies in a Subculture*, 1968)
  'Windsor Forest, Britannia and River Poetry', *SP*, 77 (1980), 283–4

Roscoe, E. S., *Robert Harley, Earl of Oxford, Prime Minister 1710–1714, A Study of Politics and Letters in the Age of Anne* (London, 1902)

Rosenmeyer, Thomas G., *The Green Cabinet: Theocritus and the European Pastoral Lyric* (Berkeley and Los Angeles, 1969)

Röstvig, Maren-Sofie, *The Happy Man: Studies in the Metamorphoses of a Classical Ideal* (second edition, Oslo and New York, 1971)

Rothstein, Eric, 'Discordia Non Concors: the Motif of Hunting in Eighteenth-century Verse', *JEGP*, 83 (1984), 330–54

Rowbotham, Sheila, *Woman's Consciousness, Man's World* (Harmondsworth, 1973)
  Hidden from History (Harmondsworth, 1974)

Russell, Nicholas Carrick, 'Animal Breeding in England, c. 1500–1770' (unpublished Ph.D. thesis, Imperial College of Science and Technology, London, 1981)

Ryder, M. L., 'The History of Sheep Breeds in Britain', *Agricultural History Review*, 12 (1964), 1–12, and 13 (1965), 65–82
  Sheep and Man (London, 1983)

Sackville-West, Vita, *The Land* (London, 1926)
  The Garden (London, 1946)

Sambrook, A. J., 'An Essay on Eighteenth Century Pastoral, Pope to Wordsworth', *Trivium*, 5 (1970), 21–35, and 6 (1971), 103–15

Sambrook, James, *James Thomson 1700–1748: a Life* (Oxford, 1992)

Sappho, *Poems and Fragments*, translated by Moira Balmer (Newcastle upon Tyne, 1992)

Scott, Mary W., *James Thomson, Anglo-Scot* (Athens, Georgia, 1988)

The Scottish National Dictionary , ed. William Grant and David D. Murison (ten volumes, Aberdeen, 1960)

Seddon, Quentin, *The Silent Revolution: Farming and the Countryside into the 21st Century* (London, 1989)

Shelley, Percy Bysshe, *Selected Poetry and Prose*, Introduction by Kenneth Neil Cameron (New York, 1951)

Shenstone, William, 'A Description of the Leasowes' in *The Works in Verse and Prose of William Shenstone, Gent* (London, 1768), vol. II, pp. 287–320

Shiach, Morag, *Discourse on Popular Culture: Class, Gender and History in Cultural Analysis, 1730 to the Present* (Cambridge, 1989)

Short, Brian (ed.), *The English Rural Community: Image and Analysis* (Cambridge, 1992)

Sitter, John, *Literary Loneliness in Mid-Eighteenth Century England* (Ithaca and London, 1982)

Skinner, J. B., D. E. Lord and J. M. Williams (eds.), *British Sheep and Wool* (Bradford, 1985)

Smith, John, *Chronicum Rusticum Commerciale, or Memoirs of Wool* [1747] (reprinted in facsimile, two volumes, New York, 1969)

Smith, Robert William Innes, *English-Speaking Students of Medicine at the University of Leyden* (Edinburgh and London, 1932)

Snell, K. D. M., *Annals of the Labouring Poor: Social Change and Agrarian England, 1660–1900* (Cambridge, 1985)

Somerville, William, *The Chace, a Poem* (London, 1735)

Southey, Robert, *The Lives and Works of Our Uneducated Poets*, ed. J. S. Childers (London, 1925)

Spacks, Patricia Meyer, *The Varied God: A Critical Study of Thomson's The Seasons* (Berkeley and Los Angeles, 1959)

Spate, O. H. K., 'The Muse of Mercantilism: Jago, Grainger and Dyer', in *Studies in the Eighteenth Century: Papers Presented at the David Nichol Smith Memorial Seminar, Canberra, 1966*, ed. R. F. Brissenden (Canberra, 1968), pp. 119–31

Spenser, Edmund, *Poetical Works*, ed. J. C. Smith and E. de Selincourt (Oxford, 1970)

Stephen, Henry, *The Book of the Farm*, fourth edition, revised by James MacDonald (Edinburgh, 1889)

Stephens, John Calhoun (ed.), *The Guardian* [1713] (Lexington, Kentucky, 1982)

Stewart, Sheila, *Lifting the Latch: a Life on the Land* (Oxford, 1987)

Stokoe, W. J., *The Observer's Book of Trees* (revised edition, London and New York, 1960)

Sutherland, James, *A Preface to Eighteenth Century Poetry* (London, 1948)

Swift, Jonathan, *The Correspondence of Jonathan Swift*, ed. Harold Williams (five volumes, Oxford, 1963–5)

Theocritus, *The Idylls of Theocritus*, translated by R. C. Trevelyan (Cambridge, 1947)

Thirsk, Joan, G. E. Mingay *et al.* (eds.), *The Agrarian History of England and Wales* (volumes I–VIII, Cambridge, 1967–85)

Thomas, Keith, *Man and the Natural World: Changing Attitudes in England 1500–1800* (London, 1983)

Thompson, E. P., *The Making of the English Working Class* (Harmondsworth, 1968)
Customs in Common (London, 1991)

Thompson, E. P. and Marian Sugden (eds.) *The Thresher's Labour by Stephen Duck, The Woman's Labour by Mary Collier: Two Eighteenth Century Poems* (London, 1989)

Thompson, Flora, *Lark Rise to Candleford*, ed. H.J. Massingham (Harmondsworth, 1973)

Thompson, Stith, *Motif-Index of Folk-Literature* (revised edition, six volumes, Bloomington, Indiana, 1966–75)

Thomson, James, *The Seasons*, ed. James Sambrook (Oxford, 1981)
  Liberty, The Castle of Indolence and Other Poems, ed. James Sambrook (Oxford, 1986)

Todd, Janet (ed.), *Dictionary of British Women Writers* (London, 1989)

Toliver, Harold Earl, *Pastoral Forms and Attitudes* (Berkeley and London, 1971)

Traherne, Thomas, *Selected Poems and Prose*, ed. Alan Bradford (Harmondsworth, 1991)

Trow-Smith, Robert, *A History of British Livestock Husbandry to 1700* (London, 1957)
  A History of British Livestock Husbandry, 1700–1900 (London, 1959)

Turner, James, *The Politics of Landscape: Rural Scenery and Society in English Poetry 1630–1660* (Oxford, 1979)

Tusser, Thomas, *Five Hundred Points of Good Husbandry*, Introduction by Geoffrey Grigson (Oxford, 1984)

Unwin, Rayner, *The Rural Muse: Studies in the Peasant Poetry of England* (London, 1954)

Vaughan, Henry, *Poetry and Selected Prose*, ed. L. C. Martin (London, 1963)

Voss, Fred, *Goodstone* (Newcastle upon Tyne, 1991)

Wallis, P. J. and R. V., *Eighteenth Century Medics (Subscriptions, Licences, Apprenticeships)* (second edition, Newcastle upon Tyne, 1988)

Warner, Alan, 'Stephen Duck, the Thresher Poet', *REL*, 8 (1967), 38–48

Wasserman, Earl R., *The Subtler Language* (Baltimore, 1959)

Watkins, Alfred, *The Old Straight Track: Its Mounds, Beacons, Moats, Sites and Mark Stones* (London, 1925)

Watson, Sir James Anderson Scott, and May Elliot Hobbs, *Great Farmers* (London, 1951)

Webb, [Gladys] Mary, *Gone to Earth* (London, 1917)
  Precious Bane: a Novel (London, 1924)

Wendorf, Richard, 'Robert Dodsley as Editor', *Studies in Bibliography*, 31 (1978), 235–48

White, R.S., *Innocent Victims: Poetic Injustice in Shakespearean Tragedy* (Newcastle upon Tyne, 1982)

Whitlock, Ralph, *A Short History of Farming in Britain* (London, 1965)

Williams, Alfred, *Folk Songs of the Upper Thames* (London, 1923)

Williams, Ralph M., *Poet, Painter and Parson: the Life of John Dyer* (New York, 1956)

Williams, Raymond, *The Country and the City* (London, 1973)

Wood, Nigel, 'Collins and the End of Shepherd Pastoral', *Durham University Journal*, n.s. 46 (1985), 25–31

Wordsworth, William, Preface to *Lyrical Ballads* (1800), in *Wordsworth and Coleridge, Lyrical Ballads*, ed. R. L. Brett and A. R. Jones (revised edition, London, 1965)

The Salisbury Plain Poems, ed. Stephen Gill (Ithaca, 1975)

Wordsworth, William and Dorothy, *The Letters of William and Dorothy Wordsworth: The Middle Years, 1806–11*, ed. E. de Selincourt, revised by Mary Moorman (Oxford, 1969)

Wright, Arthur Robinson, *British Calendar Customs*, ed. T.E. Lones (three volumes, London, 1936–40)

Wrightson, John, *Livestock Handbooks No. 1: Sheep. Breeds and Management* (London, 1919)

Yorke, Philip C., *The Life and Correspondence of Philip Yorke, Earl of Hardwicke, Lord High Chancellor of Great Britain* (Cambridge, 1913)

Youatt, William, *Sheep, Their Breeds, Management and Diseases* (London, 1837)

Young, Arthur (ed.), *The Annals of Agriculture*, vols. I–XXXIII (1784–99)

Zionkowski, Linda, 'Strategies of Containment: Stephen Duck, Ann Yearsley, and the Problem of Polite Culture', *Eighteenth-Century Life*, 13 (1989), 91–108

Paintings

Artist unknown, *Country Around Dixton Manor (Dixton Harvesters)*, *c.* 1730, Cheltenham Art Gallery, described as 'British Provincial School, Eighteenth Century'

Artist unknown, *Dixton Manor*, *c.* 1730, Cheltenham Art Gallery (an apparent companion piece to *Dixton Harvesters*)

Constable, John, *Flailing Turnip-heads*, *c.* 1812–15, reproduced in Parris and Fleming-Williams, *Constable* (1991), Plate 38 and pp. 106–7

Index

CAMBRIDGE STUDIES IN EIGHTEENTH-CENTURY
ENGLISH LITERATURE AND THOUGHT

General Editors

Professor HOWARD ERSKINE-HILL LITT.D.,FBA, *Pembroke College, Cambridge*
Professor JOHN RICHETTI, *University of Pennsylvania*